LIVE STOCK AND
DEAD THINGS

ANIMAL LIVES

Jane C. Desmond, Series Editor; Barbara J. King,
Associate Editor for Science; Kim Marra, Associate Editor

Books in the Series

LIVE STOCK

THE ARCHAEOLOGY
OF ZOOPOLITICS
BETWEEN

DOMESTICATION
AND
MODERNITY

HANNAH CHAZIN

THE UNIVERSITY OF CHICAGO PRESS
Chicago and London

The University of Chicago Press, Chicago 60637
The University of Chicago Press, Ltd., London
© 2024 by The University of Chicago
Published 2024
Printed in the United States of America

This book is supported by the Lenfest Junior Faculty Development
Grant at Columbia University.

33 32 31 30 29 28 27 26 25 24   1 2 3 4 5

ISBN-13: 978-0-226-83748-2 (cloth)
ISBN-13: 978-0-226-83750-5 (paper)
ISBN-13: 978-0-226-83749-9 (e-book)
DOI: https://doi.org/10.7208/chicago/9780226837499.001.0001

Library of Congress Cataloging-in-Publication Data

Names: Chazin, Hannah, author.
Title: Live stock and dead things : the archaeology of zoopolitics
between domestication and modernity / Hannah Chazin.
Other titles: Animal lives (University of Chicago Press)
Description: Chicago : The University of Chicago, 2024. | Series:
Animal lives | Includes bibliographical references and index.
Identifiers: LCCN 2024021801 | ISBN 9780226837482 (cloth) |
ISBN 9780226837505 (paperback) | ISBN 9780226837499 (e-book)
Subjects: LCSH: Human-animal relationships—Caucasus, South. |
Bronze age—Caucasus, South. | Livestock—Social aspects—
Caucasus, South. | Domestication—Political aspects—Caucasus,
South. | Pastoral systems—Caucasus, South. | Animal remains
(Archaeology)
Classification: LCC QL87.C43 2024 | DDC 591.9475—dc23/
eng/20240607
LC record available at https://ccn.loc.gov/2024021801

For Tuan

CONTENTS

◆

◆

◆

INTRODUCTION

This book is an attempt to give the domesticated sheep, goats, and cattle that lived thousands of years ago—and the humans they lived with—a chance to be interesting. A chance to surprise us with their weirdness. A chance to help us write new stories about the past and its relationship to the present. How does one give sheep a chance to be interesting? With living animals, it might look like the simple act of putting out an extra bowl of food. The philosopher Vinciane Despret (2006, 368) relates how retired primatologist Thelma Rowell puts out twenty-three bowls of food in front of her twenty-two Scottish blackface ewes every morning at her farm in Yorkshire. The extra bowl avoids making competition over food "the only possible response" her sheep can make. If, in the presence of the additional bowl, sheep still choose to compete, then that choice can't be explained through mere scarcity. Understanding sheep under these conditions requires asking new and more imaginative questions about their social world. The presence of the extra bowl gives sheep more choices, and researchers more interesting hypotheses.

Putting out an extra bowl is an *invitation*, one that gives the sheep "a chance" to be interesting. The twenty-third bowl pushes back against the forces—like sheep's economic importance and their tight imbrication into human worlds—that have encouraged scientific research to give sheep very few opportunities to surprise us.[1] Despret (2006, 361) notes that what is at stake in this practice is not merely resolving the question of whether sheep are "naturally" competitive or cooperative, but rather, "Do we prefer living with predictable sheep or with sheep that surprise us?" (367). Archaeologists and other scholars who study animals in the past can't put out an extra bowl of food. But we can still give animals in the past a chance to be interesting—and a chance to surprise us.

The domesticated sheep, goats, and cattle that lived in the Caucasus mountains over three thousand years ago—that I know through my study of the bones from their long-dead bodies recovered through the excavation of archaeological sites—have been full of surprises. As I spent time with these bones—touching them, examining them, counting them, weighing them, and transforming them into data in spreadsheets and graphs—I found patterns that upended easy assumptions about the differences between the modern and premodern, the industrial and traditional, and the economic and noneconomic.

When analyzing minute differences in the isotopes of carbon and oxygen atoms in the enamel of their teeth to determine when sheep, goats, and cattle were born during the year, I was surprised to find that sheep were born nearly year-round. This felt unexpectedly *modern*, because year-round milk production was supposed to be the product of refrigeration, pasteurization (and germ theory), and railroads. So why was it happening three thousand years earlier, in the Bronze Age? My perplexing data were not evidence of what sheep did naturally, but neither did they match economistic models of herding, which are concerned with increasing the output of milk while reducing the input of human labor.

Moreover, when I looked at what parts of the body were present in the faunal remains recovered from the excavations, I was surprised to find large numbers of jaw bones (mandibles) and ankle bones (tarsals). Again, simple utility didn't explain things, and the pattern was not typical of what zooarchaeologists look for: butchery waste, tool or artifact production, or even catchall categories like ritual or symbolism. Puzzling over *why* there were so many of these bones led me to question the available tools for interpreting archaeological data—tools that rested on the division between the modern and premodern, the value of dead animals as commodities and the social value of living animals, and the utilitarian and symbolic values of animals in political life.

My own attempts to extend an invitation to these long-dead herd animals, to give them a chance to be interesting, emerged in two disparate domains, one methodological and the other theoretical. But in practice, as I tacked between the archaeological data and the wider intellectual constellations I was drawing on to shape my interpretations and arguments, I found these developments were closely interrelated. The surprises that cropped up in the zooarchaeological and isotopic data pushed me to reconsider various aspects of zooarchaeological practice, and I began to look for new ways to interpret the traces of past human and animal lives. But at the same time, I also realized that rethinking what we might know about the lives of animals in the deeper past would require reworking how we think about politics and the relationships between the present and the past.

In declaring that this book is about zoopolitics between domestication and modernity, I am making two interventions. First, domestication should be thought of as a condition of, or even a technology for, plasticity—not as the origin point of a teleological trajectory toward the present. What I found in the faunal data from Late Bronze Age (1500–1100 BCE) sites in the South Caucasus looked very different from the dominant narratives that shape how scholars and publics understand the connections between human-animal relations in the present and the past. What it *didn't* look like was an embryonic form of contemporary instrumental relations between humans and livestock. The data didn't reveal that humans' relations with domesticated animals in the deep past were the prototypes for modern human-animal relations—the origin point of contemporary forms of inequality, instrumentality, efficiency, and the objectification of non-human nature. Instead, the interpretive problems I encountered pushed me to think about how humans' relations with domesticated herd animals in the deeper past were a space of potential, one in which the capacities of both humans and animals were altered through new material practices, biological transformations, multispecies labor relations, and novel forms of interspecies symbiosis.

Rather than approaching domestication as a process that necessarily led to increasingly objectifying and instrumentalizing relations with animals (and nature more broadly), a zoopolitical approach to domestication examines how living with domesticated animals enabled the emergence of new forms of labor, value, and political life in the past. Living with domesticated herd animals did not funnel toward a singular future, but instead opened up many potential paths. If we were to look more closely, we would probably find false starts, dead ends, and promising experiments that fizzled out for one reason or another. Thinking about the relations between humans and cattle, sheep, and goats "postdomestication" and premodernity as open and plastic rejects the teleological connections between the present and past that structure the metamyth that contemporary forms of inequality, objectification, and instrumental relations with animals have their origins in the deeper past.[2]

Second, zoopolitics also involves considering animals as active participants in political life in the past. Herding is not merely a way to produce food or accumulate wealth and convert it into power. Human–herd animal relations are a central part of the historical unfolding of the material-semiotic processes of social life, which in turn shape the human relations and subjectivities central to what we term "the political": membership in or exclusion from a political community and the roles of leaders and subjects.[3] Zoopolitics is, at its heart, a performative understanding of political life, in which relations between members of political communities and between rulers and ruled emerge out of everyday practices—out of the basic stuff of social (re)production. The multiple potentials, the plasticity, embedded within human–herd animal relations is shaped by herd animals' active and foundational role in shaping political life.

Zoopolitics rearticulates how we think about labor and politics. Crucially, it pushes back against the idea that labor defines the human (against the animal) and the assumption that labor is the process by which humans transform and objectify nature, creating property and inequality. Instead, it radically expands the idea of labor, defining it as the iterative acts by humans and animals that bring worlds into being, shaping political life in the process. Drawing on various Marxian critiques of work, it challenges the idea that productive labor is a fundamental feature of human nature (Baudrillard 1975; Povinelli 1993; Weeks 2011). Zoopolitics also foregrounds the importance of herd animals' reproductive labor in political life, and it does so in conversation with feminist scholars' critique of the exclusion of human reproduction from analyses of labor and politics (e.g., Federici 2021; Fraser 2014).

Zoopolitics' performative understanding of political life incorporates a key insight from critiques of capitalism: that work, in addition to producing stuff, also produces social and political subjects. But it insists that doing things produces both relations and persons (subjects) even when what is being done doesn't resemble productive activity. In doing so, zoopolitics destabilizes how we think about domestication and how our ideas about domestication connect the past to the present. It rejects the simple story that domesticating plants and animals led to the modern world, the idea that "modern political formations . . . [rise] inexorably, if not inevitably, out of roots put down in prehistory" (Adam T. Smith 2003, 17). Instead, it holds open the question of the relation between labor and domination in past—both for humans and for domesticated herd animals.

WRITING FROM AND BEYOND ARCHAEOLOGY

At its heart, this book inquires into the surprises that emerged from my zooarchaeological work on the Late Bronze Age animal bones from the

Tsaghkahovit Plain (located in the modern country of Armenia). That research was shaped by my original questions about political life in the Late Bronze Age (and the role herd animals might have played in shaping it) and by the zooarchaeological methods available for studying the material traces of past lives through bones. As I worked, I was drawn toward other, more expansive questions and problems—which pulled me into conversation with work being done in sociocultural anthropology and animal studies more broadly. I am writing from the perspective of archaeology, but the arguments I make here go beyond it. I am convinced that the potential weirdness of the past—and the potentialities of humans' relationships with domesticated herd animals—matters for questions and conversations in disciplines that, up to this point, have had only limited contact with archaeology.

In *What Is Posthumanism?*, Carey Wolfe (2010, 115) argues that "it is only in and through our disciplinary specificity that we have something specific and irreplaceable to contribute to this "question of the animal." In my case, the specificity of this contribution emerges from its beginning in zooarchaeological research on politics in the Late Bronze Age South Caucasus in four ways: (1) the centrality of the materiality of animals bodies (particularly their bones and teeth), (2) the anthropology of animals and its unique genealogy and relationship to critical animal studies, (3) the productive collision of the question of politics in pastoralist societies and in relationship to the animal, and (4) the historiographic specificity of the ancient South Caucasus.

Bones

Zooarchaeologists have developed a suite of methods for analyzing the bones of animals recovered from archaeological sites to illuminate animal and human lives in the past. Zooarchaeology's methodological specificities—which are grounded in the material remains of animals' bodies—offer an opportunity to deepen (and transform) how we understand the long-term histories of human-animal relationships. In my own work, I have focused on expanding zooarchaeology's theoretical and methodological capacity to explore the full range of herd animals' potential to actively shape political life in the past (Chazin 2016a, 2023; Chazin, Gordon, and Knudson 2019). But archaeology tends to appear in nonarchaeologists' writing about human-animal relationships only to relate the story of early domestication, ignoring its potential to make other contributions. One of the goals of my work is to take the zooarchaeology of a time and place in the deeper past—

one that is "postdomestication," but that also challenges the well-worn teleological histories linking the present and the past—and make it more accessible to other scholars who are interested in human-animal relationships past and present.

Zooarchaeology provides a unique vantage point from which to study human-animal relationships. Much of the work of zooarchaeological analysis is aimed at reading the traces of both animals' lives and animals' deaths in bones (and other material remains). Traditional zooarchaeological analyses are able to generate valuable information about slaughtering, butchery, and consumption practices. Moreover, the development of new scientific techniques like isotopic analysis has greatly enhanced the range of information about living animals that is accessible archaeologically. Zooarchaeology, by its very nature, knots together questions about animals as agentive, cocreators of social life with questions about the active participation of their bodies in social and political life after death. These strengths give zooarchaeology, at least potentially, a heightened ability to think carefully (and materially) about animals' pre- and postmortem lives—and the connections between them (see Overton and Hamilakis 2013, 116). Because of this ability, zooarchaeology can approach questions of intimacy and utility in human-animal relationships and the political potential of animals differently than other disciplines.

But at the same time, the nature of all archaeological research—consisting of the processes by which archaeologists make interpretations from the fragmentary and limited material remains of past lives—make it vulnerable to the power of entrenched narratives about the past (and its relationship to the present or lack thereof) and about humans' relations with animals more generally. Archaeological remains do not speak about the past directly. Archaeologists' interpretations are always mediated by the questions we ask, the methods we use, and the models we think with. Zooarchaeology, as a practice, is shaped by all the varied, conflicting, and competing stories that Western scholarship has written about living with herd animals. To more fully actualize zooarchaeology's potential to contribute to the histories of humans and animals and, at the same time, to make the empirical specificities of archaeological analysis more accessible to nonarchaeologists, this book is deeply concerned with the production of archaeological knowledge. Throughout, I investigate what happened in the deeper past—asking what we can discover about the relations between long-dead herds and herders in Tsaghkahovit Plain, Armenia—while carefully examining and questioning how we know it.

Anthropological Animals

This book has also been shaped by the wider anthropological conversation on human-animal relations, which formed at the intersection of the "animal turn" in the humanities and social sciences and the changes and debates internal to the discipline. As Brian Boyd (2017) notes, anthropology has had an uneven relationship with critical animal studies. While animals have always been present in anthropological writing—long before the animal turn—earlier anthropological interest in animals was primarily anthropocentric (as detailed by Noske 1989; Mullin 1999). This older anthropology of animals was content to use them as a vehicle for thinking about humans, which set it apart from the rejection of anthropocentrism by critical animal studies (a rejection driven by conversations in philosophy and political organizing around animal rights). Archaeology was no different, with its own history of actively engaging with the study of animals found at archaeological sites and interest in the depictions of animals in material media. Only comparatively recently have archaeologists begun to seriously consider animals as active social actors as well as natural actors.

Social zooarchaeology grew out of zooarchaeologists' dissatisfaction with the discipline's earlier assumption that "the only role animals played in prehistoric societies was as a food source: calories and protein" (Russell 2012, 7). These scholars expanded zooarchaeological interest beyond the environment and subsistence to consider the wide variety of ways that animals contributed to social life in the past. Social zooarchaeologists have creatively reworked the methods and theories of zooarchaeological analysis to make the noneconomic roles of animals archaeologically visible (e.g., Orton 2010b; Overton and Hamilakis 2013; Russell 2012). Some scholars have extended this critique, pushing social zooarchaeology beyond its inherited anthropocentrism. They insist that "the recognition that animals are not just an 'economic' resource is not enough; instead it is vital that we acknowledge that animals are agentic entities that engage in human-non-human social relationships" (Overton and Hamilakis 2013, 114). I take up the challenge to work toward forging new theories and methods that consider animals as something other than economic or symbolic resources or raw materials (Overton and Hamilakis 2013; Boyd 2017; Oma and Birke 2013).

I do so by thinking about human–herd animal relationships as forms of what Despret (2004, 122) calls *anthropo-zoo-genetic practice*: practices that mutually "construct animal and human," transforming both in the process. This entails developing ways to see the ongoing entanglement of human and animal histories as they are lived in everyday life and their unfolding consequences in the past (through the archaeological record). In doing so, I am aided (and inspired) by the ethnographic work done by scholars who tell stories about the deadly serious stakes of living with and caring for herd animals and other companion species (e.g., B. Campbell 2005; Law 2010; Fijn 2011; Govindrajan 2018; Sharp 2019; Blanchette 2020).[4] These stories highlight how humans' relationships with animals constantly mingle mundane encounters and sustained relations, representations of and judgments about those relationships, the generation of wealth, and processes of material destruction and death. What I find interesting about herd animals is that their connections to the "darker" side of companion species—race, sex, money, death—are more readily apparent. Yet our stories about living with herd animals often smooth over the complex knotting of care and exploitation, thus drawing a stark line between trust and domination.

Ethnographic work on human–herd animal relationships among contemporary pastoralists and herders draws our attention to the complex imbrication of love and use in ostensibly traditional and nonindustrial forms of animal husbandry (B. Campbell 2005; Fijn 2011; Govindrajan 2018). But at the same time, scholars studying human-animal relations in high-tech industries like industrial meat production and biotechnology also see tangles of care and exploitation (Blanchette 2020; Sharp 2019). This inverts our assumptions about the differences between modern and traditional lifeways and between exploitation and coexistence. As I reflected on the issues of archaeological interpretation I was struggling with, this ethnographic work led me to question some accepted connections (and assumed differences) between the contemporary world and the deeper past. Sociocultural anthropologists' new insights about contemporary human-animal relations revealed interesting homologies between past and present, which tended to blur the (default and tacit) binary distinction between modern and premodern.

Rather than any one-to-one correspondence between the human-animal relationships described in ethnography and those I was examining in the deeper past, what emerged from the resonances across time periods were a number of intriguing questions. These questions, in turn, were connected to classic themes in anthropology: gifts and commodities, value, kinship, ritual. To illuminate the *anthropo-zoo-genetic* practices that shaped political life in the past, the interpretations presented in the second half of the book remix archaeological models, anthropological debates, and contemporary ethnographic and historical accounts of human-animal relationships. As I tacked back and forth between archaeology and sociocultural anthropology, three key themes emerged as crucial for thinking about human–herd animal relations outside the typical divisions and distinctions: eating and feeding, labor and reproduction, and pre- and post-mortem lives.

From Pastoralism to Zoopolitics

My interest in politics began with questions about the transformations in political life in the Late Bronze Age that archaeologists were reading out of the archaeological landscapes of the South Caucasus. In that context, thinking about politics meant thinking about pastoralism. Over time, I came to appreciate that pastoralism—as a category mobilized by anthropologists, archaeologists, and historians—was an unstable welding of human–herd animal relations and the idea that pastoralists were politically other to sedentary, agricultural societies (an idea accepted as the norm in political theory). Long-standing narratives and imaginaries placed pastoralists outside modernity as well as outside mainstream historical teleologies of progress and civilization (as reviewed by A. Porter 2012; Sneath 2007).

Recent scholarship on pastoralism in Eurasia has challenged the idea that pastoralist politics are defined by a lack of stability or a failure to accumulate wealth. Instead, archaeologists and historians have conjured a picture of pastoralist mobility as a powerful political technology that could create great empires, novel political experiments, and powerful elites (Frachetti 2012; Honeychurch 2015; Honeychurch, Wright, and Amartuvshin 2009; A. Porter 2012; Sneath 2007). From the beginning of my work on this topic in graduate school, I found this theoretical reversal hugely exciting—and it was a large part of why I decided to work in Eurasia rather than in the Americas, where I had first done archaeological fieldwork.

Over time, I became frustrated by the limited picture of human-animal relations these new models offered—reducing the stakes of living with herd animals to pastoralist mobility—and the limited agency afforded to herd animals themselves. That's because while I was reading about the political stakes of pastoralism in theory and in history, I was also reading rich ethnographic accounts of contemporary herders (B. Campbell 2005; Fijn 2011; Govindrajan 2018). Those books and articles brought into focus a wider range of human-animal relations—feeding, care, sacrifice, reproduction, labor—and sketched out their political stakes. The hours I spent reading the debates about pastoralism in the anthropological literature—how to define it, whether it was a unique lifeway, and what were its political consequences—convinced me it would be useful to think about the specificity of living with domesticated cattle, sheep, and goats.[5] It led me to consider what might make these animals—and our relations and our histories of relations with them—different from other animals that are lumped together under the category of domestication.

To weave in another strand of my thinking about politics, archaeologists are also beginning to actively consider how nonhumans, especially things and landscapes, might have a key role in shaping the ordering of political life. This conversation has one foot in the ongoing, wider intellectual re-engagement with the nonhuman world (sometimes glossed as the "material" and the "ontological" turns), and another in disciplinary-specific conversations about how to study politics in the past through its material traces.[6] Objects have received the most attention, reflecting a harmony between the interest of the material turn in the category of the thing or object and the prosaic ubiquity of material things—artifacts (pots, tools, figurines, etc.) but also things like architecture, soils, and rocks—in archaeological interpretations. More recent interest in ontologies in archaeology, driven by a broader engagement with a wide range of posthumanist theories, has brought animals more firmly within the conversation on politics as members of larger collectivities of humans and nonhumans, using theoretical apparatuses like assemblages, machines, and publics (e.g., Bauer and Kosiba 2016; Crellin et al. 2020; Kosiba 2020; Adam T. Smith 2015; Swenson and Warner 2012).[7]

Herd animals intersect the larger problem of the exclusion of animals from political theory in a specific way. Not only are the political potentialities of animals (and their relations with humans) different from those of clay pots or stone walls, but the shape of their prior exclusion is also different.[8] As domesticated herd animals, the cattle, sheep, and goats at the center of this book have a unique and complicated relationship to the metamyth of objectification (see chapters 1 and 2). Reincorporating herd animals into our accounts of political life means grappling with the stories we tell about domestication as an origin point. It also requires examining carefully what objectification—with its connections to ideas about property, accumulation, and labor—means specifically for animals in both our theories and our interpretations of the past.

This also requires different analytical tools, built from the performative approaches developed by scholars of gender and science and technology studies (STS), to analyze the material-semiotic, historically emergent, and power-laden nature of social life (see chapter 3).[9] To say that politics is *performative* is to insist that relations of inclusion and exclusion and of authorization and subjection emerge from and are transformed through the creative and constrained repetitions of practices in everyday social life. To think about politics performatively is to look for the ordering practices that produce political orders. In addition, as Karen Barad (2003, 2006) has emphasized, the performative practices of politics are necessarily elaborate assemblings of humans and a wide variety of nonhumans (Chazin 2016a).

Thinking about animals as political actors also requires changes in how archaeologists approach the material traces of the past. It means addressing Lindsay Montgomery's (2020, 62) call for "broadening the types of information that we consider relevant and embracing anomalies as data in and of themselves rather than as abnormalities within an established pattern in need of explanation and testing." Across the book, I examine the surprises in my data—and I use that sense of the unexpected as a way to drive forward interpretations. Not to resolve the tension between data and models but to move away from, and critically examine, the accepted acts of classification entailed within archaeological methods and in prior interpretations of the data. My work shares with Montgomery's analysis of Indigenous critical philosophy as archaeological praxis a common critical stance toward the broader comparative project of anthropology and archaeology and their disciplinary histories of engaging with alterity. My specific contribution is to question and rework the Western "ontostories" about domestication, examining the sense of history that they craft through establishing teleological connections between the present and the past, within their larger role in colonial dispossession and violence (K. Anderson 1997; Tsing 2018).

South Caucasus

Exploring how humans, sheep, goats, and cattle lived together in the ancient South Caucasus is a chance to think about human–herd animal relationships in a context that is not the originary process of domestication but also quite distant from contemporary human-animal relationships. Archaeology, in general, has the potential to extend the horizon of the conversations about the history of human-animal relations. As Boyd (2018, 251) notes, conversations in sociocultural anthropology and animal studies have a limited time depth: "'Deep history' is not and should not be confined to the study of the past few centuries of colonialism and capitalism; though this timespan may constitute deep history for sociocultural anthropology and human-animal studies as currently formulated, this timescale is not sufficient for long-term analysis of human-nonhuman relations."

In extending this critique, it is also important to avoid skipping directly from the histories of the (relatively) more recent past to the beginning of Western textual traditions (in the classical world and the ancient Near East) and from these textual traditions to the early processes of domestication.[10] It's worth considering what stories we are missing in the rush to connect Çatalhöyük, ancient Sumer, and Aristotle. This is not to say that archaeologists haven't been hard at work studying postdomestication societies across the map—in addition to thinking very carefully about the meaning of domestication as a process (e.g., Leach 2003; O'Connor 1997; Russell 2002). Rather, what is curious (and troubling) is that the new data and theories have not coalesced into a new story. They have left older stories about the inevitable connection between domestication and the more recent past relatively undisturbed.

While grappling with the analysis of animal bones, it has become clear to me that the linear narratives connecting domestication and modernity don't do much to help understand the data from the South Caucasus. The Late Bronze Age is "postdomestication," putting it at a remove from both the question of origins and the pernicious "search for firsts" (see Sterling 2011, 181) *and* also from the useful rethinking of domestication now underway in archaeology. But it is also early enough that it doesn't seem to be obviously connected to the later, better documented histories of human-animal relationships of the past five hundred years or so. Being early is not a strictly temporal fact: it has more to do with the sense that the Bronze Age South Caucasus is peripheral to, but not totally isolated from, what is usually taken to be the main plot of the development of Western civilization," the state, or modernity postdomestication.

Archaeologists and historians working in Central Asia and Africa have argued that the models of state formation and the development of different types of political organization that take the ancient Near East and Europe as the norm are unable to account for the histories of either region (Fleisher and Wynne-Jones 2010; Guyer and Belinga 1995; Honeychurch 2015; Sneath 2007). But often, the corrections to these assumptions are made in the form of an alternate model that presumes the difference of pastoralists from an assumed norm.[11] In writing about the ancient South Caucasus, I use insights from archaeologists working in Inner Asia and Africa who challenge normative political models that were developed in the study of ancient societies in Southwest Asia.

But I am not using these insights to merely assert the peculiarity or non-normative nature of political life in the South Caucasus. Nor am I universalizing models developed to explain the specific local histories of politics in Inner Asia and Africa. Rather, ethnographic, historical, and archaeological accounts from these regions have expanded how I think about the plastic potentials of humans' relationships with herd animals. Taking and reworking these crucial insights to suit different questions arising in a new historical context pushes back against the implicit tendency to diminish how much these alternative models challenge normative ones. Rather than accepting pastoralism as something that makes, and marks, the difference between the West and Inner Asia or Africa, this book explores what we are missing when we presume that difference.

OUTLINE OF THE BOOK

This book explores the ways in which postdomestication, premodern herding societies were spaces of potential—ones where the capacities of both humans and herd animals were altered through novel material practices, multispecies labor relations, and forms of interspecies action that created value beyond calories or cash.[12] The unexpected nature of the entanglements that emerge from the analysis of animal remains from Late Bronze Age sites in the Tsaghkahovit Plain, Armenia, highlights the fact that humans' relations with domesticated herd animals in the deeper past did not funnel toward a singular future marked by instrumental exploitation and inequality. The chapters in the first half of the book challenge the metamyth that contemporary forms of inequality, objectification, and instrumental relations with animals have their origins in domestication, thus rejecting the teleological connections this myth establishes between the present and the past.

In chapter 1, I argue that the temporal structure of domestication stories, which produce, and reproduce, the ontological distinction between culture and nature, human and nonhuman, and the present and the past, renders large swathes of the past uninteresting—as the historiographic equivalent of flyover country. But recent archaeological work on the history of early domestication and theoretical discussions of domestication in human-animal studies destabilize the traditional story, pushing back against the dismissal of the deeper past. Moreover, entrenched domestication narratives obscure how much of our understanding of deep history is actually shaped by Western ideas (and concerns) about civilization and political order. In chapter 2, I argue that in light of this difficulty, we need to replace the question, Were animals objectified? with the question, What kinds of relations of use existed in the past? I untangle the ways in which objectification muddles together property, accumulation and commodities, labor, and the ethical issue of "making killable" (sensu Haraway 2008), thus producing teleological relationships between the present and the past. To trace histories of relations of use, I propose using *eating and feeding*, *labor and reproduction*, and *pre- and postmortem value* as the major lenses through which to think about human–herd animal relations.

If herd animals' status as objectified property isn't the foundation of the connections between the present and the deeper past, how should we think about animals when considering them as potentially efficacious participants in political life? In chapter 3, I argue that taking a performative approach to politics by emphasizing material-semiotic, historically emergent, and power-laden assemblages of humans and animals makes it possible to see herd animals as political actors. Specifically, I argue that we can trace archaeologically how herd animals contribute to: (1) performative practices that shape political groups, communities, or publics by whom they include and exclude, while rendering people within groups as similar or different; and (2) the performative activities that generate legitimate authority by calling into being the relationships between, and the categories of, the rulers and the ruled.

In the second half of the book, I present an extended archaeological case study examining the political possibilities of human–herd animal relations at two Late Bronze Age sites in the Tsaghkahovit Plain, Armenia. While the scope of the theoretical argument in the first half of the book is quite broad, the archaeological data I consider is much smaller in scale (in both time and space). This is a deliberate methodological and analytical choice meant to highlight the potential for new possibilities of interpretation, both locally and more broadly. I have worked to shape my discussions of archaeological data to meet the different needs and interests of readers from archaeology and from other disciplines. In the later chapters, detailed information about the archaeological data and methods (above and beyond what is essential to know to follow the argument) will be found in boxes in the text (e.g., box 5.1) or in the endnotes.

In chapter 4 I set the scene by introducing readers to currently available evidence and interpretations of social and political life in the South Caucasus during the Late Bronze Age. There I highlight certain interpretive habits that shape how archaeologists have read the record for evidence of political inequality and hierarchy and outline how a performative approach to politics opens a space for new interpretations. From this foundation, the subsequent chapters present a detailed consideration of the archaeological evidence for human–herd animal relationships, drawing on zooarchaeological and isotopic data. I weave contemporary and more recent historical examples of human–herd animal relations into my efforts to interpret the archaeological data. I use these accounts to draw connections between the present and the past in ways that are perhaps less typical for archaeology. Rather than using them directly to build models to take to the archaeological data, these examples help me shape questions about the practice of archaeological interpretation and the stories archaeologists (and others) tell about the past.

I use this method to help me interpret the zooarchaeological and isotopic data from the Tsaghkahovit Plain, which depart from the tacit expectations of traditional archaeological analysis. In chapter 5, I use the history of industrialized milk production to rethink the interpretation of expanded seasonality of sheep reproduction in the Late Bronze Age Tsaghkahovit Plain. Rather than focusing on the production of resources (meat, milk, wool), I explore how we might interpret the data as evidence of human and animal labor (and coreproduction). In chapter 6, an ethnographic analysis of contemporary intensive pork farming (Blanchette 2020) helps me think about how to trace the pre- and postmortem value of herd animals to account for the anomalously large numbers of jaw and ankle bones found at these sites. Rather than an ideal-typical distinction between the value of living animals as culturally specific forms of wealth and dead animals as economic resources, I use the idea of value-in-action to analyze the political potential of the circulation of living animals and their bodies after death.

Chapter 7 traces the divergent trajectories that emerge from in-depth analysis of the spatial distribution of isolated bones within the walls of Late Bronze Age sites and questions the utility of binary categories like economic/symbolic, public/private, and ritual/secular. An ethnographic analysis of contemporary animal sacrifice and legal battles over animal protection in India highlights the important political roles of both everyday and extraordinary practices involving herd animals (Govindrajan 2018). In the conclusion, I weave together all these lines of evidence into an account of the ways in which Late Bronze Age human–herd animal relationships created cross-cutting forms of felicitous authority. Political authority was composed through competing practices that generated value from the co-labor of herds and herders, the value of living and dead animals in transforming social spacetimes (sensu Munn 1992), and the circulation of isolated skeletal elements. The proliferation of values hints at the tumultuous

terrain of political action in the Late Bronze Age Tsaghkahovit Plain, complicating the story about the centralization of political power within the
walls of fortresses in the Late Bronze Age South Caucasus—and highlighting how human–herd animal relations in the deeper past opened potential
trajectories, rather than channeling a course toward a singular future.

• 1 •

FLYOVER HISTORY
AND DOMESTICATION AS
AN ONTOSTORY

Domestication is powerful story, or genre of stories, about living with animals. It is a story of cosmogony: of worlds ending and worlds being brought into being. Traditional narratives of animal domestication present it as a series of events and actions where animals were objectified and transformed into property, and humans gained an ever-increasing mastery over (and separation from) nature.[1] Domestication is an *ontostory*, a particular type of cosmogonic narrative foundational to Western ontologies (Fowles, cited in Alberti et al. 2011, 899). Ontostories endlessly redivide culture from nature, the human from nonhuman, and the present from the past in their retellings. As the domestication ontostory works to separate these categories, it simultaneously produces an awkward suturing of the *process* of domestication and the *category* of domesticated animals (as differentiated from wild animals).

Domestication as a *process* refers to the myriad actions and activities that, over time, changed humans' relationships with different species of animals and plants. Archaeologists use the material traces of these processes—animal bones, seeds, phytoliths, chemical traces in soils—to help us see these past actions in the present. Thinking about *process* leads to questions like, What are the similarities and differences between domesticating plants and domesticating animals? Is cultivating a swidden plot similar to taming a wild goat? What led people and plants and animals to change how they relate to one another? How long did that take? Was it fast or slow? How did it change the bodies and habits of people, animals, and plants? Were some animals more likely to participate in becoming domesticated? Why did domesticated maize become bigger but domesticated cattle become smaller? In contrast, domestication as a *category* refers to the binary distinction between domesticated and wild animals and the mapping of different species, histories, and individuals into these opposing categories. The category of domesticated animals points to the question, Is this animal domesticated or is it (still) wild? These categories are primarily ontological in nature, even as they appear to refer to (and emerge from) the process of domestication in the past. The categorical separation of the domestic and the wild is foundational to Western thinking about animals, as is evident from any cursory survey of either the anthropological or animal studies literatures.[2]

Domestication, as an ontostory with categorical implications, is "the imposition of a particular interface between what happened and that which is said to have happened" (Trouillot 1995, 12)—simultaneously a diverse set of practices and events that happened in the past and also a way of organizing our stories about the past (and the past's relationship to our present and possible futures). One of the powerful effects of the domestication ontostory is the way in which it collapses domestication as process into domestication as category. Specifically, because the category of domesticated animals serves as a bridge between the present and the past, it promotes a teleological sense of inevitability in domestication narratives. The basic temporal structure of the traditional domestication narrative establishes: (1) the initial rupture created by early practices of plant and animal domestication—which set human history on a new path and separated humans (further) from nature—and (2) the basic continuity between the practices that created that rupture in the Neolithic and the contemporary world. Sometimes there is an intermediate step in the narrative, which helps span the gap between the distant Neolithic and the present. This bridge takes different forms in different accounts: the invention of selective breeding, the origins of civilizations in places like ancient Assyria and Babylonia, or the classical traditions of ancient Greece and Rome. This continuity was originally framed as the triumphant and ongoing extension of human mastery over the nonhuman world. But it can be told as a positive story about civilization or as a troubling one of increasing objectification of (and withdrawal from) the natural world (and animals in particular).

This narrative structure, along with the idea that modernity finds its origins in domestication, persists despite widespread transformations in how scholars understand domestication. Archaeological research indicates that the initial process of domestication was not the progression of human mastery that the older stories promoted. It was messy and diverse, and humans were only one player in a multispecies ensemble. People in the deeper past didn't set out to master nature or become civilized. In fact, it looks increasingly like they may have just been playing around (cf. Graeber and Wengrow 2021, 211). Anthropologists and others have brought attention to the many human-animal relationships in the contemporary world that strain the boundaries between the domestic and the wild (Bocci 2017; Cassidy and Mullin 2007; Lien 2015; Parreñas 2018; Swanson, Lien, and Ween 2018). Yet even though scholars are increasingly skeptical that the old stories about domestication apply to the contemporary world or to the early period of domestication, the middle ground is left undisturbed. The old story continues to be readily available as scaffolding for how we think about herd animals (especially in the Old World) from sometime after the early Neolithic until the present.

Domestication ontostories transform vast swathes of the past into historical flyover country. The stories don't deny that things continued to happen between the Neolithic and the time of ancient Greece or between the time of ancient Rome and the industrial revolution. But it does deny that anything important happened—or that we might gain something other than a filling in of minor details in the larger ontostory if we were to investigate the terrain more closely than from thirty thousand feet.[3] This assumption is wrong: it would be well worth our while to be more curious about what might have been happening in flyover places and times. But this isn't the only problem. The dismissal of eras and places also produces a set of obstacles to thinking about human–herd animal relationships in the past. The easy acceptance that modern attitudes toward animals are our inheritances from "the Hun, and Scythian horsemen, Mediterranean goat- and ass-keepers, Semitic cattle breeders, Persian shepherds, and Arabian camel-lovers" (Shepard 1998, 154) obscures the extent of the connections between contemporary ideas about herd animals and our stories about domestication as a form of civilizational progress.[4] One of the benefits of rethinking the plots of our domestication stories is that it makes it easier to talk about humans' specific histories with herd animals in new ways, departing from the usual story of domestication. Separating out specific histories of peoples' relationships with herd animals and how they changed over time makes it possible to think about the tensions, gaps, or contradictions between smaller-scale, more local histories of herd animals and long-term or grand narratives about human-animal relationships.

Archaeology holds considerable potential to contribute to our understanding of the real and long-term histories of relations between groups of humans and groups of herd animals. These histories have left their marks on bodies, both human and animal, and on the surface of the world we coinhabit today. But unlocking that potential means accepting the pos-sibility that even in the post-Neolithic histories of Southwest Asia and Europe, we might find evidence of different kinds of human–herd animal relationships than those offered by the old ontostories. In this chapter, I map the way that thinking about herd animals trails certain stories about domestication along behind it. These stories about domestication as a pro-cess and a category limit the questions we ask by narrowing our focus to questions about objectification and instrumental use. Then, in the next chapter, I explore how becoming curious about the flyover country in sto-ries about domestication pushed me to bring forward new questions to ask about the long-term history of human–herd animal relationships, moving away from stories about instrumental relations and objectification toward histories of *relations of use*.

WHAT IS A HERD ANIMAL?

The research I discuss in the following chapters emerged, in part, through my engagement with the category of pastoralism—a category that has caused anthropologists no small amount of intellectual indigestion (see Arbuckle and Hammer 2019; Dyson-Hudson and Dyson-Hudson 1980). Pastoralism focuses our attention on certain kinds of human-animal rela-tionships. But from another angle, it focuses on humans' relationships with *certain kinds of animals*. By way of a shorthand, I use the term *herd animals* to refer to the kinds of animals involved in the human-animal relationships to which the label *pastoralism* draws our attention. I like the fact that the modifier *herd* is both a broad ecological term and also strongly linked to our intuition that pastoralism is something specific and distinct. In some usages, *herd* simply refers to a social group of animals of the same species (wild or domesticated) and the way they behave together. In others, *herd* points to the human-animal relationships we associate with pastoralism (hence the terms *herding* and *herder*).

While older definitions of (nomadic) pastoralism focused on groups' relative dependence on herd animal products for subsistence or mobility, more recent work expands the definition of pastoralism beyond the limits of nomadic or mobile pastoralists. Arbuckle and Hammer (2019, 393), in a recent review of the archaeology of pastoralism in Southwest Asia, offer a simple definition: "the husbandry of domesticated ungulates including cattle, sheep, goat, camels, horses, and donkeys, with no specification of the relative importance of animals in the overall economy, level of incorporation into market economies, degree of mobility, or forms of community social organization." This definition is useful. But I also want to linger a moment and think about what, exactly, might be specific or different about the husbandry of domesticated ungulates such that we might want to think about them separately from the category of domesticated animals more broadly. Is it because of the characteristics (whether physiological or ethological) that define ungulates as a group? Is it something specific about the character of the husbandry that makes it useful or necessary to separate domesticated ungulates from other forms of livestock (pigs, chickens, ducks, rabbits, etc.)? Is it both? How are we to make sense of, and talk about, the ways that humans' relationships with domesticated ungulates may substantially overlap with other kinds of human-animal relationships—and that there were, and still are, many different ways that humans can live with domesticated ungulates? A sheep like Dolly, the first mammal cloned from an adult somatic cell,[5] may be entangled with humans in ways that are more akin to lab mice working in a laboratory today than to the lamb found that was buried next to a person within a house at Çatalhöyük some nine thousand years ago.[6]

In its original context, Arbuckle and Hammer's (2019) definition put the impetus on archaeologists to specify the details about mobility, herding practices, production orientation, and social life that are often subsumed into, or presumed by, the use of the term *pastoralist*. But they did not explore the ways that broadening the definition of pastoralism might cross other boundaries, those between the past and the present or the ancient and the modern. Some readers may feel uneasy about a definition of pastoralism that stretches to accommodate both free ranging pigs roaming in the forests of Borneo and a concentrated animal feeding operation (CAFO) in the plains of the Midwestern United States. Rather than offering terminology that resolves these tensions cleanly, this chapter embraces the ambiguity in the term *domesticated herd animals*. Explicitly acknowledging the ambiguity illuminates the messiness that is otherwise excluded by our categories (and by some domestication stories). The taxonomic exactitude of the category of domesticated ungulates obscures two sources of this ambiguity. First, some domesticated herd animals simultaneously establish and occupy an important central location within the larger conceptual terrain of domestication. And second, different domesticated ungulates have both different histories of relationships with humans *and* also different relationships to the category of pastoralism and the domestication ontostory.

The way I want to use the term *domesticated herd animals* is not as a tax-onomic category, nor as a term that categorizes a specific type of human-animal relationship. It might be better described as the space at the center of the overlapping circles in a Venn diagram, one that encompasses both the histories of human-animal relationships *and* the histories of Western accounts of human-animal relationships (figure 1.1). Four characteristics define the space I am mapping out:

- Species that have a long history of being domesticated and living with humans (especially species that were involved in the early domestica-tion processes in Southwest Asia)
- Species that have had key roles in more recent histories of industrial-ization, capitalism, imperialism, and colonialism[7]
- Species (and their histories of domestication) that are the conceptual origins of many aspects of traditional ideas about domestication as both a process and a category
- Species whose relationships with humans are deeply entangled in eth-ical debates about instrumentality, intimacy, and killing animals

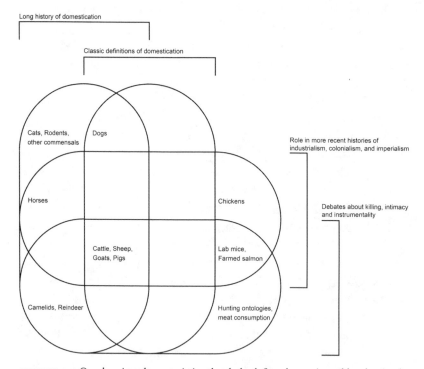

FIGURE 1.1 Overlapping characteristics that help define domesticated herd animals.

The first two categories probe how and when thinking about herd animals makes conceptual or historical linkages between the more recent and the deeper past. Does the history of early domestication of ungulate species in Southwest Asia ten thousand years ago tell us something about the history of the last five hundred years and the roles of herd animals in it? Or vice versa?

The third category emerges out of the tension between recent anthropological thinking about domestication and the older, master narrative, which still holds much intellectual and emotional currency. The traditional Western story of domestication is one that sees it as a process of human control or mastery over nature, which thereby transcends it. These stories see domestication as the origin of things like domination and property and envision a process of selective breeding as a form of engineering (Ingold 2011b) or a process of degradation turning once noble beasts into grotesques (Tuan 1984). Finally, the last category highlights how pastoralism and hunting (as forms of instrumental relationships with animals) are also deeply caught up in questions about how to understand the ethical stakes of killing animals. Anthropology, in particular, has troubled over the tension between emic and etic understandings of these dilemmas.

Considering these overlapping domains helps to clarify which animals all four of these characteristics apply to. We could think of them as Domesticated Herd Animals. Domesticated cattle, sheep, and goats are firmly at the center of this terrain. They are some of the earliest domesticates, they play a key role in histories of industrialization and colonization, and they are the creatures that inspired many of the traditional ideas about domestication. As livestock, they are caught up in the moral politics of instrumental use in the present (meat-eating, factory farming, etc.). Other domesticated ungulates that fit the broader definition of pastoralism—animals like reindeer, camels, alpacas, yaks, and donkeys—fit less neatly in the center, and perhaps most importantly, they are peripheral to the stories about domestication and herd animals that I am trying to unravel and reweave.[8]

What about horses and pigs? Horses have a slightly different relationship to the story of domestication and our imaginaries of human-animal relationships. Horses, much like dogs, are generally thought to have especially intense and intimate relationships with people. Moreover, horse domestication, as it is currently understood, is a different story than the domestication of cattle, sheep, and goats. Archaeological and genetic evidence agree that one initial center of horse domestication was the Central Asian steppes. Archaeological evidence from the mid- to late fourth millennium BCE from Botai in Kazakhstan suggests that these early domesti-

cated horses were bitted and milked and appear to have been domesticated
to hunt wild horses, in addition to providing food in the form of meat and
milk (Olsen 2006; Outram et al. 2009).[9]

The other thing that makes horses unusual is the importance horseback
riding plays in scholarly work on human-animal relations. Horseback riding (and also horse-drawn transport) is an important pastoralist technology (Anthony 2007; Bökönyi 1994; Kohl 2007) and is a critical part of the
classical mounted pastoralism that is at the heart of our imaginaries of wild
and free nomads. At the same time, horseback riding has taken a central
place in discussions of animal agency and the intimacy of humans' relationships with domesticated animals (e.g., Argent 2013; Armstrong Oma
2010; Brittain and Overton 2013; Despret 2004).

Pigs can be placed in the central terrain I am sketching out here. They
are among the earliest domesticated animals in Southwest Asia and have
been important players in colonial expansion in the Americas and the
transformations of human-animal relationships seen in industrial agriculture. Yet pigs are often excluded from discussions of Domesticated Herd
Animals, for two differing reasons. First, pig husbandry is omitted from
conversations about pastoralism. Pigs are usually understood as a sedentary species and have been used as a proxy measure for the presence or
absence of sedentary or mobile communities (Hesse and Wapnish 1998;
Price 2020).[10] As omnivores, their dietary needs are different from those of
cattle, sheep, and goats and overlap more with human diets. This contrast
shapes a different terrain of potential human-animal relationships. Moreover, in certain archaeological frameworks, pigs are seen as valuable only
for their meat rather than for secondary products that can be harvested
without killing the animal.[11] This excludes them from stories about the
role that secondary products have played in shaping human–herd animal
relationships and human history more broadly (see chapter 5).

Second, despite their long-term history of domestication in Southwest
Asia and their role in shaping the traditional narratives of domestication,
other lineages of pigs elsewhere in the world offer up models of human-
pig relationships that look rather different. Ethnographic descriptions of
pigs allowed to roam freely, with extremely porous boundaries between
wild and domesticated pigs, are common (see the sources cited in Price
2020 and Russell 2012). While these are relationships with domesticated
animals, they are not central to the traditional story of domestication. Describing the "no fences, no prohibitions" style of human-pig relationships
in the Meratus Mountains in South Kalimantan, Indonesia, Anna Tsing
(2018, 236) asks, "Would you call these arrangements 'domestication'?

Regardless of your answer, clearly they have not been *world historical*. They have not set a course for progress. Indeed, they distinguish themselves as marginal" (emphasis mine). Unpacking what gets lumped together under the umbrella of *herd animals* highlights local histories—wild and domesticated horses at Botai, unruly domesticated pigs that roam the forests in Indonesia—that are in tension with the domestication ontostories that shape how we understand the long-term histories of human–herd animal relationships. Some of this tension comes from the way these stories tangle the categorical division between the domesticated and the wild with the process (or processes) of being or becoming domesticated. Histories that don't separate cleanly between the wild and the domestic, between the human and the nonhuman, trouble the easy connection between origins and outcomes in our domestication stories.

"IT'S SOMETHING WE DID TO THEM": RETHINKING DOMESTICATION

The original domestication ontostory establishes a connection between the deeper past and more recent history, as it narrates the separation and purification of nature and culture.[12] It tells the story of a process driven by human needs and desires, which is either implicitly or explicitly cast as a sequence of conscious intervention in, or the engineering of, nature through human mastery and control. When we discuss the history of human-animal relationships, terms like *domination*, *mastery*, and *objectification* are shibboleths for this story, which presents domestication as a process that necessarily exploits animals. Archaeology and sociocultural anthropology, as academic disciplines, were shaped by these stories. In turn, they helped to enliven these stories for, and enshrine them in, wider scholarly and public imaginations.

Anthropologists and archaeologists have begun to challenge the original version of the domestication ontostory. Driven by methodological innovations and changing theoretical orientations, domestication has been a subject of lively debate and under continual revision in archaeology for a very long time.[13] Alongside this long-standing and fairly continuous archaeological conversation, sociocultural anthropologists' interest in human-animal relationships and multispecies approaches has opened up parallel (and sometimes intersecting) discussions about what kinds of animals count as domesticated and what kinds of relationships count as domestication (Cassidy and Mullin 2007; Swanson, Lien, and Ween 2018). As the victim, perhaps, of earlier successes, new thinking on domestication in archaeology and anthropology has of yet not gained as wide a circulation or made as durable an impact as traditional domestication stories.

In this animated series of conversations, the original version of the domestication ontostory is under revision from two directions: domestication maximalists and domestication minimalists. The maximalists, as they rethink the stories we might tell about domestication, seek to expand the category beyond the traditional bounds established in the original story. In contrast, the minimalists contend that domestication is essentially defined by its power to sever (or attempt to sever) culture from nature, both in practice and in the stories we tell about that practice. They argue for a smaller, stricter definition of what kinds of human-animal relationships count as domestication. In considering these opposing positions, what emerges is the extent to which definitions of domestication are unstable and contested in large part because of how the process of domestication is sutured to the categorical distinction between domesticated and wild animals through the ontostory of domestication. The maximalists' interest in the possibilities of the processes and practices of domestication deform these ontological categorizations in certain ways (see, e.g., Lien 2015, 164–65). The minimalists, in contrast, place the active process of dividing between culture and nature and between wild and domesticated at the center—the *onto* in the ontostories—thus consciously excluding other practices and histories from the term.

As their name suggests, the domestication maximalists have expanded, sometimes radically, the scope of what domestication might encompass. For instance, the imprecision that Helen Leach (2007, 72) identified in the term *domestication* and its use moved her to broaden the scope of what the term might encompass. She notes that domestication simultaneously refers to both the early coevolution of humans, plants, and animals in the Neolithic and later practices of selective breeding or artificial selection. Her response is to subdivide domestication (as a *process*) into four stages, defined by different mechanisms of genetic selection: two early stages defined by unintentional selective pressures on plants and animals (and also humans) and two later stages where selection is intentional and human-driven. These stages are arranged into a more or less traditional sequence of increasing human control over animal and plant reproduction, one that strongly resembles the narrative of domestication as the origin of modernity.

Yet in other important ways, Leach's approach is a departure from business as usual. First, it undercuts the narrative of human mastery and separation from nature (cf. Plumwood 1993) by insisting that early domestication was more or less unintentional and that it radically reshaped humans in the same ways that it did plants and animals.[14] Moreover, Leach's first stage of domestication is quite broad and encompasses human-animal relationships, like those between humans and the house mouse and house sparrow, that are excluded from more traditional approaches to domestication. More subtly, this approach tentatively departs from the temporality of traditional domestication narratives. In Leach's schema, the first and second stages continue to exist in the present, rather than being superseded by the later ones.[15] It also gives an analytical framework that might help us think about how two species, say sheep and mice, have moved between stages at different tempos and along different trajectories.

A recent edited volume consisting of chapters by sociocultural anthropologists (Swanson, Lien, and Ween 2018) also critically engages with the legacy of traditional narratives of domestication as a process in ways that expanded its remit as a category. These scholars were inspired by the ongoing archaeological work of recasting narratives about early domestication, which emphasize that domestication as a process was gradual, multidirectional, multiple, mutual, and unintentional and that it fundamentally should be understood as a multispecies relation (e.g., Boyd 2018). Starting from this perspective, the authors collected in the book turned toward ethnographic questions and contexts through an approach the editors of the volume called "decentering domestication": (1) attention to domestication practices, not just domestication stories and (2) attending to domestication from its margins (in terms of species, practices, times, and places) rather than its center (Lien, Swanson, and Ween 2018, 19). This enabled the authors to both find "unexpected relations" in the usual places we think of when we think about domestication (farms, cages, villages) and domesticatory relations in places and landscapes that might otherwise seem like the wild, or at least beyond the scale of domestication as we commonly think it.

New thinking about domestication has not been limited to expanding the species, times, places, and relations that might count as domestication. Other anthropologists have pushed the envelope further in developing less anthropocentric approaches. Terry O'Connor's (2018, 8) focus on the long history of commensalism between humans and other animals has led him to characterize domestication as "just one part of a spectrum of affiliative relations arising from the coevolution of people and other species— relations that are subject to ongoing negotiation and change, and not all of which are intentional." Using terms like *commensalism*, *synanthropy*, and *mutualism* to assess interspecies interaction situates domestication as one process among many. It pushes against the anthropocentrism of traditional narratives (O'Connor 1997, 2018). Nevertheless, despite this less anthropocentric terminology, O'Connor (2013, 127) distinguishes between wild commensals and domesticated animals, defining as *domesticates* those that are owned (as property), captively bred, and used as either material or social resources. In essence, what O'Connor presents is a fairly nonanthropocentric approach to thinking about domestication as a process and a practice, while his category of "domesticates" retains more of a traditional ontological framework.

More provocatively, John Hartigan (2014, 37–38) has suggested that domestication, and indeed culture more generally, is not limited to humans. Hartigan extends the practices of cultivation (and therefore domestication) to species beyond the human, including the ants (*Duroia hirsuta*) that carefully tend monoculture plots of trees in the Peruvian rainforests. Suggestively remixing the entanglements of cultivation and culture, he argues that what is important is not meaning, which is often the wedge used to separate human culture from animal nature, but *care*. He suggests we think about culture as "the capacity to care for—to domesticate—other species: to render them plastic and mutable rather than the fixed types we so often imagine natural objects to be."

This perspective extends agency to animals, but in a different way than the arguments suggesting humans were not alone in having agency in early domestication. Though he does suggest that much of domestication is driven by unconscious choices and processes, Hartigan (2014) isn't interested in adjudicating whether domestication is necessarily exploitative or mutual. He merely notes that his radically expansive definition retains the sense of asking "who's doing what to whom?" (2014, 38), a question that animates much of the contemporary debate. Instead, his main intervention is to remove the reigning anthropocentrism at the heart of the concept. He argues that animals (at least some of them) are capable of forms of care that reform others and that this reformation is the same sort of thing (if not quite exactly the same thing) as what humans have been calling domestication.

The domestication maximalists, despite the meaningful differences in their positions, all productively question the diversity of practices and relations that can be awkwardly lumped together under the term *domestication* (see also Losey 2022). Moreover, they highlight the issue of anthropocentrism in the original ontostory and its descendants. This anthropocentrism seems less tenable now due to our changing understanding of the data on early domestication processes and because the exclusion of animals from the heart of the action (agency) that is a feature of certain Western onto-logical commitments seems both less secure and more parochial than it once did.

Pushing back against these radical expansions of what might count as domestication, domestication minimalists insist that the term is better re-duced to, and isolated as, the "world-historical" process (Tsing 2018) that was the origin of a Euro-American "natural order of things" (Lien, Swan-son, and Ween 2018, 2).[16] This line of thinking argues that the correct re-sponse to the gathering critiques of the master narrative of domestication is to restrict the word by applying it only to species, times, places, and relations that were the origins of, and helped to entrench and expand, the master narrative of domestication. For instance, Kay Anderson (1997, 473) offers a nuanced account of the intellectual, social, and material histories that shape the "politics of domestication," which provides a sharp critical perspective on the master narratives of domestication. For her, domestica-tion is, by definition, a practice that had rooted within in it the major tenets of the traditional story: "The practice of domesticating animals had em-bedded within it an edifice of ideas surrounding the control, elaboration, and 'improvement' of wildness (into service and products)." Her focus is the history, and the heart, of the master narrative, and she doesn't explic-itly invoke or discuss any of the multispecies relations that exist outside that particular "edifice of ideas."

In contrast, Anna Tsing (2018, 232–33) is explicit in her move to ex-clude a wide range of multispecies relations from the term *domestication*. She argues that the cost of expanding the definition of domestication is twofold: (1) it reduces our ability to understand the "historical force" of certain forms of interspecies dependence and (2) it runs the risk of inflect-ing our understanding of human-nonhuman relations with overtones of "civilization" and "home," regardless of whether they are appropriate. In essence, her intervention is to assert that the master narrative of domes-tication is not merely a trope, but rather a specific historical process that "sets world history into motion." Tsing's framing of domestication as a "progress concept" is a claim, not that the master narrative is built on the wrong trope, but rather that we need to look for how "progress becomes inscribed into interspecies relations."

The minimalists' position highlights the crucial role of the categoriza-tion of people, places, and species as domesticated or wild in shaping the world over the past few centuries (see also Norton 2015). They remind us that the stakes of being wild—and not being human—are often those of life or death. Feral (i.e., domesticated) goats in the Galapagos Islands have been subjected to an extensive and violent eradication campaign to protect the habitats and food sources of the wild species (Bocci 2017; see also Govindrajan 2018). In the regulation of scientific lab work, domesticated animals that are classed as livestock are not subject to the same strict regulations as more charismatic "wild species" like monkeys or domesticated, nonlivestock species like dogs and cats (Sharp 2019, 64).

Anderson traces how domestication, in the narrow sense that she and Tsing are staking out, produced the category of the wild (and its related categories of savage and primitive)—categories that were applied to people during imperial expansion and colonization. The categorization that the minimalists are concerned with is the "history of real people, real power, real practices, and real geographies," not merely intellectual taxonomies (K. Anderson 1997, 475). They draw our attention to the profound ways the domestication ontostory has given shape—through the histories of imperialism, colonialism, industrialization, and modernity—to the contemporary world. At the same time, however, the minimalists remain wedded in certain ways to the temporal suturing of deeper pasts and the present in the original ontostory.

THE PERILS OF FLYOVER HISTORY

The stories that Tsing and K. Anderson tell about world-historical domestication retain the familiar narrative structure that identifies the origins of modernity in a deeper past. They begin with the creation of the *domus* in the Neolithic, and then leap forward in time: Anderson (1997, 471) to the ancient Greeks and Tsing (2018, 240–43) to the roles of rice, sugar, and cattle in the history of states and empires over the past five hundred years. Tsing suggests that the examples of relationships between humans and domesticated plants and animals that she draws from more recent histories can be extended backward in time. This possibility rests on understanding the state as a transhistorical political formation. She writes: "States capitalized on and transformed the political economy of domestication. . . . Relatively recent histories can make the point" (240). Though Tsing does not explicitly make the claim one way or the other, it strikes me as important that her polemic is plotted as a linear historical sequence: from Neolithic origins to historical states and empires, with no stops in between.

I value the ways in which the domestication minimalists take the cosmogonic actions of the domestication ontostory seriously and insist on tracing its terrible, tangible impacts on human and animal lives in more recent history and the contemporary world. Nevertheless, I am skeptical

of the connections these scholars make between the category of domesticated, its role in the history of the last five hundred years or so, and the
much earlier histories of the processes of domestication that produced domesticated herd animals. That they do so is perhaps not surprising. Seeing
a link between the transformation of the relationships between humans and
cattle ten thousand years ago in the valleys and foothills of ancient Mesopotamia and Anatolia and the arrival of cattle in New World after 1492 is
intellectually comfortable. The narrative arc holds the customary shape of
our thought in the way an old pair of jeans holds the shape of one's body,
having been molded through repetition over time.

As I sketched out in the previous section, currently our stories about domestication are caught between the rising chorus of archaeologists—who
are busily recrafting our narratives of pre-Neolithic lifeways and the processes of early domestication, emphasizing mutuality and contingency—
and the tenacity of the "overarching evolutionary trope of the shift from
wild to domestic, from nature to culture" (Boyd 2017, 306). This tension
helps explain the role of one particular archaeological account of early domestication in the work of the domestication minimalists. Both Tsing and
K. Anderson cite Ian Hodder's (1990) book, *The Domestication of Europe*,
which tells the story of domestication as the establishment and evolution
of the *domus*.[17] Hodder examines early domestication in Europe as a social
and symbolic phenomenon rather than a scenario driven by rationality or
utilitarian progress, offering his interpretation of the archaeological evidence from across Europe. In doing so, Hodder (1990, 41) argues that
that the idea of "home," or the *domus* (in contrast to the wild), was both
a potent social metaphor and "the mechanism of change" that led to both
the development of agriculture and the "creation of larger social units."
Hodder's *domus* is simultaneously the space of Neolithic settlements and
homes (diligently excavated by archaeologists) and the symbolic separation of the *domus* and the *agrios* (wild; 1990, 86) beyond. Accordingly,
the categorical separation of wild and domesticated was made real and
durable (as well as archaeologically visible) through Neolithic practices
and material culture.

For scholars like Tsing and K. Anderson, Hodder's *domus* continues to
suture together the history of the process of domestication (as a history of
changing human-animal relationships) and the history of domestication
as a category that divides the domesticated from the wild and the human
from the rest of nature.[18] The story Hodder proposes is not quite the old
master narrative. It abandons the functional explanations and the emphasis
on the protoscientific engineering of nature that marked older ideas about

domestication, while retaining the sense that domestication was a world-historical event. As a result, stories about the *domus* perpetuate what Boyd (2017, 306) diagnoses as the "cryptic structuralism" of many Neolithic transition stories, maintaining a reliance on the coordinates of modern, Western ideas about nature and culture, and about the domesticated and the wild.

Recent archaeological work on early animal and plant domestication has pulled back sharply from the idea that domestication was a process of human mastery. Archaeologists now place much more emphasis on the mutual shaping of relations, contingencies, and unintentional consequences. These new stories about the very earliest domestication practices—describing multiple, experimental processes of creating new ways of living with plants and animals that emerged in various forms about ten thousand years ago—disrupt the straightforward narrative paths that place the origins of the human-animal relations privileged by the master narratives of domestication in the deeper past. The idea of *domus*, and its development out of Neolithic lifeways, makes it possible to reanchor the narrative, allowing it to retain a deeper time origin, at the price of a more restricted narrative horizon and a slightly shallower historical depth.

Not all archaeologists agree with Hodder's story about the *domus* in the Neolithic. It has been critiqued on numerous grounds (e.g., Davis 1992; Halstead 1996; Tringham 1991; see also Pluciennik 2002), and Hodder (1998) himself partially reconsidered the matter in a later paper. This matters because it means that we have good reason to question whether the *domus*, as the foundation of the ontostory of domestication, began in the Neolithic. But more than that, we should be skeptical that all we need to do is trim the Neolithic from the narrative, leaving the latter part of the sequence more or less in place. Yes, the old ontostories came from somewhere. But we must also recognize that identifying them as our inheritance from the ancient Assyrians, Babylonians, Greeks, or Romans conforms to certain narrative expectations. The emplotment of modernity's origins out of the ancient past retains the sense of inevitability, the teleology, that the traditional narratives of domestication trafficked in so effectively. In this way, domestication narratives run parallel to how archaeologists and other scholars have thought about the origins of inequality and political complexity in the past (Graeber and Wengrow 2021). They channel our thinking about human-animal relationships in the deeper past, pushing us to focus on points of similarity (qua continuities) and to ignore the bits of evidence that don't quite fit.

This is not to argue that modernity is a rupture with the past. That would replace one problematic story of modernity's origins with another, equally troubled one. Rather, I am saying we need to treat the stories that claim historical links across large gaps of space and time with a greater intellectual curiosity and a higher evidentiary standard. If nothing else, even if something like the *domus* did emerge in the Neolithic in certain places, that doesn't mean it persisted unchanged (or changed in one direction only). The domestication ontostory obscures how much of our ideas about the long-term history of human-animal relations is shaped by relatively recent, Western ideas about human nature, civilization, and the nature of political life. In effect, it works to naturalize certain questions that emerge from modern concerns, making it hard to ask new questions about the past. Hopefully, a fresh take on how we think about our relationships with cattle, sheep, and goats in the past will help us develop our curiosity and kickstart new ways of telling stories about human-animal relations in the past.

✦ 2 ✦

HERD ANIMALS AND RELATIONS OF USE

"The objectification of animals is not new and can be traced back more than 10,000 years. At this time, humans intervened in, and started to exercise control over, the lives of animals to use them for food. . . . The emergence of 'walking larders' fundamentally altered how people viewed and treated animals."

Rhoda M. Wilkie, **"Animals as Sentient Commodities,"** 2017

Traditional domestication stories pose two major problems for understanding human-animal relations in the past. To start, they reduce large swathes of the past to flyover country. More perniciously, they lead us to ask the wrong questions about the past—questions that narrow how we think about human-animal relations and present history as a teleological trajectory from the past to the present. Domestication stories suggest that *objectification* is the self-evident bridge between human-animal relations in the present and the deeper past. They claim that the formation of new kinds of (instrumental) relations with (objectified) herd animals in the deeper past was a critical ingredient of the development of the modern world—a world indelibly shaped by inequality, hierarchy, and the state. Yet in actuality, this narrative has more to with the events of the last five hundred years than it does with what went on the Neolithic. The concern with objectification has its foundations in ongoing debates within the West about the nature of political order and power.

The question, Are these animals objectified? only makes sense in light of the assumptions encoded in the domestication ontostory—assumptions that prevent us from exploring the full diversity of human-animal relationships postdomestication and premodernity. The objectification of animals is one of the major themes of the traditional story of domestication, and it sounds the strongest note when we think about our relationship with livestock animals. It's not that this question is never appropriate. But it shouldn't be the first one we turn to when contemplating human–herd animal relations in the deeper past. Instead, I draw together anthropological, STS, and archaeological perspectives on human-animal relationships of all kinds (not just involving herd animals or pastoralism), and highlight three themes that shape my inquiry into human–herd animal relationships across the rest of the book: eating and feeding, labor and reproduction, and animals' pre- and postmortem lives.

To challenge objectification as the bridge between human-animal relations in the present and the past, I take up Donna Haraway's (2008) distinction between *objectification* and *relations of use*. Objectification refers to treating animals as nonsubjects, reducing them to the status of things or biological machines and viewing them as "raw material" for human social life (Noske 1993, 185). It rests on the ontological distinction between humans and animals (also subjects/objects, mind/body, nature/culture, and many others). Objectification is indelibly linked to the issue of oppression (cf. Haraway 2008, 74). In contrast, the concept of relations of use gestures at the kinds of instrumental relations between humans and animals that involve labor, use, and killing but do not produce objectification (and don't rest on Cartesian dualisms).[1] Haraway's distinction interrupts the domestication ontostory (along with its claim that the instrumental relations of early domestication are the source for modern forms of objectification)— by insisting that "instrumental relations of people and animals are not themselves the root of turning animals (or people) into dead things, into machines . . . who have no *presence*, no *face*, that demands recognition, caring, and shared pain" (71).

Telling new stories starts with asking new questions: questions about what kinds of potentials there are in human–herd animal relationships. and questions about what might have gone on within the gaps of the flyover histories we've inherited. Every sheep and every shepherd is, in some way, shaped by the histories that connect them back to the early populations of sheep and humans that participated in new forms of relations in the foothills of ancient Mesopotamia and Anatolia. But they're not all connected in the same way, nor can we arrange them in a linear sequence between then and now—not, at least, without ignoring many more interesting stories and connections.

BREAKING DOWN OBJECTIFICATION

The domestication ontostory has its origins in a larger set of philosophical and ethnographic claims about non-European Others that emerged

directly from early modern European debates about order. Michel-Rolph
Trouillot (2003) labeled this conceptual apparatus "the Savage slot." He
argued that the intellectual terrain eventually occupied by anthropology,
the source of the field's *raison d'être*, originally arose from European anx-
ieties about order—both political and ideological. Trouillot's diagnosis
raises two key points for my argument. First, the material-semiotic practices of capitalism, colonialism, and the modern state on the ground ne-
cessitated ideas about order that were universal and absolute, thus lodging
questions about the universal legitimacy of power and its relation to order
in the heart of Western metanarratives. This apparatus provided the foundation for knowledge of the Other, a category that encompassed both contemporary non-Western peoples *and also* Europeans' ideas about the past
(see also Cobb 2005). Second, Western metanarratives drew links between
contemporary issues and the deeper past to bolster the ideological claims
being made and paper over any differences: "Greece did not beget Europe.
Rather Europe claimed Greece" (Trouillot 2003, 21).

Partisan salvos in European debates about the nature and legitimacy of
order naturalized certain ideas about human nature and social life. These,
in turn, have constrained scholars' questions about the past. In a 2021
book, David Graeber and David Wengrow argue that the question, What
is the origin of inequality? only makes sense within a specific Western
metanarrative about the nature of inequality and authority and its historical development—one articulated in the wake of Indigenous critiques of
European societies in the sixteenth and seventeenth centuries. Focusing on
the origin of inequality has excluded other questions we might ask about
the past, but it has also strengthened the teleological claims about the inevitability of the world we live in today. The metamyth of objectification
has produced a similar problem by narrowing our ability to investigate past
human-animal relations.

To rethink humans' relations with herd animals, I start by separating
the concepts that have been knotted together by domestication stories.
Traditional narratives of domestication draw together ideas about property, instrumental relations, and objectification to explain how we got
from *there*—relations with wild animals—to *here*—domesticated livestock
as objectified property in instrumental relations within capitalism. The
concept of objectification slides across multiple analytical frames: property, accumulation and commodities, labor, and making killable. Each
of these frames has their own intellectual histories and assumptions, and
teasing them apart helps to diagnose what ideas are naturalized when we

accept certain teleological framings of the relationship between the present and the past.

Property

Property regimes and the objectification of domesticated animals have been essential to the role of herd animals in colonial expansion and the industrialization of livestock production.[2] The category of property, including how we think about its relationship to the subject/object and human/animal divides, is indelibly shaped by the teleological histories of property that emerged in European thought in the eighteenth and nineteenth centuries, when Europeans used imaginaries of the Other to debate questions about order. One of the questions that concerned them was whether the desire for private property is a virtue or a vice. Contributing to the debate, French and Scottish intellectuals began writing stadial (or conjectural) histories, speculative arguments that crafted a logical sequence of social development centered around property. They depicted a three-stage sequence whereby societies went from hunting (no property), to herding (animals as movable property), and then to agriculture (landed property) (Adam Smith [1672–73] 1978; Blackstone 1803, 3–8; Dalrymple 1757, 86–88; Ferguson 1767, 124; Helvétius 1810, 424–25; Kames 1792, tract 3, 88-156).

Regardless of whether one agrees with Helvétius (1810, 426; see also Kames 1792, 103) that "the preservation of property is the moral divinity of empires" that makes "equity flourish" and that justice "may be reduced to the maintenance of the right of property," the widespread acceptance of stadial histories established a durable teleological trajectory from no property to modern property laws. The sense of historical inevitability this trajectory would acquire is largely a result of the way these conjectural histories "peeled back" features of contemporary ideas about property (Rowley-Conwy 2007, 139). They worked backward from fixed (private) property in land (agricultural fields) to mobile property without landed property (pastoralists' herds), and arrived finally at the conclusion that hunters lacked any conception of property beyond mere possession. In these original formulations, herds emerged as the intermediate step between no property and landed property. The emphasis on pastoralist mobility (and the absence of the attachment to land) comes mainly from this process of working backward, and it resonated with the culturally salient distinction between movable and immovable property. These early accounts are different from nineteenth- and twentieth-century historical narratives because they are not organized directly around production (or the division between foraging and herding or farming). Instead, most of the early stadial theories see pastoralists as truly intermediate, whether judged in terms of private property, hierarchy, or government.

Stadial theories seeded the idea that different features of society interrelated with one another and, above all, with subsistence (Pluciennik 2001). At the same time, they also established the idea that human progress or development could be tracked through the (unidirectional) trajectory between forms of subsistence. In the subsequent history of anthropology and archaeology, this initial sense of interconnections between different aspects of society would be transformed by the emergence of new ideas about social evolution and the major disruptions in European ideas about history and the deeper past provoked by prehistoric archaeology. Despite these upheavals, many of the depictions of hunters and herders in these early texts would remain available to writers as a kind of ethnological and historical common sense, reemerging at regular intervals.

What does it mean to say that herd animals are property? Is it equivalent to saying they are objectified? The short answer is no, not necessarily. The equation of property and objectification in Western thought and legal frameworks is not universal or even monolithic. But perhaps more important is the recognition that the category of property haunts, and is haunted by, both racism and anthropocentrism (both conceptually and in the actual histories of exploitation; see Bhandar 2018). In *Being Property Once Myself*, Joshua Bennett (2020, 1) succinctly characterizes enslaved Black people in the United States and the animals they lived and worked alongside as "twin captives, affixed by modernity's long arc." He explores how the African-American literary tradition envisions animals (and Black people's relations with them) as the promissory source of "a vision of human personhood rooted not in the logics of private property or dominion" (4).

What does the relation between "modern" chattel slavery and "modern" human-animal relations have, if anything, to do with the question of property and human-animal relations in the deeper past? Our ability to answer is constrained by how we understand property and its relationship to the question of domination and the human/nonhuman divide. Owning a chair doesn't generally figure in a lot of ethical quandaries, but both the conceptual possibility and actual instances of owning animals and human beings have been the sites of fierce debates. At the heart of the issue is the idea that ownership properly renders *someone* a *something*. This idea of ownership, of property, stems from a peculiar feature of Roman law, which was later was taken up by Europeans as they shaped their own legal codes. Ownership, in Roman law, was understood as the absolute rights in *rem*—that is to say, things. Crucially, these absolute rights include the right to destroy the thing you own. This sense of ownership underlies the idea that considering animals as property renders them fundamentally killable (sensu Haraway 2008).

Yet the anthropological literature on pastoralist human-animal relations suggests it would be a mistake to equate being property with the absence or denial of personhood (or being killable, as discussed later in the chapter). Both archaeological and ethnographic studies reveal societies where domesticated herd animals were forms of property but not objectified (see, e.g., Armstrong Oma 2010; B. Campbell 2005; Ingold 1988; Orton 2010a). It is precisely this contention that provides the foundation for Ingold's (2011b) much-cited essay, "From Trust to Domination," in which he uses the contrast between trust and domination to sketch out three different kinds of human-animal relationships:

- Hunting: social relationship between human and animal persons based on trust (autonomy and dependency)
- Pastoralism: social relationship between human and animal persons based on domination (social control over subject-persons)
- Ranching: human control of animals as "object-things"

Ingold splits pastoralism off from hunting, but also from the forms of human-animal relationships found in modern, capitalist livestock production. In doing so, he separates the idea of domination from objectification, thus departing from the teleological framework of the domestication ontostory.

Ingold's argument that domestication (as domination) is a form of social relation and not a relation between subject and object specifically invokes human slavery. He suggests that in the ancient slavery-based societies, "the parallel between the domestic animal and the slave appears to be self-evident," and he cites the Roman terms *instrumentum genus vocale* (slaves) and *instrumentum genus semi-vocale* (cattle). He then cites Yukata Tani's (1996) work, which suggests that the castration of slaves (to make them eunuchs) in the Mediterranean derived from the practice of castrating selected male animals and using them as guide-wethers.[3] Tani (1996, 2017) argues that there is distinction, similar to Ingold's distinction between trust and domination, dividing "Western" approaches to animal husbandry from "Eastern" ones, and he argues there is a separate "Siberian-

Mongolian" tradition that maintains the autonomy of animals (both wild and domesticated).

Tani (1996, 406) suggests that Sumerian texts provide evidence of an analogical extension of practices between humans and animals to human subordinates. He further argues that the analogy between humans and animals rests on the existence of a group of humans that stands "over and above both subordinated humans and animals" and refers to that group using the Roman term *dominus*. This brings us back to Roman law codes and the question of slavery. Tani's argument suggests that the Roman equation of cattle and slaves is the outcome of a longer regional history of domination. But there is reason to question this aspect of the argument.[4] Orlando Patterson (1982, 22), in his book *Slavery and Social Death*, argues that the idea of ownership as conferring absolute rights over things was a legal fiction that emerged in Rome *in the wake of needing to deal with the social issue of slavery*. He contends that this fiction was necessary to artificially separate the social relations of slavery from their obvious continuity with the social relations of marriage and other forms of kinship, as "claims and powers vis-à-vis other persons with respect to a given thing, person, or action" (see also Miers and Kopytoff 1977, 12).

Not only does this suggest that property's relation to objectification is an open historical question, this line of investigation also takes us back to the *domus*. Romans' need for the legal fiction of *dominium* emerged from the problems posed by their reliance on slaves as a key form of wealth. But the concept of property and ownership that they developed also reflected the specific characteristics of Roman society—specifically, the idea of the *domus* as a functional, productive unit that was, at least in its ideal form, isolated from the rest of society (Patterson 1982, 29). This underscores that the twining of the house, the family, and taming in the idea of the *domus* in the domestication literature has much less to do with the historical legacy of the Neolithic and much more to do with the specific history of Roman society, politics, and law (see Hodder 1990, 45).

Crucially, what the Roman legal fiction of property as a relationship between person and thing does is sever any relationship between violence and care within the social relation of property (cf. Graeber and Wengrow 2021, 161). The Roman legal fiction of person-thing relations is what allows the domination of the *pater*, who is now able to destroy what belongs to him because he has no obligation to care for it. Accepting the Roman view of property as given—and ignoring the specific historical trajectory of its uptake in later European legal and social ideas about property— obscures what is actually at stake in the unequal relations between people and between people and animals in the past. Just as scholars of human slavery have argued that defining slavery through the idea of property and ownership hinders our ability to understand it both historically and cross-culturally (Patterson 1982; Miers and Kopytoff 1977), it similarly constrains our ability to ask questions about the relationships between care and violence, kinship and exploitation, and domination and freedom in the past, across species lines.

Accumulation

Rousseau's *Discourse on the Origins of Social Inequality* was an attempt to explain, as Graeber and Wengrow (2021, 65) vividly put it, how

> Europeans are able to turn wealth into power; turn a mere unequal distribution of goods—which exists, at least to some degree, in any society—into the ability to tell others what to do, to employ them as servants, workmen, or grenadiers, or simply feel that it was no concern of theirs if they were left dying in a feverish bundle on the street.

The stadial theories that emerged in Europe around the time Rousseau wrote his essay offered one explanation for this—an explanation that would eventually naturalize and universalize both European ideas about private property and also material accumulation. As they sought to explain the development of private property, European writers asserted that the accumulation of material wealth, first in the form of herds and later in landed property, led to social inequality and the need for government. Adam Ferguson's (1767, 124) conjectural history anticipated later developments, inasmuch as he argued that the achievements of so-called civilized societies were driven by the desire to labor (leading to the progressive development of industry) and desire to acquire possessions.

Stadial histories, and the evolutionary narratives of human history that developed from them in the nineteenth century, located pastoralists as the middle term between "civilized" (settled agriculture) and "savage" (mobile hunter-gatherers). Originally, this location hinged on the logic of herds as an intermediate form of property, in between no property at all and landed property. The ordering was retained even as the logical sequence between stages was reimagined as a historical and evolutionary sequence, one that depended primarily on subsistence practices (Pluciennik 2001). However, by the mid-twentieth century, the pastoralist had mutated into a protorational actor, the precursor to economically modern

man (*Homo economicus*). The transformation of the pastoralist into an individual who maximizes reflected the changing nature of the questions about
order animating Western interest in the Other. Rather than defending private property as a virtue of civilization, the new project was to determine
to what extent the rest of the world deviated from the norms defined by
neoclassical economics (Gregory 2015). Pastoralists retained their intermediate position, but in place of the teleological development of property,
the rationality of the self-interested individual was universalized by being
projected backward in anthropological spacetime.

Within the larger teleological progression, humans' relations with domesticated animals became an anthropological shorthand for where their
society fell in the teleological array of political complexity. Societies that
had supposedly "failed" to domesticate animals (see Norton 2015) and
plants were unable to accumulate wealth and thereby develop complex
forms of politics (and persistent inequality). But settled agricultural societies that treated domesticated animals and plants as commodities to be
accumulated through maximizing productivity were capable of becoming
states and empires. Pastoralists were both intermediate and aberrant, assumed to be both poor (incapable of accumulation) and free (lacking permanent forms of inequality) (but see Asad 1978; Sneath 2007 for critiques
of this idea).

Archaeology's focus on surplus production is a reflection of this broader
emphasis on material accumulation as the motor of historical change and
development. The idea that surplus production (and its redistribution) is
the main economic aspect of political power remains common, even among
archaeologists who otherwise disagree on how to study political life in the
past. In part, this reflects the outcome of the importance of surplus production to Western ontostories (e.g., Childe 1951; Sherratt 1981). Thinking
about surplus and accumulation leads to thinking about domesticated animals as resources (or capital) that are incorporated into the larger project of
turning material resources into power (deFrance 2009). But the idea that
animals are the stuff of politics is reinforced by the tendency in traditional
political theory to reduce animals to the category of property, thus centering questions of possession and ownership (Adam T. Smith 2015, 72).
While recent work has begun to explore how animals' symbolic value was
important to political projects in ancient polities (Grossman and Paulette
2020; Arbuckle and McCarty 2014), models of political life that reduce
animals to resources in the past and the present limit our theoretical imaginations (Boyd 2017; Overton and Hamilakis 2013).

Labor

The subsistence fault line created by the teleological accounts of human history written by nineteenth-century evolutionary anthropologists married humans' relationship to animals and plants to Western ideas about (productive) labor. Definitions of labor put forward by Western philosophers simultaneously produced an anthropocentric division between humans and animals via domestication as mastery and separated and ranked humans on the basis of their labor. Locke's (1980) influential definition of labor emphasized the transformation of nonhuman entities through human action and intentionality, linking the development of private property to human labor. Defining labor in this way empowered a dismissive attitude toward the activities of hunters and foragers (Povinelli 1993) and conformed to the domestication ontostory—narrating the inevitability of the increase and expansion of private property through intentional, transformative labor, culminating in capitalist modernity.

While Marx was intensely critical of capitalism and offered a counternarrative to the stadial histories' explanation of property and inequality, his ideas about labor, and many of their subsequent elaborations, were anthropocentric and excluded forms of production, including reproduction, that did not produce material goods. Marx (1977, 284) explicitly identified labor as an "exclusively human characteristic," writing that "what distinguishes the worst architect from the best of bees is that the architect builds the cell in his mind before he constructs it." Feminist critiques have highlighted Marx's failure to consider the "hidden abode" of the household and the domestic and reproductive labor that made capitalist wage work and accumulation possible (Fraser 2014; Weeks 2011). Sylvia Federici's (2021) work demonstrates that the divisions between production and reproduction, public and private, and men and women emerged within the specific history of the transition to capitalism. The Marxian tradition is not alone in excluding reproduction from their understanding of productive activity. Hannah Arendt (1958) makes a tripartite division between labor, work, and action—though her distinction between work and labor differs from Marx's. In Arendt's schema, labor reproduces biological life, work creates the object world around us, and finally, action is political activity (explicitly set off from the other two).

Like the feminist philosopher Kathi Weeks (2011, 15), I find the exclusion of reproduction and production from the political sphere contrary to how I want to think about the political. Not only does the exclusion of reproduction from the conversation about labor stymie our understanding of human political life, it also is a problem for any attempt to build a nonanthropocentric approach to labor. As I discuss in chapter 5, thinking about animals as beings that work expands our ability to think about human-animal relations in productive ways. But it is important to acknowledge that much of the work done by herd animals falls under the heading of reproductive labor. Sociocultural anthropologists have begun to analyze the relationship between animal labor and capitalism in the contemporary world (Barua 2019; Besky and Blanchette 2019; Porcher 2017a). But archaeologists have not yet fully grappled with how to think about animal labor in pre- and noncapitalist pasts (Chazin 2023). To do so, we will have to untangle the ways in which definitions of work and labor contain historical narratives because of their entanglement with Western ideas about property, accumulation, and the histories and ideologies of capitalism.

NEW QUESTIONS TO TELL NEW STORIES

The question, Are these animals objectified? doesn't serve us well. It is too indebted to the domestication ontostory, which muddles together property, accumulation, and instrumental relations while simultaneously alleging a necessary and inevitable historical connection between early animal domestication and modern human-animal relations. Framing the question this way hinders our ability to think about the long-term history of human-animal relations, and political life more generally. Instead we should ask, What kinds of *relations of use* existed between humans and animals in the past? This releases us from the teleology of objectification. It makes it possible to see postdomestication human-animal relations as spaces of potential, not stops on a one-way train to modernity. In doing so, it makes it possible to discover experiments and dead ends, thus opening us up to the potential strangeness of the past.

Moving from objectification to relations of use also changes how we think about the status of killing within humans' relationships with domesticated herd animals. In her exploration of the instrumental relations between humans and laboratory animals, Haraway (2008, 79) distinguishes between killing animals and making animals killable and meditates on the difference between the commandments "Thou shall not kill" and "Thou shall not make killable." The problem for Haraway is that "Thou shall not kill" simultaneously fuels the problematic separation of people and animals into those that can't be killed and those that can, as well as the fantasy of living without any sort of killing at all. "Thou shall not make killable" shifts the moral calculus around death, acknowledging that "eating and killing are an unavoidable fact of the relations that tie together all mortal companion species" (Despret 2016, 85; see also Plumwood 1999).

The idea of making animals killable opens space for me to think about relations of use between humans and herd animals in the past—relations that involved killing without necessarily rendering animals killable (or conforming to the ontologies of contemporary industrial agriculture). The category of livestock suggests relations with animals where killing and eating them doesn't require much in the way of justification. This is often explained by asserting that domestication produces or requires the objectification of animals, allowing the living animal (and its carcass) to be treated as an object and not a subject. If animals are objects, then their killing is an ethical nonevent.

But if we question objectification as a way to organize the history of human–herd animal relations, we can ask instead, When, where, and how were domesticated herd animals made killable? The archaeological record is full of animals that were killed by humans. When the dead animals are domesticated, there is the tendency to assume they were already made killable, which rendered their deaths a nonevent by their ontological categorization. But we shouldn't necessarily assume that domesticated herd animals were objectified even if they were property or involved in relations of use. Instead, we should ask questions about eating and feeding, labor and reproduction, and pre- and postmortem value to investigate the ways in which humans and herd animals worked together in the past and the political stakes of those relations for both humans and animals.

Eating and Feeding

Contemporary anthropology offers at least two models for thinking about relations of use that involve killing animals and using their bodies and do not require the assumption that killing requires objectification or making killable: (1) gift relations between humans and animals and (2) familiarizing predation. I draw the idea of gift relations between humans and animals from ethnographic explorations of Northern peoples' relations with the animals they hunt. Paul Nadasdy (2007) argues that people in Kluane country in the southwest of the Yukon, Canada, have relationships with the animals they hunt that are very much like the relationships of reciprocity among humans that anthropologists call gift exchange. In this exchange, prey species feed human hunters by willingly and consciously giving them their bodies to eat and otherwise use.[5]

Thinking about human-animal relationships as gift exchanges does not imply that the cross-species reciprocity is selfless giving. Giving gifts, whether within or between species, creates social relations that can produce competition, animosity, and hierarchy as well as social integration and equality.[6] The polemical framing of Ingold's (2011a) distinction between trust and domination obscures the possibility of multiple kinds of social relations across species lines within pastoralism (see also B. Campbell 2005). Rather than diagnosing relations as trust or domination, it may be useful to consider how we might attune our investigations to the possibility of different modalities of interpersonal relations across species lines. Emphasizing gift relations rather than trust per se pushes me to consider the dynamics of eating and feeding—the exchange of food as a specific kind of gift exchange—in a much wider frame than the focus on objectification would allow.

By focusing on eating and feeding, I also find entry into the other model for relations of use: familiarizing predation, which has emerged out of recent ethnographic and historical scholarship about hunting peoples in Amazonia (Vivieros de Castro 1998; Fausto 2007; Descola 2013; Kohn 2013; Weismantel 2015). Anthropologists and historians argue that for some people in South America, predation is a form of relations between humans and animals—one that is fundamentally social (see Fausto 2007, 500).[7] It is crucial that, in these societies, human beings are not the only persons and that they can be both predator and prey (depending on the context, or rather, the outcome of relations and encounters between human and nonhuman beings).[8] Hunting is merely one form within a wider set of predatory relationships between human and nonhuman persons. Fausto categorizes these relationships as familiarizing predation, which consists of a set of practices that work to incorporate humans and nonhuman others as kin. A key component of the model is the idea that eating is both a risky and a consequential act. Feeding is an important part of making kin—both within and across species (Fausto 2007; Strathern 2012; Fausto and Costa 2013; Norton 2015). Fausto (2007, 503) also draws a distinction between "eating and sharing food in order to produce kinship" and "eating as a way of identifying with what is eaten," two practices that are at odds because of the susceptibility of persons to other persons' agentive capacities.[9]

What I take from these discussions is the intuition that thinking differently about feeding and eating would shake up our assumptions. Doing so interrupts the binary oppositions between modern/nonmodern, traditional/industrial, subsistence/intensive production, and animals as persons/animals as objects that shape much of our analysis of human–herd animal relationships.[10] Thinking about feeding and eating focuses analytical attention on the importance of practices of care in shaping human–herd animal relationships (cf. Sykes 2014, 30–31).[11] Recent ethnographic works have richly detailed the world-making nature of the difficult relationships of care—with their life and death stakes—between humans and livestock (Blanchette 2020; Bocci 2017; B. Campbell 2005; Govindrajan 2018).

The archaeology of human–herd animal relationships, as well as the tools of zooarchaeology, have a tendency to emphasize the ways in which herds feed humans. When archaeologists do consider how humans feed herds, the act is often taken as evidence of increased human control or couched in functionalist or economistic frameworks that emphasize the economic efficiency of certain forms of husbandry (see chapters 5 and 6). For studies of pastoralism specifically, feeding is often reduced to the question of pasture availability as a variable shaping mobility practices. In my own work, isotopic analyses revealed previously unknown details of what herds ate and how they were fed in the South Caucasus during the Late Bronze Age. These methods made it possible to learn about foddering practices and other forms of care that were previously invisible in the archaeological record. They provided the foundation that allowed me to address how relations across species lines were being made and unmade through feeding and eating herd animals.

Labor and Reproduction

Livestock work for us, but we also work for them. This is perhaps most easily seen in the intimate relations of care seen in ethnographic accounts of human–herd animal relationships somewhat outside capitalist (or at least industrial) forms of agriculture. But ethnographic work on industrial livestock also highlights the fact that humans labor for and alongside herd animals. Human labor that maintains the reproduction and labor of animals in industrial agriculture is unevenly distributed (geographically and by employment type), and in many ways, it is well hidden in contemporary life (Blanchette 2018, 2020). Within and beyond capitalism, human and herd animal labor cocreate each other's social and material reproduction.

Anthropologists and archaeologists have developed analytical tools to think about the relationship between labor and reproduction in pastoralist practices. These methods help us examine the differences between intensive and extensive herding systems, various forms of pastoralist mobility, and production systems oriented toward different products like meat, milk, and wool. But these tools are formulated in ways that tacitly assume the objectification of animals, bypassing the question of what kind of property or kin herd animals might be. I want to develop the understanding that the arrangements of labor and reproduction in pastoralism matter by using other ways of thinking about human–herd animal relationships, ones that more explicitly articulate the focus on labor and reproduction.

Herd animals' labor necessarily encompasses reproduction. While reproductive labor is not the only kind of labor herd animals do, it is a foundational part of both cohabitation and care across species lines *and* in relations of use. There are strong resonances between thinking about animals as doing work and feminist scholars' focus on the devaluation of human reproductive or maintenance labor (cf. Battistoni 2017, 20; see also Montón-Subías and Sánchez Romero 2008; Weeks 2011; Fraser 2014). If "women's work" is traditionally isolated from, and obscured by, theories of labor that prioritized and overvalued production for the market or the public sphere, then the reproductive labor of herd animals is doubly obscured. Not only are herd animals reduced to background conditions through the category of natural resources, but the importance of herd animals in sustaining everyday forms of human life is also devalued. Starting from the position that herd animals work—because of the obvious primacy of reproductive labor—makes it much harder to assume that the biological-social reproduction of animals, let alone that of humans, is outside either labor or politics.

Returning to the idea that what matters when we think about property is not so much ownership, but instead complex social relations between persons (not necessarily limited to humans), then focusing on labor and reproduction makes it possible to investigate the relationship between care and violence in new ways (cf. Graeber and Wengrow 2021). Here I draw on Nerissa Russell's (2007) suggestion that the "new kinship" theory in anthropology offers a useful way of thinking about domestication. There is a powerful homology, if not an outright identity, between the ways kinship mixes (and produces) what we think of as society and nature in complex ways and the interrelation of material and social reproduction of both humans and herd animals. The material aspects of reproduction, diet, ethology, and ecology do matter, but they are not necessarily determinative, nor are they in a determined relation to social life. Kinship also gives models and examples for the different ways human–herd animal relations might mix intimacy, power, and forms of property relations. Herd animals offer an especially interesting case for thinking about feminist scholarship's critique of the distinction drawn between production and reproduction in economic and political theory.

Thinking about labor and reproduction also changes how we think about the politics of work—and the question of domination—across species lines. In her book, *The Problem with Work*, Weeks (2011) argues that in contemporary society (and contemporary political theory), it is hard to see and talk about the politics of work for reasons similar to why it can be hard to see and talk about the politics of domestic life. She attributes the relative invisibility of politics in these domains to old ideas about property (and its relation to politics) and our insistence that work and domestic life are sites of individual relations rather than collective experiences. Weeks's argument is concerned with the specific problems of contemporary work. Her critique goes beyond decrying the exploitation of waged labor under capitalism and joins other antiwork and antiproductivist thinkers in their suspicion of the general reification of (unalienated) labor in Western thought. These scholars argue that seeing labor as the fundamental and transhistorical feature of humanity reproduces, rather than challenges, the ideologies of capitalism (e.g., Baudrillard 1975; Tronti 1979; Weeks 2011). In this line of thinking, the question of domination comes to the forefront of the discussion of work and labor—which in turn, intersects with the question of the relation between domestication and domination. As Naisargi Dave (2019) argues, when thinking about animal work, we must also consider the refusal to work (see also Despret 2015).

What does this critique imply for thinking about animal and human labor and work outside capitalism? Do the arguments of Weeks and Dave about the necessary relation between work and domination hold for pre- and noncapitalist times and places and for any kind of reproductive labor undertaken by domesticated herd animals? Weeks argues that to think clearly about the politics of contemporary work, we need to attend to the ways through which work, in addition to producing stuff, also produces social and political subjects. She focuses on the ways in which our working lives are key terrains for both gender relations and the experience of domination, and what that means for politics. As I discuss in the next chapter, archaeologists should also attend to the important role of labor in shaping the political life, beyond its production of material goods. But the claim that doing things produces relations and persons (subjects) holds true even when doing things doesn't resemble productive activity (Povinelli 1993). It is, in fact, the basic premise of performativity—which I use as the foundation for my approach to thinking about the political possibilities of human–herd animal relations (chapter 3).

But where does that leave us with regard to the question of domination and that of its relation to labor in human-animal relations in the past? To address this issue, we need to focus on the difference between labor-as-activity and labor-as-domination. By labor-as-activity, I mean the wide range of activities or tasks that create historically specific forms of value and shape social persons through relations. The concept of labor-as-activity organically reunites production and reproduction and holds much potential for a nonanthropocentric approach to labor. It also refuses teleological narratives about production (cf. Baudrillard 1975). Nevertheless, taking the antiwork critique seriously means that in addition to this expansive view of labor, we must also look at labor-as-domination, which focuses our analytical attention on the question, What forms of work reproduced (or transformed) what kinds of domination (or power or authority) in the past? Of course, it is crucial that we avoid putting labor-as-domination in an *a priori* relationship with modernity or capitalism (Chazin 2023).

The relationship between human and herd-animal labor varies across time and space. It is probably best understood as a spectrum of variation; one where the labor required to grow animals—which, in turn, makes both herd and human reproduction possible—is variously apportioned and channeled. Herding can be extensive or intensive; it can be oriented toward producing meat or secondary products. These labels point to different arrangements of human and animal labor, defined not so much by requiring more or less input of human labor or allowing for more or less efficient production, but by different choreographies of human and animal effort in time and space. Foddering gives an example of how this approach might change interpretations of human-animal relationships in the past. Rather than thinking about feeding animals as emblematic of the human control involved in domestication, my approach takes feeding as a site for negotiation between animals' labor and humans' appropriation.

The relations of eating and feeding that I highlighted in the previous section can be thought of as the foundation of human–herd animal relationships. Herders rely on herds for their own social and material reproduction and are also responsible for a broad array of labors of caring that foster herds' social and material reproduction.[12] The default imaginary of pastoralism in Eurasia emphasizes grazing on pasture, seeing it as the impetus for mobility, the explanation for pastoralists' "marginal" location, and evidence of the lack of a certain form of human control. Yet in reality, even highly mobile pastoralists may also provide food to animals through a variety of foddering practices. Shifting our perspective, we might think about foddering as a transfer of some form of labor from herd animals themselves to human beings. Foddering can be connected to forms of pastoralism that involve more day-to-day interactions between herds and herders. This labor on behalf of nonhuman others can produce deeply intimate forms of relating and care (B. Campbell 2005; Armstrong Oma 2010; Govindrajan 2018).

Yet feeding doesn't always create relations of intimacy or kinship between humans and herd animals. Feeding has also been a key part of the intensification of production in commoditized agriculture. Within the context of industrialized agricultural production, providing specialized feed is meant to enhance efficiency and productivity by engineering animals into ideal forms (e.g., Lien 2015). Labor is shifted from animals to humans and technology (fertilizers, tractors, factories): for example, high-protein feeds in intensive dairy production (DuPuis 2002, 137; Smith-Howard 2014, 112–14) and the use of barley to finish calves for beef production (Wilkie 2010).

The contrast between the stories we might tell about feeding herd animals opens up new questions. When thinking about human–herd animal relations in the past, we should ask how shifting labor from animals onto humans or shifting the types of labor required from humans and herds might have impacted both human-animal and human-human relations. Making this shift in my own analysis of the expansion of sheep birth seasonality revealed the complexity of labor practices in the Late Bronze Age South Caucasus, which were shaped by the labor of both humans and animals. It reframed the political stakes of milk production, moving them away from accumulation and toward the performative enactment of political authority and belonging.

Pre- and Postmortem Lives

Thinking broadly about eating and feeding also leads me to focus on the pre- and postmortem lives of herd animals. One of the key insights I've drawn from the anthropological and archaeological literatures on pastoralism is the idea that herd animals are simultaneously *objects of* and *producers of* value. Human–herd animal relationships are shaped by this tension, and prior archaeological and ethnographic work suggests ways in which we might look for it in the archaeological record. But my sensibilities and experiences as a zooarchaeologist—whose investigation of human–herd animal relationships begins with the physical remains of dead animals— led me to expand on that insight by explicitly tracing the connections between the pre- and postmortem value of herd animals and the pre- and postmortem itineraries of herd animals' bodies. This approach makes explicit the long-standing, implicit work across life and death histories that is common in zooarchaeological practice and interpretation.[13] Using a combination of zooarchaeological and isotopic data to examine life and death histories enables me to consider the importance of the materiality of herd animals' bodies.

Ethnographers and archaeologists have a long history of attending to the ways in which herd animals' bodily materiality and ethological proclivities shape human–herd animal relationships, and also humans' relationships with each other. Perhaps the earliest instance of this analytical attention is the recognition of the immense value placed by African cattle pastoralists on living animals themselves rather than on those animals' capacity to produce meat or other resources. Viewed through European categories and values, the emphasis on large herds in many pastoralist societies looked irrational—it appeared alternately as waste, inefficiency, or the ur-form of the tragedy of the commons. Ethnographic work challenged that view, seeking to account for the kinds of value embodied by living animals (and their difference from monetary or market value). Out of this scholarship emerged the insight that the circulation of living animals created and sustained different kinds of social relationships from those forged through the circulation of dead animals (e.g., Hall 1986; Ingold 1988; Reid 1996).

Meanwhile, zooarchaeologists were also paying attention to the materialities and ethologies of herds as they attempted to interpret the information provided by the archaeological analysis of animal bones. Drawing on the fact that fewer males are needed for the demographic reproduction of herds, they argued that the early slaughter of males represented more intensive, efficient forms of production that were linked to the needs for animal resources of political elites and state bureaucracies (Crabtree 1990). Models assessed the relative transportability and perishability of pastoralist products like meat, milk, and wool, arguing that wool and meat on the hoof were much more suitable than milk for paying tribute or centralized redistribution (Wapnish and Hesse 1988; Wattenmaker 1998; Zeder 1988). Different parts of the body were assessed for the amount of meat or marrow they carried and how they might have been processed during butchery to account for the differential distribution of body parts in archaeological sites. Zooarchaeologists also paid close attention to the ethological differences between cattle, sheep, and goats: their mobility, need for pasture and water, relative fecundity, meat and milk yields, ability to cope with drought and other stressors, and so on. They wove these factors into interpretations that explained the relative success or failure of the centralized control of economic activities, the emergence of intensified production of meat or wool in what they termed "complex" societies, and the relative

balance of power between bureaucrats in urban centers and nomadic pastoralists on the margins of ancient city-states (e.g., Arbuckle 2012; Wapnish and Hesse 1988; Zeder 1991).

Although these interpretations differ in their historical contexts and
animating assumptions, when taken together, they underline the importance of tracking human–herd animal relationships across the boundary
between life and death. They also suggest ways in which the materiality
and ethological proclivities of domesticated herd animals shape, without
necessarily determining, the terrain of human–herd animal interactions.
Living animals represent the possibility of future wealth and social action,
as well as the capacity to materialize and perpetuate social ties between
people through time and space. Postmortem, animal bodies became food
and other materials, which were useful for growing human bodies, forging
social relationships, and enshrining hierarchies. Zooarchaeologists have the
tools to consider these questions because they have always been deeply
attuned to the ethological and material specificity of animals. Our ideas
about the differences between animals of different species, sexes, and ages;
between the material properties of milk, meat, and wool; and between
the different parts of the body are all useful to help us understand how
the value of living and dead animals shaped production, circulation, and
consumption in the past.

But we need to change our assumptions about the rationality of production and the division between subsistence production, viewed as inefficient, conservative, and small-scale, and intensive animal economies,
which are viewed as efficient and linked to political complexity. That division replicates the logics of stories linking early domestication to the emergence of industrial agriculture, which obscure more than they illuminate
(Porcher 2017b). Asking new questions about herd animals' life and death
histories is a step toward telling different stories about human–herd animal relationships. Thinking about pre- and postmortem value expansively
and creatively allows me to consider practices and activities in the Late
Bronze Age South Caucasus—activities that would normally fall under
the category of production—in a new way. Working outside the teleological accounts that necessarily link political authority to the accumulation
of material goods reveals practices that trafficked in the different values of
living and dead animals without assuming how they were valued.

These new themes, and the new questions they raise, challenge the
central assumptions of the old ontostory of domestication, which presumed
that domestication was the origin of the instrumental relations with herd
animals and that those relations were either the seed of civilizational prog-

ress or the first step toward the problems of contemporary life. The temporal structure of this story, along with the relationship it asserts between the past and present, hinders our ability to explore the long-term history of human–herd animal relations. In contrast, thinking about relations of use pushes us to consider how living with herd animals is one part of the larger political struggle over value—not merely to accumulate it, but to define what value is and how it should shape the lives we lead (Graeber 2013; Munn 1992). But to fulfill that promise, we also need to transform how we think about politics.

• 3 •

HOW TO DO THINGS WITH HERDS

The title of this chapter, "How to Do Things with Herds," is a tongue-in-cheek reference to the book *How to Do Things with Words* (Austin 1975), in which J. L. Austin played with the commonsense distinction between speaking and doing by exploring how some speech acts actually do things in the world. In substituting *herds* for *words*, I am questioning the commonsense idea that herd animals and their relationships with humans are peripheral or secondary to human politics. But what does it mean to do things with herds? Is it to wield them as a tool or a weapon? Or is it to work together with them, the way we might "do something" with another person? Even in reference to human-human relationships, "doing something" with someone (at least in English) is ambiguous.

To investigate how living with herds shaped political life, we need a way around the difficulty that political theory has in seeing animals as political actors (Donaldson and Kymlicka 2017). Many approaches leave little space for animals as participants. Either nonhumans—animals, but also objects, landscapes, and so forth—are excluded as immaterial to politics or they are reduced to the merely economic.[1] Traditionally, when not excluded entirely, herd animals entered political theory as property or resources, which rendered them the stuff of politics. While archaeologists are increasingly willing to consider (and incorporate) the idea that animals might be useful to political projects because of their symbolic value (Arbuckle and McCarty 2014; Grossman and Paulette 2020), the view of animals as economic and symbolic resources continues to limit how we envision the political possibilities of living with herds (Boyd 2017; Overton and Hamilakis 2013).

Moving beyond this limitation requires a different way of thinking about politics, one that enhances our capacity to consider how animals are part of political life. An anthropological approach to value offers one route forward. Two key points form the foundation of this approach. First, it starts from the premise that politics can be broadly understood as "the struggle to establish what value is" (Graeber 2001, 88)—encompassing the accumulation of value, but also the conflict between and convergence of different forms of value and different projects to create and control it in social life (Munn 1992; Graeber 2013). It is important that value is not merely economic value (cash or calories) but also encompasses "all those creative actions whereby we shape and reshape the world around us, our-selves, and especially each other" (Graeber 2013, 223).[2]

When thinking specifically about domesticated herd animals, we need tools capable of tracing how herd animals are simultaneously objects of value and producers (or creators) of it. Keeping both in our analytical sights necessitates a sense of political life that encompasses both *accumulation*, the political impact of the value produced by herds, and *labor*, the political impact of herds as they create value. Other scholars have considered how including animals in the analysis changes how we think about categories like commodities, capital, and biopolitics under capitalism and in contemporary life (e.g., Haraway 2008; Saha 2017; Shukin 2009). For precapitalist and noncapitalist times and places, we need tools to investigate the practices that generated, circulated, transformed, and accumulated values in the past, tools that aren't forged from business-as-usual, teleological stories about the premodern origins of labor and accumulation under capitalism (see chapter 2).

Rather than measuring ancient politics with a modern ruler—matching archaeological evidence to models derived from political theory tied to the modern nation-state, sovereignty, or biopolitics—archaeologists would be better served by developing our capacities to look for and describe the ordering practices that produced political orders in the past. To abandon the limiting teleologies of Western ontostories, we need analytical frameworks that help reveal their diversity. Performativity theory, as developed in the work of Karen Barad (2003, 2006) and Judith Butler (2006, 2015), has a great deal of potential to assist in this particular task.[3] The concept of performativity emerged from scholars' engagement with Austin's examination of "performative utterances" ("doing things with words"), which coalesced into a broader theoretical approach, which accounts for how performative actions create the "social facticity" of social worlds and subjectivities (Nakassis 2012, 625). Performativity enables scholars to account for the material-semiotic, historical, and power-laden nature of social life. In doing so, it provides a path toward thinking about animals as taking part in political life—as something other than symbolic or economic resources.[4] I supplement the open-ended framework of performativity with a flexible and expansive approach to the basic parameters of political life, defining politics as: (1) practices that construct social groups and subjectivities, producing both belonging and exclusion (*relations of affiliation-distinction*) and (2) practices that shape how some people are enabled to control the actions of others and create relations between ruler and ruled (*relations of authorization-subjection*).

THE BASIC FRAMEWORK

What I mean by *a performative approach to politics* is the idea that the relations between members of a political community and between rulers and ruled fundamentally emerge out of forms of "iterated doing" (Barad 2006, 57). This approach envisions the political as ordering practices that produce what we commonly think of as political orders.[5] The human relations and identities central to definitions of the political—membership in or exclusion from a political community, the roles of leaders and subjects—come into being and transform through the historical unfolding of the material-semiotic processes of social life. Crucially, as Karen Barad's (2003, 2006) work highlights, these performative processes are elaborate assemblings of materials, persons, animals, spaces, and discourses (Chazin 2016a). I am drawn to a performative approach because it emphasizes the possibility (and the necessity) of thinking about politics in a way that can account for the material and semiotic aspects of social life concurrently.

Performativity is not the only possible way to chart a path that doesn't divide between the material and the discursive. Assemblage theory and Peircean semiotics are other routes taken by scholars in archaeology (e.g., Crellin et al. 2020; Crossland 2014; Hamilakis and Jones 2017; C. Watts 2008). However, a performative approach has certain advantages for thinking about politics in particular. First, performativity gives us clear language to describe how power and authority emerge from practices that are intrinsically material and semiotic, without falling back on the idea that the material either merely encodes or is inscribed with human social relations (Joyce 2015b) or that it masks or hides human relationships of exploitation and domination (Kosiba 2020, 16). Second, performativity's insistence that relations and roles emerge from practices foregrounds the generative (and not merely the repressive) nature of power, avoiding a simplistic distinction between "power over" and "power to" when think-ing about political life in the deeper past. Finally, a performative approach makes it possible to analyze how the practices that shape political life si-multaneously generate and transform both the context of political life (the political order) *and* the participants' subjectivities (Nakassis 2012, 625).

Performativity offers a model for thinking about how politics *works*—about how political life emerges in the doing of politics. It is especially well suited to thinking expansively about the politics of everyday life. But the breadth of the analytical framework fits awkwardly with the way po-litical theory tends to think about politics, namely, as a specific domain of social life or certain types of properly political relationships. Thus, it is also necessary to establish how I frame the political. I define politics as the set of multiscalar and interwoven relations of affiliation-distinction and authorization-subjection. Thinking metaphorically, we could consider relations of authorization-subjection as the warp threads and relations of affiliation-distinction as the weft threads, which together form the fabric of political life through their interrelation. This metaphor highlights the ways in which the political comprises both sets of relations simultaneously and also that the qualities of the political fabric emerge from the rela-tionships between them (as well as from the characteristics of the threads themselves).

Using the analytical framework of relations of affiliation-distinction and relations of authorization-subjection focuses our attention on differ-ent aspects of what is generally encompassed by the political. The pair *affiliation-distinction* points to the ways that groups, social identities and subjectivities, communities, and publics are shaped by whom they include and whom they exclude, as well as the ways people within groups are made similar or rendered distinct. Crucially, political groups, communities, and publics are not categories that we can take for granted within our analysis. Rather, they emerge through performative practices that generate both affiliation and distinction. The pair *authorization-subjection* points to the ways in which people are differently empowered. This does not happen through membership in static categories, but through performative activity that creates and maintains the relationships between ruler and ruled (and the categories of ruler and ruled).

I draw these two pairs of relations, authorization-subjection and affiliation-distinction, from my reading of recent approaches to politics in archaeological thought.[6] This literature is primarily concerned with human-human relations, though the definition of politics is often paired with other theories that propose a more active, central, or even agentive role for material things in political life (Honeychurch 2015; Johansen and Bauer 2011; Adam T. Smith 2015). I start from the premise that nonhumans (both inanimate and animate) are key to performatively creating and maintaining these relations between humans, but also that herd animals themselves were in relations of affiliation-distinction and authorization-subjection as well.

AFFILIATION-DISTINCTION ACROSS SPECIES LINES

Thinking performatively about relations of affiliation-distinction focuses analytical attention on the ordering practices that produce political and social orders through the material-semiotic practices that include and exclude. These ordering practices are not limited to the human—they can and do create politically salient relations across species lines. Animals can be crucial participants in the relations of affiliation-distinction that play a key role in producing, challenging, and transforming political life. For example, Radhika Govindrajan's (2018) ethnographic work in Kumaon, in Uttarakhand, India, shows how cross-species relations between humans and cows are simultaneously key to national political projects of cow-protection and violent Hindu nationalism and also the source of the local resistances to that project and its failures.

Local distinctions between those who live in the mountains (*pahari*) and those from elsewhere draws together some humans and some animals while excluding others. The term *pahari* encompasses the humans *and* the animals that emerge from, and are enmeshed in, the more-than-human social worlds of the mountains. But not all cows in Kumaon are *pahari* cows. Other cows, which are descended from the cross-breeding of local breeds with Jersey cows (as part of development projects to expand milk production in rural areas), are excluded from the category. The exclusion of these cows is not a simple mapping of a semiotic category onto the passive bodies of cows. Rather, the salient material-semiotic distinction between *pahari* and non-*pahari* emerged from villagers' everyday experiences of living with, working with, and caring for both kinds of cattle.

The difference of Jersey cows was constituted through and experienced in everyday interactions. Their foreignness was evident in their different manner of conception (artificial insemination through state programs), the different rhythm of their walk, their preference for manufactured livestock feed over local plants, their increased levels of milk production, the "watery-ness" of their milk (and urine and dung), and their gentleness (in contrast to the "quarrelsome" *pahari* cows). In addition to the embod-

ied difference of Jersey cows, Govindrajan (2018, 85) emphasizes that the
kinship between villagers in Kumaon and their *pahari* cows was materialized through everyday experiences, including rituals using the cows' milk,
dung, and urine. Villagers formed loving relations built through daily acts
of caring labor with both *pahari* and non-*pahari* cows, but while Jersey
cows were considered "good cows," they were also generally understood
to be "spiritually effete."

It is this difference in cows' ability to be effective participants in ritual
acts through their skilled participation and production of ritually efficacious bodily substances, and thereby, members of a more-than-human
community, that lies at the heart of their deep impact on political life. The
material differences between local cows and foreign Jersey cows also mat-
tered to people involved in national campaigns for cow-protection, projects
deeply connected to exclusionary Hindu nationalist politics. They maintained that the local, *pahari* cows were uniquely capable of producing the
milk that was, in turn, responsible for the physical and moral health of the
(exclusionary) Hindu nation. Yet when it came to the question of slaughter, the distinction between local and foreign cows was displaced. Jersey
cows were included in the nation in need of protection from foreign bodies
while non-Hindu citizens were excluded from the nation (defined as cow-
mothers and cow-protectors) and subjected to violence.[7]

Despite the legal bans and violence against those suspected of being
cow-killers, people in Kumaon continued to send economically nonproductive cows to be slaughtered. While others explain this by citing the
economic difficulty of supporting large numbers of nonproductive cattle
in poor rural areas, Govindrajan (2018, 89) highlights the tension between
nationalist claims and villagers' lived experiences of bovine difference:

> The distinctiveness of different bovine bodies matters a great deal to those
> villagers who are called on, in the law and in the discourse of *gau-rakshaks*
> [cow-protectors], to unquestioningly accept kinship with cows at large. For
> them, to be related to a pahari cow is a materially, symbolically, and affec-
> tively singular experience that cannot be replicated in the connection they
> share with Jersey cows.

But the moral and legal debates around slaughter were not the only way
in which cows are salient actors in politics in Uttarakhand. Jersey cows'
lack of ritual power was part of the reshaping of local commensal politics between castes. Ritually powerful milk from local cows, which was so
deeply connected to the moral and physical health of the people who con-

sumed it, was also understood to impact the health of cows as well. Milk from those cows was not served to people of the lower castes because doing so was thought to endanger the health of the cow. Lower-caste guests would be served tea made with packaged milk, a much-resented form of caste "humiliation" (Govindrajan 2018, 88). However, the arrival of Jersey cows changed the situation in more ways than one. Jersey cows' lack of ritual power precluded their use in rituals. But it was precisely the lack of connection between the Jersey cows and the person who consumed their milk that made it safe to sell to dairies, where it might be consumed by a distant, unknown customer who could be of any caste or religion. This lack of connection also meant that higher-caste villagers would serve fresh milk from their Jersey cows to lower-caste visitors, thus transforming the micropolitics of caste between neighbors.

Distinctions across Scales

What emerges from Govindrajan's depiction of the complexities of relations between people and cows in contemporary Uttarakhand is the way in which the ordering practices producing political life are necessarily complex, but also *multiscalar*. In that example, the inclusion of certain cows within the logics of the cow-mother and cow-protection, as part of the political project of Hindu nationalism, shifted depending on the context and the particular political issue at stake. The exclusion of Jersey cows from some cow-protection practices and inclusion in others should not be read as a "careless confusion nor a regrettable inconsistency" (Gal 2002, 77). Rather, it highlights the important role of the movement of relations of affiliation-distinction across scales in shaping politics.

This movement across scales does a particular kind of political work. The shifting distinction between cows that are included and those that are excluded from the project of Hindu nationalism—moving from the connection between the moral and physical health of the individual milk drinker and the individual cow providing the milk to the claim that any cow's death threatens the nation—highlights the relative nature of these positions. As the distinction moves across scales, Jersey cows are outside the relevant moral-political community relative to the discourse about the superiority of *pahari* cows but inside it when juxtaposed with non–upper-caste or non-Hindu citizens accused of cow-slaughter and beef consumption. The shifting nature of these divisions is an example of the powerful semiotic process of *fractal recursion* (Gal 2002, 81).[8] As distinctions shift between scales, calibrating the relative position of people, animals, objects, "activities, identities, institutions, spaces and interactions," they collapse into one another, naturalizing them and allowing them to disappear from notice (91).

In addition to helping account for the way in which relations of affiliation-distinction structure political life, the concept of fractal recursion also highlights an important methodological point for understanding human-animal relations in the past. Gal (2002, 85) notes that social science theory also participates in the process of fractal recursion around the public/private divide, mistaking "fractal embeddings" for "reified 'objects' of the social world that seem solid and distinct." The same can be said of the categorical distinction between wild and domesticated. Kerry Harris and Yannis Hamilakis's (2014) discussion of the multispecies colonization of Crete in the Neolithic period highlights the problems caused by retrojecting the contemporary distinction between domesticated and wild into the past. When humans voyaged to Crete from the mainland, around 7000 BCE, they were accompanied by a range of animals, some considered "domesticated" and some considered "wild." Affixing these labels to the animals recovered from archaeological contexts is commonplace, but it immediately raises a number of intellectual issues. The division of taxa into these two categories simultaneously reflects their ongoing salience for zooarchaeological practice *and* also the different histories of these animals prior to their arrival on Crete. Yet as Harris and Hamilakis note, the practice of transporting deer and other wild animals in close quarters with people challenges typical definitions of "wild."

When archaeologists consider what happened on Crete after its colonization, the accepted categories of domesticated and wild collapse and erase meaningful differences between the evidence of the kinds of relations people have with cattle, goats, and deer. Harris and Hamilakis (2014, 108) suggest that managed interactions with "wild" fallow deer may have been part of the larger project of participating in a wider Mediterranean ecumene by facilitating local political strategies. They consider zooarchaeological evidence that some domesticated cattle were specifically bred to be larger (and perhaps more aggressive) to be used in bull-leaping performances. They draw a parallel between hunting agrimi (feral descendants of the domesticated goats that were first brought to the island) in the wider landscape and the evidence for spectacular interactions with large bulls:

By referencing hunting thus, these bull-leaping performances would have temporarily produced a heterotopic locus, a space of wilderness structured by ancestral and genealogical time. If bull-leaping is a ritualized performance of bull-hunting, it references and cites earlier, originary times, perhaps the times of the first colonization of Crete. As Knossos is one of the earliest sites occupied by the first, Neolithic settlers on Crete, this may go some way to explaining the apparent long-standing significance of cattle for this particular site. Indeed, the emergence of the monumental "palaces" of Crete, such as the one at Knossos, celebrated and materialized history (Hamilakis 2013). They were established at these specific locales because of their long occupation, and thus their ancestral and genealogical weight, and the equally long history of embodied and sensorial performances, including the rituals of commensality.

As this example from Crete shows, archaeologists need to be careful that we are not reifying distinctions in our interpretations of archaeological evidence because they seem natural to us, given the socially salient ideas about the difference between domesticated and wild animals in contemporary society. Instead, we should strive for approaches that help us see instances of locally salient and historically significant forms of fractal recursion in the past.

FELICITOUS AUTHORITY

Relations of affiliation-distinction help orient us to the way political groups are brought into being. But this framework needs to be complemented by an analysis of the ways in which individuals and groups—as well as various kinds of nonhumans—are differently empowered to "do things." Through the elaborate assembling of people, materials, animals, spaces, discourses, landscapes, and so forth, the "iterated doings" (Barad 2006) of political life call into being the relations between rulers and ruled— relations that are simultaneously those of affiliation-distinction and of authorization-subjection. Relations that authorize people and practices weave together power and legitimacy (Adam T. Smith 2003). Approaching authority as grounded in relations emerging from performative actions retains the important insight that authority is relational in nature, rather than a characteristic or power possessed by individuals (Crumley and Marquardt 1987, 610; Fleisher and Wynne-Jones 2010; O'Donovan 2002, 20). In addition to avoiding the reduction of legitimacy to a quality or status of individual humans (something they possess), we also must avoid thinking about legitimacy as residing merely within human-human relations of authorization-subjection.

So how to incorporate animals in our understanding of authority? We can do so by attending to the way herd animals contribute to the success (and sometimes the failure) of practices that produce authorization and subjection. That is to say, we should attend to how people successfully did things with herds. To do this, I need to rework the concept of felicity—borrowing it from Austin's *How to Do Things with Words* (1975, 89)—by insisting that felicitous authority is necessarily material, emplaced, and embodied. *Felicity* was originally used to describe the success (or failure) of the subset of speech acts that have the force of actions themselves, rather than merely describing actions.[9] Austin was primarily interested in words, but he noted that these words need help to achieve success. In his example of a judge pronouncing a verdict, the performative force of the statement relies on many other things beyond the judge's speech act. It requires proper clothing (a robe, not a bathing suit), the proper setting (in a courtroom, at the bench), and the successful completion of various statements, cross-examination, the introduction of evidence and witnesses, questioning, and so forth (all of which entail their own required materials, actions, etc.).

Felicity, as I am using the term, refers to practices and relations that are politically consequential in a specific way—they successfully authorize some individuals and subject others. Felicitous practices of authority achieve their ends: subjects pay taxes, feed dead ancestors, or bring their herd animals to the temple as sacrifices, producing both ruler and ruled through relations. Other practices might be infelicitous either because they didn't work as expected or because they no longer produced legitimate authority. The dynamics of authorization-subjection cannot be fully encompassed by reference to relationships between people. They depend on places (architecture, landscapes), many different kinds of material objects (tools, technology, clothes, bodily adornment, etc.), and other nonhuman entities (including animals, plants, spirits, ghosts, and ancestors).[10]

Gabriel Rosenberg's (2020) discussion of "scrub sire" trials in the early twentieth century in the United States offers an example where herd animals played a key role in establishing felicitous authority. As part of the "Better Sires—Better Stock" campaign, the US Department of Agriculture (USDA) encouraged its agents to organize mock trials of a "scrub sire," that is to say a bull of unknown or mixed lineage (in distinction to ostensibly superior purebred animals). The campaign, and the scrub trials in particular, comprised a set of performative practices that shaped the relations of authorization-subjection between the state and US citizens, working to legitimate and justify increasing state control and intervention in both human and animal reproduction. Rather than determining wrongdoing in the case of a crime already committed, these trials sought to convince Americans of the felicity of the state's authority to adjudicate the value (or lack thereof) of "eugenically unfit life," a category that spanned the species boundary between humans and livestock (Rosenberg 2020, 381).

The USDA campaign combined educational materials and programs (like the trials) with more coercive forms of state intervention. The specific felicity of the trials—as public spectacles that brought together scrub bulls, lawyers, and large local audiences—emerged from the wider field of eugenics. Rosenberg (2020, 364) details how eugenicists, scientists, and policymakers alike routinely used examples and ideas from livestock breeding to support the need for interventions into human reproduction and political life (in the form of immigration restrictions, compulsory sterilizations, etc.). Scrub cattle emerged as a powerful, material example of eugenic principles for lay audiences—and scrub as a category came to encompass both humans and livestock. This was possible because intensive livestock breeding was already a part of the everyday worlds of many Americans, as well as a key source of wealth.[11]

These trials promoted the power of the state to govern reproduction, both human and animal. They drew on the felicitous practices of the US legal system, using literal courtrooms and following the ritual procedure of a trial with all its niceties. Some of the potential felicity of these trials relied on the use of didactic proceduralism to enshrine the necessity and fairness of legal structures (as they were publicly exhibited). But the trials also played parodically with the absolute difference between humans and livestock, to establish the legitimacy of the state's control over the reproduction of both (Rosenberg 2020, 385).

The relations of authorization-subjection between the state and citizens that the USDA campaign sought to establish, in the terrain of reproductive control, were interwoven with the relations of affiliation-distinction between the eugenically fit and those deemed unfit (which crisscrossed distinctions made on the basis of race, class, and disability), as well as the shifting and unstable connections and divisions drawn between humans and livestock—both important weft threads in the weaving of US politics in the early twentieth century.[12] At times, the connections drawn between humans and livestock were a potent source of felicitous practices of authorization, yet they were always haunted by the specter of failures of felicity that could emerge from those same linkages. The equation of humans and animals in eugenic demonstrations could be infelicitous if the wrong lessons were taken from the comparison or if the comparison was refused by audiences who were perturbed by the equation of humans with animals.[13]

Felicity offers the possibility of moving beyond approaches that limit the role of the nonhuman to mediation—to merely constraining relationships between people or to being material surfaces inscribed by immaterial relations and ideas (Y. Marshall and Alberti 2014, 24). Mediation suggests the existence of relationships that are above, beyond, or outside the "iterated doings" that involve humans and the rest of world. As I mean it, felicity is a characteristic describing the outcomes of certain kinds of performative practices that we associate with the political. It does not merely describe an immaterial relation between people, but the iterated doing of relations that calls into being people, animals, and objects in a specific time and place. Put another way, relations of affiliation-distinction that produce social "positions"—that give specific form to both power and legitimacy—are themselves the product of the contextual production of efficacious and legitimate acts and practices (Butler 1997, 146, 156–57). Thus, an archaeology of politics requires attending to how we might investigate the conditions of felicity for both sets of relationships and how they interlace to form the weave of political life.

POLITICAL ANIMALS

A performative approach makes it easier to consider how "animals condition political and cultural possibilities not just as immaterial metaphors but as particular actors with complex lives, histories, and characters" (Govindrajan 2018, 89). There are (at least) two places where we can begin to look for domesticated herd animals' role as key participants in local life. First, we can consider the "labor politics" of working with and working for humans. An expansive understanding of labor adds questions about "appropriate social relationships of compensation, care, and value" (Battistoni 2017, 21) to the more typical view of herd animals as a form of wealth that can be converted into power over people. Thinking about labor challenges us to assess the political possibilities (and implications) of relations across species lines, which highlights the plastic space of social and material interdependence.

Labor, as the concept is used here, combines the politics of care and reproduction across species lines with the recognition that working together is an important arena for relations of affiliation-distinction and authorization-subjection. While herd animals' status as objects and producers of wealth is certainly important, it doesn't exhaust the political possibilities of living with them. Archaeologists should not ignore how the act of (re)producing also makes its makers and makes the world. The embodied persons produced by work and the relations between embodied persons made through labor are also potential threads within the fabric of politics.[14] Beyond working with and for humans, herd animals are imbricated in a wider suite of performative practices of political life. Expanding out from the daily work of care and reproduction, herd animals participate in other iterative actions that maintain, challenge, and transform relations of affiliation-distinction and authorization-subjection. Thinking about animal labor and thinking about how animals participate in social life beyond the work of production and reproduction are necessarily overlapping and complementary analytical frames, not frames that are mutually exclusive or clearly bounded.

In the chapters that follow, I return to the surprises and mysteries posed by the archaeological data from Late Bronze Age sites in the Tsaghkahovit Plain. Examining a wide range of archaeological data, I consider how we might read it as evidence of the iterated doings of political life in the Late Bronze Age—and how we might see herd animals as actively shaping relations of affiliation-distinction and authorization-subjection. Drawing on isotopic data, in chapter 5, I read the evidence of human intervention into sheep diet and reproduction, not as the production of resources, but as a negotiation of human and sheep collective labor, which forms a key site for the work of political authority and relations of affiliation-distinction. Using zooarchaeological data to trace the itineraries of animals' bodies postmortem highlights the extent to which herd animals' bodies circulated widely after death. Rather than representing the typical waste of quotidian butchery, cooking, and eating activities or large-scale communal feasting events, the faunal remains from these sites provide evidence that isolated skeletal elements were circulating into sites in highly unusual ways.

Chapter 6 uses this evidence to explore the value of living and dead animals, which it locates in value-in-action. The insistence with which performativity establishes the material-semiotic nature of political orders and authority resonates productively with anthropological approaches to value (and the relation between value and politics), leading to new ways to think about the value of herd animals in the past. In chapter 7, I investigate how political authority emerged from different choreographies of value that integrated living and dead herd animals into relations of authorization-subjection. I read the circulation of bones as traces of different choreographies of value, which move beyond a binary distinction

between public and private or quotidian and ritual activities. Taken together, what emerges is an exploration of how the pre- and postmortem
lives of herd animals were entangled with practices in which pastoralist
labor (both human and nonhuman) and value (of living and dead animals)
played a critical role in establishing the conditions for felicitous authority
and shaping the ordering practices that produced new political orders.

UNEARTHING POLITICS IN THE TSAGHKAHOVIT PLAIN

Imagine you are standing in a high meadow, in a valley ringed by mountain peaks. The tops of the highest ones are still covered in snow, despite the warmth of the summer sun. Closing your eyes, you can hear the buzzing drone of insects and smell the grassy, floral mix of the plants crushed beneath your feet. If you stand there long enough, you might hear (and smell) a flock of sheep moving past you—the sound of many legs moving through the grass, punctuated by a bleat here and there. If you open your eyes and turn to your left, you can see a meadow pocked with small hillocks, some larger than others, interrupting the relatively flat expanse of grasses on the valley floor—the familiar trace of ancient burial mounds. To your right, as your eyes move up the slopes, you can see lines ringing one hilltop and rocks visible here and there, poking out above the turf—the visible remains of a walled site dating to the Bronze or Iron Age (figure 4.1).

What we know about the past emerges from archaeologists' ongoing encounter with material traces in the present day. Archaeological landscapes, constituted through the actions and interests of archaeologists in the present, bind together past and present because they are composed of the accumulating (and dissipating) material traces of past actions and events (Joyce 2015b). These traces are part of a very real, material landscape that can be seen, touched, smelled, and heard (not to mention surveyed and excavated) in the here and now. Some of these traces, such as large stone walls, are immediately obvious. Others are very subtle, requiring many nonhuman assistants to perceive them, such as the minute differences in the isotopes found in a piece of bone or urine or dung in a dirt

FIGURE 4.1 Archaeological landscapes of the Tsaghkahovit Plain. Upper photo: Tsaghkahovit Fortress, courtesy of Adam T. Smith. Lower photo: Gegharot Kurgan 3, with excavations at Kurgan 2 visible in the upper right; photo by author.

floor. Archaeologists use these traces to suture together past and present, object and interpretation, by working to cohere the accumulated material traces that archaeologists perceive (and attend to) into questions and narratives. Both the pleasures and the perils of archaeological interpretation come from the basic fact that these material traces are often ambiguous and our judgments are rarely totally certain.

Archaeological narratives emerge from the ongoing struggle to stabilize the material traces gathered by archaeologists into stories about life in the past. This struggle is defined by the tension between the questions and answers that arise from the examination of archaeological traces and the work needed to bridge the gap between details and data and explanations and interpretations. Two material traces are the most immediately visible in the Tsaghkahovit Plain today: the fields of tombs and the hilltop sites enclosed by large stone walls (often referred to as fortresses). Tombs and walled sites, as the material traces of past activity, point to questions like, What instigated these actions? What were they intended to do? What were they a response to? What responses did they engender? As a locus for open-ended inquiries, these traces shape new possibilities for archaeological interpretation and narratives. Nevertheless, there is a countervailing tendency for habits of interpretation to displace the questions provoked by material traces.[1] On one hand, this is a normal, necessary step in archaeological knowledge production. Without gathering together traces into interpretation and stories, how can we say anything about the past? If every material trace is only a question, how can we form an answer?

Yet the stability and fixity that archaeological interpretations provide can be an ambivalent power. Habits of interpretation render some archaeological traces symbols of particular stories, substituting an answer in the place of questions.[2] They are often sites of inertia, not least because they provide a crucial stable point from which to tackle the spiraling uncertainty of questions and assumptions in archaeological interpretation. The inertial tendency of narratives (and their material correlates) can foreclose interpretive paths—even when based on limited or provisional material evidence or ambiguous interpretations. In this chapter, I work my way out from the material traces recovered from the people and herds living in the Tsaghkahovit Plain in the mid- to late second millennium BCE to present what we currently know about life in the South Caucasus during the Late Bronze Age—and suggest a few ways of shaking up habits of interpretation and reading the available archaeological traces against the grain of the current understanding.

CONTEXTUALIZING THE SOUTH CAUCASUS

Late Bronze Age societies in the South Caucasus are somewhat mysterious—but not in the *Ancient Aliens, Who really built these pyramids?* kind of way. It's rather that we know far less about their lives than we might like to know, and comparatively less than we know about some other ancient societies. We don't know what they called themselves or what languages they spoke. Archaeologists refer to the *Lchashen-Metsamor material culture horizon*, which encompasses the people who lived in the Tsaghkahovit Plain at this time along with other people living in the South Caucasus.[3] This name bundles together some of the people living in the region from the mid-second to the mid-first millennium BCE (encompassing both the Late Bronze and Early Iron Ages), who are united by the style of pottery and other objects they made and named after the archaeological sites that established this node of people and things in space and time, but not necessarily homogeneous in terms of characteristics such as language, genetic descent, or culture more generally.

A look at the map shows that the South Caucasus is situated between Anatolia, Mesopotamia, and Persia to the south and the North Caucasus and Pontic-Caspian steppes to the north (figure 4.2). This geography has shaped how archaeologists have understood the ancient Caucasus, which they place on the peripheries of other world regions. Scholars have long been interested in how people, domesticated animals and plants, and technologies like chariots and metalworking moved through the Caucasus on their way to less peripheral places. Scholars studying the ancient civilizations of Mesopotamia, the Levant, the Anatolian Plateau, and ancient Persia—an intellectual community with a distinct history shaped by the early history of the discipline and practices of institutionalization in the nineteenth and twentieth centuries (B. Porter 2010)—have emphasized the material evidence for the flow of people, animals, and material culture between the Caucasus and these regions.

The connections between the South Caucasus and Anatolia, Mesopotamia, and Persia were strong at certain times and much weaker at others. The Early Bronze Age Kura-Araxes culture (3500–2500 BCE) extended from the edge of the Caspian Sea west to the Mediterranean coast in Syria and Israel. Two millennia later, the Urartian empire was both a neighbor and a rival to the Assyrian empire, with references to it appearing in Assyrian-language inscriptions in the second and first millennia BCE. Sandwiched in between, the Late Bronze Age (1500–1100 BCE) period, the focus of this book, lacks these obvious material connections with other

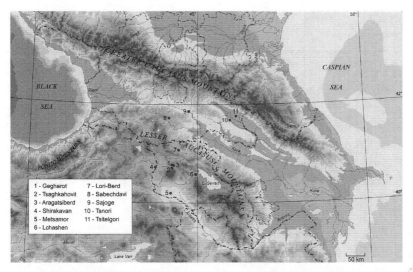

FIGURE 4.2 Map of the South Caucasus showing the Late Bronze Age archaeological sites mentioned in the text. Base map produced from open-source map on Wikimedia (https://commons.wikimedia.org/wiki/File :Caucasus_topo_map-blank.jpg, original creator: Borrichon, CC-BY-SA 4.0).

regions. While an occasional artifact, like the Mitannian cylinder seal found at Gegharot, suggests limited contact with other regions, scholars have long puzzled at the lack of obvious ties and interactions between the South Caucasus and regions to the south and west in the centuries preceding the rise of the Urartian empire. Charles Burney and David Lang (1971, 128) sum up the general mood, writing that Urartu appears "suddenly from the murky prehistory of a backward region, so close, as the crow flies, to centres of the ancient Near East and so little influenced by them" (see also Kohl 1992, 134; Sagona and Zimansky 2009, 248).

To scholars outside the region, the South Caucasus was peripheral not only because of its geographic location but also due to its perceived differences from Near Eastern civilizations—shaped by its distinctive forms of material culture (large burial mounds called *kurgans*, wheeled vehicles, and metal artifacts that connected it to the steppe regions to the north), social organization, and importantly for my work, the long-term history of human–herd animal relations (glossed under the label of pastoralism). The sense of otherness of the ancient South Caucasus twines together narratives about the long-term histories of humans' relations with herd animals and narratives about the development of more "complex" and permanent forms of social inequality and hierarchy (discussed in chapter 2).

In some respects, these interwoven narratives about the deeper past reflect the ongoing inheritance of nineteenth-century evolutionary theories that linked the narrative arc of civilizational and political progress to the development of animal husbandry and plant agriculture (Pluciennik 2001). Both Soviet and Anglo-American archaeologists inherited those frameworks, particular those of Lewis Henry Morgan (see Bulkin, Klejn, and Lebedev 1982; Dolukhanov 1995; Trigger 2006). Though Soviet and Anglo-American archaeology developed along different lines, they overlapped in their understanding of the archaeology of the South Caucasus. In both regions, archaeological evidence from the South Caucasus was taken into larger debates about the historical evolution of inequality and hierarchy and the role that technologies like metallurgy and chariots played in ancient civilizations.

For Soviet archaeologists, this question emerged through efforts to bring archaeological work in line with Marx's five stages of socioeconomic evolution, progressing from primitive society to slaveholding society, followed by feudalism, capitalism, and finally socialism or communism (Lindsay and Smith 2006; Trigger 2006, 341). Soviet scholars debated about how unequal nomadic pastoralist societies in Central Asia were, splitting between those who thought they could be classed as feudal and those who thought the pastoralism was incompatible with class society (Sneath 2007; Gellner 1984).[4] By the 1940s, Boris Piotrovskii (1941, 320) had identified the Urartian empire as a slave-based society. This meant that earlier Bronze Age societies in the South Caucasus were necessarily assigned to the category of primitive society which constrained the range of questions that might be asked about political and economic organization in the millennia preceding the Urartian empire. Within these constraints, as intellectual space opened up in the post-Stalin era, Soviet archaeologists' examinations of local sites and regional sequences explored the relationships between economic activities, technological developments, and social inequality and hierarchy (e.g., Kushnareva 1997; Martirosian 1964; Khachatrian 1975; Khanzadyan, Mkrtchyan, and Parsamyan 1973).

Outside the USSR, archaeological materials from the Caucasus occasionally featured in large-scale (both temporal and geographic) accounts of the development of complex societies in Eurasia written by Anglo-American archaeologists. In these accounts, the Caucasus features as a corridor for the flow of goods and technology, especially wheeled vehicles and metals. The most widely influential of these accounts is Sherratt's (1981, 1983, 1997) "secondary products revolution." Sherratt argued that the increased exploitation of nonmeat animal products like milk, wool, and animal traction after initial domestication produced social inequality and hierarchy (see chapter 5). Sherratt draws archaeological data from the Caucasus into the larger argument, tracing the diffusion of wheeled vehicles, milking, and the plow from Southwest Asia to the rest of Eurasia.

Soviet and Anglo-American archaeologies compared the archaeological data from the South Caucasus to the history of ancient societies in neighboring regions, looking for direct connections and influences with the aim of developing theoretical frameworks. The Caucasus often serves as a foil to models of political and social evolution that emerged from the study of states and empires in Anatolia, Mesopotamia, and Persia or Europe. Ristvet and colleagues (2012, 321) draw a poetic parallel between the way the archaeological record of the South Caucasus in the Bronze and Iron Ages challenges the orthodoxies of Near Eastern archaeology and the successful challenges people in peripheral places like the South Caucasus posed to states and empires in the ancient past (see also Badalyan, Smith, and Avetisyan 2003; Lindsay and Greene 2013). The distinctiveness of the ancient South Caucasus was linked to its long regional tradition of pastoralism (cf. Lindsay and Greene 2013; Masson 1997)—encompassing both the forms of material culture that evinced similarities between, and direct contact with, steppe pastoralists as well as the deep history of human–herd animal relations in the region. But the category of pastoralism has largely served as an answer for the differences in political and social life in the South Caucasus, rather than a source of questions about the details of humans' relations with herd animals.

Despite the upheaval in local scientific institutions caused by the collapse of the Soviet Union, it also led to collaborations between local and foreign scholars in the South Caucasus that have built a vibrant scholarly community that brings these different intellectual traditions together. This collaborative work extends from the trowel's edge—thanks to the growing number of collaborative field projects bringing together Armenian, Georgian, and Azerbaijani archaeologists with archaeologists based in the United States and Europe—to a profusion of edited volumes, international conferences, and regional journals. My own zooarchaeological work in the Tsaghkahovit Plain is part of this larger story as I contributed to the collaborative work of Project ArAGATS, a long-running field project that has generated a large corpus of archaeological data about life in the Late Bronze Age (along with other periods).

EXCAVATING TSAGHKAHOVIT AND GEGHAROT

Project ArAGATS, the joint Armenian-American Project for the Archaeology and Geography of Transcaucasian Societies, has undertaken archaeological research in the Tsaghkahovit Plain since 1998 (figure 4.3).[5]
In the first couple of years, the project completed an archaeological survey
of the plain and identified a large number of prehistoric sites (Adam T.
Smith, Badalyan, and Avetisyan 2009). The survey identified and mapped
an extensive Late Bronze Age archaeological landscape that includes the
remains of walled hilltop sites, smaller sites located on high peaks, and
numerous clusters of Late Bronze Age burials.[6] After completing the survey and making limited test excavations at different walled sites, Project
ArAGATS began systematic and extensive excavations at Gegharot and
Tsaghkahovit. Initial excavations at both sites revealed traces of complex
histories of occupation.

Early excavations on the citadel and terraces at Tsaghkahovit revealed
that later construction had disturbed the Late Bronze Age strata almost
entirely, which led the project to shift its focus to a series of rooms (the
Tsaghkahovit Residential Complex) outside the site walls that had intact
Late Bronze Age living surfaces. There, excavators encountered the remains of walls enclosing small rooms, and within them, they encountered
multiple floor layers. In one of the excavation units, the floor layers were

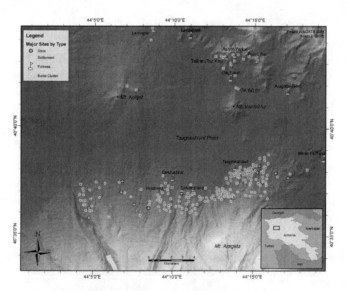

FIGURE 4.3 Distribution of archaeological sites in the
Tsaghkahovit Plain. Courtesy of Adam T. Smith.

separated by large accumulations of dirt (10–40 cm; Badalyan et al. 2014, 194). But the radiocarbon dates for those layers indicated that all were constructed within the same phase of occupation. The accumulation of dirt between the floor surfaces suggests that these spaces were occupied intermittently, as people left and returned to them over time.

Excavators at Gegharot encountered a thick layer of destruction debris filled with charcoal, charred beams, and burned artifacts. Continuing down, they encountered similar debris filling pits and the gaps between walls. Adding to the complexity and confusion is the Late Bronze Age occupants' tendency to cut into the remains of the Early Bronze Age site when constructing their own walls and pits, leading to places where later floors were found below earlier occupation levels (giving the appearance of violating the basic principles of stratigraphy). What these traces revealed is that Gegharot was destroyed twice during the few hundred years during it was occupied in the late second millennium.

In addition to working out the basic facts of the chronology and spatial organization of occupation at both sites, the extensive excavations turned up large quantities of a wide variety of archaeological materials: countless broken pieces of pottery, some whole and partial ceramic vessels, thousands upon thousands of animal bones, charred seeds, burned beams, a wide variety of broken bone and stone tools, molds for casting jewelry and small ornaments, and various odds and ends of personal adornment that were lost or thrown away over the life of the site. Collectively, these materials hold immense potential to reveal traces of past activity, giving access to what life might have been like in the Late Bronze Age at these sites. Members of the Project ArAGATS team have made detailed analyses of the animal bones and charred seeds and other plant materials (Badalyan et al. 2008, 2014; Chazin 2016b, Chazin n.d.), as well as the production and distribution of ceramics (Greene 2013) and the material traces of human biographies and mortuary practices revealed through the excavation of burials near both sites (M. Marshall 2014).

The long-term archaeological research in the Tsaghkahovit Plain has produced detailed and multivalent datasets that are generally not available for other sites from this period in the region (see box 4.1 later in this chapter). As a result, the work of members of Project ArAGATS has had a key role in filling in the details of interpretations of social and political life. But at the same time, the complicated depositional histories of Gegharot and Tsaghkahovit highlight that we are missing traces of things we would like to know more about—and that the archaeological materials from the sites retain important forms of ambiguity and uncertainty. Furthermore, the interests and expertise of project members mean we know quite a bit about some things (animal bones, ceramic production) and less about others (microstratigraphy and soils analysis, ceramic forms and uses). Nevertheless, the data accumulated over the past more than twenty years of research have given us useful, and occasionally highly detailed, information about Late Bronze Age lives in the Tsaghkahovit Plain.

The material traces uncovered by members of Project ArAGATS reveal that the sites of Gegharot and Tsaghkahovit were deeply interconnected with one another—and that they were likely important places for people living elsewhere in the plain. Based on the spatial distribution of sites, an early hypothesis was that there were two communities or polities in the plain (Badalyan, Smith, and Avetisyan 2003; Adam T. Smith, Badalyan, and Avetisyan 2009, 395). This division was suggested by the appearance two discrete clusters of burials and walled sites. The map produced by the archaeological survey reveals an empty area between Gegharot and Tsaghkahovit (figure 4.3). However, despite the gap on the map, the people living in and around Gegharot and Tsaghkahovit were closely integrated with one another. While there are noticeable differences in how the work of making pots and raising animals was organized across the two sites, those differences are not necessarily more important than the differences identified within each site itself.

Gegharot is located on top of a foothill at the end of the Pambakh range, sitting above the modern village (figure 4.4). In the late second millennium BCE, on approaching the site, you would have seen a fortification wall encircling the top of the hill. Below this wall, buildings and open spaces would be visible on the western side, encircled by the lower terrace wall. At the bottom of the hill, which is now covered by modern houses, you would see clusters of tombs surrounded by stone circles (*cromlechs*), and if you turned to look to further away to the southeast, you would see a group of burial mounds (*kurgans*) sprouting from the relatively flat area of the plain and nestled against the slopes of Mount Vardablur. It is less clear what you would have seen had you gone within the walls enclosing the site, since the complicated stratigraphy and repeated destruction have obscured many of the details of spatial organization. Excavators have found traces of rooms, some with features like platforms or basins, and a number of pits, including one where excavators found a number of complete vessels and other intriguing objects. That room, and others like it, form the nucleus of a habit of interpretation that labels these spaces "shrines" (Adam T. Smith 2015, 162; Adam T. Smith and Leon 2014).

Radiocarbon dates indicate that the first period of occupation at

FIGURE 4.4 Map of Gegharot. Courtesy of Adam T. Smith and Project ArAGATS.

Gegharot was between about 1422 and 1246 BCE and lasted somewhere between one hundred and two hundred years (S. Manning et al. 2018). The Late Bronze Age occupation at Tsaghkahovit began at roughly the same time. At Gegharot, this first period of occupation ended in a conflagration that burned much of the site. People returned to the site and removed and relocated the debris behind walls and in pits, rebuilding the site with a new layout. The second period of occupation at Gegharot was shorter, lasting between forty-five and one hundred years sometime between 1264 and 1186 BCE. This phase of occupation ended when the site

of Gegharot was again destroyed by fire, which produced the thick layer
of destruction debris encountered by Project ArAGATS team members.
Tsaghkahovit and Aragatsiberd (another walled site near Gegharot) were
abandoned around the same time.

Approaching Tsaghkahovit in the latter half of the second millennium
BCE, you would have seen a stone wall encircling the top of a conical
hill that rises some eighty meters above the plain, on the edge of a spur
of the Aragats massif (figure 4.5). The lower portion of the hill was covered in terraces bounded by a series of stone walls. To the southeast, you
would see aggregated groups of buildings with short stone walls topped by
wattle and daub or possibly felt tents. Further out, you might have seen
animals penned in corrals and clusters of tombs stretching out along the
slope of Mount Aragats. Immediately to the southeast of the hill, there

FIGURE 4.5 Map of Tsaghkahovit. Courtesy of Ian
Lindsay, Adam T. Smith, and Project ArAGATS.

would have been a series of rounded buildings built on terraces descending down the slope of the hill below the walls encircling the central citadel and terraces—the area that excavators labeled the Tsaghkahovit Residential Complex (TRC).[7] The material traces recovered here show that people processed crops and foods (toasting and grinding them), as well as storing them in small quantities. People worked in and used these buildings intermittently, routinely abandoning them long enough for dirt to accumulate and cover up the traces of activity on the floor surfaces. The arrangement of rooms in this area of the site shifted over time, responding to the changing needs of the inhabitants. After the rooms were no longer used for such purposes, animal bones and broken ceramics, along with other ephemera of daily life, were deposited within the walls until the site was abandoned at the end of the twelfth century BCE.

THE BONES

Luckily for me, digging into Gegharot and Tsaghkahovit has turned up large numbers of fragmented animal bones (over 100,000 specimens have been analyzed). This has produced an archive that holds an immense potential to inform us about the lives and deaths of herd animals. The vast majority of these faunal remains are what we might assume were trash, bones that seem as if they were discarded after cooking, eating, or the manufacture of things like bone tools and leather. Animal bones were deposited in various places across the sites as a result of different practices of discard (with varying temporal rhythms and social meanings). Things accumulated around the site over time, but a large proportion of bones at both sites come from *middens*; that is to say, contexts where materials like bones and pottery fragments accumulated relatively quickly and in large quantities. The two largest assemblages of Late Bronze Age faunal remains, which are my main focus through the rest of the book, come from Gegharot (n = 44,676) and the Tsaghkahovit Residential Complex (n = 14,452).[8] Other assemblages from other areas or sites were too small for in-depth analysis. While over 50,000 bones is a large quantity, the nature of archaeological traces means that even with such a rich assemblage, I still find myself with unanswered questions and missing information.

Because of the complex set of actions that led to the accumulations of bones across the site and the equally complex history of what happened to these bones after being apparently thrown away, it is crucial to attend to how we might separate one set of traces from the other. Careful examination shows that the patterns we see in breakage, body-part representation, and other aspects of the faunal data from these sites are largely the result of Late Bronze Age activities (rather than a result of things that happened postdeposition; see chapter 6 and Chazin 2016b for details of this analysis). Surprisingly, despite the differences in the architecture, items, and history of occupation and use at Gegharot and Tsaghkahovit—and the differences in how faunal remains accumulated within these sites—the patterns we see in the animal bones at the two sites are remarkably similar. This suggests that what we have recovered are the material traces of a similar mix of activities happening within and around both sites.

MULTISPECIES COHABITATION AND CARE

For the people living in the Tsaghkahovit Plain in the mid-second millennium BCE, sheep, goats, and cattle (and to a lesser extent, pigs and horses) would have been woven into the fabric of everyday life in countless ways. People would have regularly heard, smelled, and seen these animals—moving across the plain; in and out of the walled sites, pens, and corrals; and likely in and around tents made of the hair of sheep and goats. Many people, if not all, would have regularly touched the bodies of living animals—while milking, herding, or shearing wool—and touched and tasted the products of those bodies like wool, milk, dung, urine, and blood. Cattle, sheep, and goats would likewise have lived lives in some proximity to human beings, but also to the other species of herd animals and dogs, seeing, touching, smelling, hearing, and occasionally tasting each other in a multispecies cohabitation that stretched across the built environment of walled sites and the wider landscape of the plain. Working together would have involved many forms of embodied interaction—some casual and individual, others routinized and collective—within daily and seasonal rhythms of movement and activities.

These material and sensory engagements between and among animals would likely have varied over the course of the year. In the summer, some cattle, sheep, and goats, accompanied by human herders, appear to have left the plain to graze on the grass growing at higher elevations—and people may have collected special plants or hunted animals found in those places. Less common among the bones found on-site, but certainly encountered in the landscape, were a wide range of wild animals: red deer, foxes, badgers, hares, voles and other rodents, tortoises, toads, snakes, and many species of birds. Male and female herd animals were kept together or apart at different times of the year to manage the animals' reproductive labor and humans' herding labor (see chapter 5). In the winter, the harsh weather meant that animals were at times dependent on people for fodder and may have spent time together in close quarters—breeding intimacy but also possibly conflict and tension. Animals born during the winter months or weakened by the cold and snow may have been brought inside human dwellings, enabling intimate forms of cross-species socialization and care (Fijn 2011; Oma 2013).

Some people would have had daily active and embodied engagements with these animals. Herders would have moved with them over the course of the day and the season, spending time watching the herds—getting to know them as individuals and as a collectivity that changed over time as new animals were born and others died or were slaughtered (cf. Panopoulos 2003). The herding of some animals may have been a task for younger or older people who were not occupied with other responsibilities or seen as appropriate work for people of certain ages, genders, or status (cf. Fijn 2011; Govindrajan 2018). The people tasked with caring for the herds would have been attentive to the differences in needs and proclivities of the sheep, goats, and cattle, as well as differences in the personality and demeanor of individual animals. This would be especially important for those animals that were milked or sheared—tasks that require close bodily contact and cooperation. These relationships would be formed over multiple years, and herders may have formed deeper relationships with animals that lived longer lives. Cattle, on average, lived longer than sheep or goats, which may have shaped the other ways their lives and afterlives differed from the lives of sheep and goats, in terms of what they ate, where they went, when they were killed, and how their bodies were broken down and circulated after slaughter (as I discuss in the following chapters).

Herders would also have had to balance the different needs for water and pasture among the cattle, sheep, and goats with the labor required to manage the herds. They would have had to make decisions about how to provide the herds with water and food, especially in the cold and snowy winter months—would they move animals to places with better pastures or provide fodder instead? Isotopic analysis reveals that herders in the Tsaghkahovit Plain tended to choose foddering over long-distance movement to lower pastures in the winter (Chazin, Gordon, and Knudson 2019, Chazin n.d.). There is isotopic evidence that some animals were fed with stored fodder over the winter months. In addition, the overall lack of isotopic variation in the samples from other animals points to a more homogenous diet than if they had been grazing in wild pastures. We also can see that certain individual animals were fed differently from others. One sheep at Gegharot was fed a special diet, likely consisting of millet, over the winter of its first year of life. Foddering was more than a technical solution to the problem of deep snow cover and limited pastures. Feeding animals with cultivated or gathered plants appears to have been a widespread and common form of care that people provided.

People would have also had a range of embodied, sensorial engagements with herd animals after death. Looking at the bones found at the sites, we can say that animals of varying ages and sexes were slaughtered, likely for a variety of reasons. Some deaths may have been more quietly quotidian—animals slaughtered to provide meat for everyday meals or special celebrations or that were unlikely to survive the winter (cf. Fijn 2011). Other deaths may have occurred at moments of heightened awareness and scripted performance, like the slaughter of sheep and goats that were buried alongside the human dead in the burial mounds (*kurgans*) south of Gegharot. People who butchered the carcasses and prepared food would have the most immediate engagement with herd animals' bodies postmortem, but nearly everyone would likely have eaten their meat, milk, and blood at some point. When eaten and drunk, the bodily substances of herd animals were incorporated into the substances of human bodies. But people also would have had intimate, skin-to-skin contact with herd animals' bodies—wearing clothing made of fleece, woolen textiles, felt, and leather. Some would have made and used tools and objects crafted from animal bones, sinews, skin, and viscera. Moreover, the ubiquity of animal bones in the archaeological deposits and their material durability indicates that in general, animal bones were also a commonly encountered aspect of everyday life.

A serendipitous discovery expanded my understanding of the multisensorial nature of the interactions of Late Bronze Age people with the bodies of herd animals after death (Hamilakis 2014, 2017)—and illustrates how the smallest detail can shift archaeological interpretations. One cold and blustery March day in Brussels, a dear friend, her eight-month old baby, and I had taken refuge for the afternoon in the Museum of Musical Instruments. Wearing headphones attached to audio guides, we wandered through the beautiful Art Nouveau building, looking at the objects on display and listening to recordings of the instruments being played. As we entered the exhibit on the history of musical instruments in Europe, a case at the front of the room stopped me in my tracks.

Inside the case were two small, unassuming objects—two ungulate toe bones (first phalanges), one large and one small, each with a hole drilled into one side of the shaft. The small black card in the case informed me that these were whistles from France and that they dated to 18,000–

12,000 BCE.[9] Yet I had seen them before. We had excavated practically identical bone objects somewhat regularly at Gegharot, but nobody knew what they were or why they had been made. Until I read the label, I would not have known, and more to the point, *did not know*, that these objects were whistles—despite the fact that they were very familiar to me. With my mind whirling at the discovery, I punched the label number into my audio guide and heard a sharp and somewhat breathy whistle echoing in the headphones.

These toe bones with the mysterious holes were part of a larger group of faunal remains from Gegharot and Tsaghkahovit—united by the way they raised questions of What? and Why? and resisted easy answers relying on ready-to-hand habits of interpretation. This included some ankle bones (astragali) from cattle, sheep, and goats that were somewhat unusual. They had clearly been altered—holes bored, surfaces scratched, edges polished—but they didn't seem to be tools or any other typical category of bone objects. And they also didn't seem to be merely butchery waste or the remains of meal preparation or eating. Moreover, when we excavated places, sometimes we would find groups of them in pits or on floors. Also strange was how there seemed to be many more ankle bones and jaw bones (mandibles) than we would expect. Both the ankle bones and jaw bones raised tricky questions of what they might be evidence of since they didn't seem like everyday butchery or consumption waste. These bones were initially troublesome, but eventually, the questions they provoked shifted my thinking in consequential ways. As these bones unsettled my expectations, they pushed me to explore how they might reveal traces of the performative practices of felicitous authority.

LIFE WITHIN AND BEYOND THE WALLS

Broken pieces of pottery, charred seeds, discarded tools, buttons, and pins expand what we can say about life in the Late Bronze Age Tsaghkahovit Plain. Many of the materials recovered from the excavations give us a window into what people were eating—both in terms of their general diet, as well as what specific foods were eaten and how they were prepared. Overall, people in the plain ate a plant-based diet, supplemented with meat from their herds and the occasional hunted animals—but they don't appear to have eaten much fish (M. Marshall 2014). They grew a variety of plant crops—barley and different kinds of wheat, along with emmer and rye. They also probably ate grapes and millet imported from elsewhere, since we find the remains of those crops as we excavate but they would have been difficult to grow in the plain, requiring a milder climate (Badalyan et al. 2014, 185). People almost certainly collected a wide variety of wild plants from the wider landscape, using them as both foods and medicines.

Of the small number of people for whom we have detailed dietary information, some ate more meat than others, but they are too few for us to know whether eating more meat was connected to age, gender, or other forms of status and distinction. One person whose teeth were analyzed appears to have eaten more dairy products than the others, probably because they needed to eat a special diet after suffering some fairly severe injuries—this individual was missing most of their teeth and their face and jaws showed signs of healed fractures (M. Marshall 2014, 384). It is interesting that people in the Tsaghkahovit Plain seem to have eaten differently from people living around the same time in the Shirak Plain to the west—they had fewer cavities, which suggests they ate less soft or sugary food (M. Marshall 2014, 263–64).

It is difficult to say exactly how meat was prepared, but the bones found at the site suggest that roasting joints of meat and toasting bones to extract the marrow was not particularly common (at least for the remains of meals discarded within site walls). Perhaps people in the Late Bronze Age preferred to barbecue al fresco. Fresh milk from cattle, sheep, and goats was likely processed into a wide variety of other dairy products—sour milk, curds, yogurt, clarified butter, soft cheeses, and maybe even alcohol. One ceramic vessel, which was found on the western terrace at Tsaghkahovit, might have been used to make butter (Adam T. Smith, Badalyan, and Avetisyan 2004, 14).[10] The choice to turn milk into something else was probably based both on practical considerations of spoilage and storage and on gustatory preferences for milks that varied in flavor and butter fat—both between species and across the seasons. We can say a little bit more about one very specific meal or dish eaten by people in the Late Bronze Age. In one of the graves near Tsaghkahovit, mourners included a large black jar filled with the remains of a cereal porridge made from barley, wheats, and emmer and sheep or goat meat—a porridge that certainly could have been enhanced by a dollop of butter, cream, or yogurt.[11]

Even more common than fragments of bones, ceramics are the most ubiquitous item recovered from the archaeological excavations at Gegharot and Tsaghkahovit. The most common type of ceramic container in the plain was jars, mostly small ones, but we have also found bowls, cups, pots, and other, more specialized, forms. How ceramics were made, as well as how they were used, provides some insight into life in the Late Bronze Age. Examining the production and distribution of pottery reveals a complicated palimpsest of different work activities and networks, giving us a glimpse of the complicated relations between the manufacture and use of these items (Greene 2013). Similar-looking vessels found in the same place on a site often were made at different production sites around the plain and possibly through different intermediate technical processes, suggesting they were made by different groups of potters. Clays from a single source were used in different production activities and moved along different networks of production and consumption.

Once made, people brought these ceramic containers, presumably filled with a variety of things—perhaps cooked porridges and stews, yogurt, soft cheeses, or wine or beer—into both sites.[12] The pottery found at Gegharot was made at multiple production sites from around the plain, some nearby and some further away. In contrast, the pottery at Tsaghkahovit was much more likely to have been produced from the clay sources closest to the site. Yet most of the wares produced near Gegharot and transported across the plain to Tsaghkahovit were coarser, everyday ceramics—not fine wares (Lindsay and Greene 2013, 707). Overall, what we know about the manufacture and distribution of ceramics highlights that it was *not* a tributary system; there is no evidence that the people in power were administering a system of centralized collection of goods nor signs of large-scale storage in ceramic containers (Greene 2013, 179). The archaeological data resist the durable archaeological habit of looking for the accumulation of the "stuff of politics" to understand political authority and inequality. There are no dramatic differences in the kinds of ceramics found within or outside the walls of sites or, intriguingly, between the ceramics used by the living and the dead. Providing the necessary equipment for mortuary rituals may have represented a considerable proportion of pottery production. Greene estimated that upward of 17,000 vessels might have been deposited in the approximately 5,400 burials found in the necropolis on the northern slope of Mount Aragats (2013, 179).

LIVING AMONG THE DEAD

The landscapes through which the living moved in their everyday lives were visibly inhabited by the dead, though unlike in the Early Bronze Age, the dead were not buried within the sites' walls. Instead, they were interred in large groups of tombs scattered amid the walled sites and open pastures of the plain. There were two kinds of mortuary architecture in the Late Bronze Age, and members of Projects ArAGATS have excavated both kinds of tombs (Badalyan et al. 2008; Badalyan and Smith

2017; Chazin 2016b; M. Marshall 2014). Sometimes the dead were buried in chambers dug into the ground, surrounded by large stone circles, and covered by an earthen mound—a style of burial common across Eurasia.

The small number of kurgans excavated by members of Project ArAGATS share a broadly similar pattern in construction and burial practices, though they varied in the particulars of tomb construction and in the items that accompanied the dead and their arrangement in the tomb's chambers.[13] One or more dead individuals adorned with beads or beaded clothing were placed in a chamber in the center of the stone circle beneath the earthen mound, along with ceramic vessels, bronze objects (including weapons), and beads (see chapter 7). Sometimes mourners placed "head and hoof" deposits (the skulls and lower limbs) of horses in the central chamber. Next to the chamber where the deceased was interred, mourners dug another, smaller chamber. They placed the bodies of very young lambs and kids at the bottom of the pit and then filled the rest of the chamber with a large number of ceramic vessels of varying shapes and sizes, portions of the carcasses of slaughtered herd animals, and other objects such as bronze daggers and obsidian arrow heads.

Other tombs in the plain were somewhat simpler and smaller. The deceased was placed in a pit dug into the ground, which was then sealed with stone slabs and surrounded by one or two smaller stone circles. This second type of burial is called a *cromlech* (see Adam T. Smith, Badalyan, and Avetisyan 2009, 106). Burial rites were even more flexible for those interred in the cromlech tombs. Chambers were constructed in a variety of ways, differing in how they were dug out and how they were placed in relation to the other tombs nearby (M. Marshall 2014). The dead in a cromlech cemetery near Tsaghkahovit (TsBC12) were generally accompanied by a moderate amount of grave goods—mostly pots (typically four or five, but ranging from none up to seven) and parts of herd animals' bodies, but occasionally other items like a bracelet or bone toggle pin. There were also variations in how the living interacted with the dead. Some tombs show signs that the human remains were handled and moved around postmortem. Maureen Marshall suggests this might be evidence that people in the Late Bronze Age were concerned that the dead be physically located in the correct place and perhaps that the presence (or transit) of the dead was necessary to constitute a place correctly or effectively (M. Marshall 2014, 286).

While there are some obvious commonalities in mortuary architecture and grave goods, the way people treated the dead seems not to have been governed by a strictly defined set of practices that had to be closely adhered to. Maureen Marshall interprets the diversity of mortuary practices, which was substantial but not unlimited, as evidence that the rituals surrounding the interment of the dead were not hegemonic practices, reflecting sedimented forms of felicitous authority or relations of affiliation-distinction. Instead, the flexibility of mortuary practices suggests that people were actively constructing and claiming group membership for the deceased while simultaneously differentiating individuals and groups from others in the larger community (M. Marshall 2014, 226). She also notes that these variable traces of past actions are ambiguous—they could be evidence of a shift in practices over time or of different traditions resulting from the history of earlier performative practices that generated relations of affiliation-distinction within the community buried in TsBC12. Marshall draws our attention to the timing of the establishment of a new cluster of burials at TsBC12 that was visually distinct from prior tombs, in the latter part of the site's occupation in the late second millennium, beginning around the same time that Gegharot was reoccupied after the first destruction event (M. Marshall 2014, 229).

Despite the quantitative and qualitative differences between the kurgan and cromlech burials, herd animals were incorporated into mortuary rituals in very similar ways in both. Late Bronze Age tombs, kurgans and cromlechs alike, contain domesticated animals in three different forms: (1) whole animals (young lambs and kids), (2) "meat units" (articulated remains, suggesting a butchered portion of a carcass), and (3) disarticulated bones found inside pots (M. Marshall 2014, 208). These traces hint at the important roles that animals played in mortuary rituals, which were potent sites for performatively producing relations of affiliation-distinction and authorization-subjection (chapter 7).

Box 4.1 Mind the Gap: The
Tsaghkahovit Plain in Context

The work of Project ArAGATS has slowly illuminated, trace by trace, some glimpses into the lives of people living in the Late Bronze Age Tsaghkahovit Plain. It is one of the clearest and most detailed pictures of life in mid-second millennium BCE in the region, and as such, it has played an outsized role in archaeologists' developing ideas about the Late Bronze Age in the region and in our ideas about the Lchashen-Metsamor material culture horizon (e.g., Sagona 2018). But there is an inherent tension

between using the data and interpretations from the Tsaghkahovit Plain to tell stories about the wider region based on the material similarities that form the basis for the material culture horizon
and accounting for the evidence of the diversity of everyday life
within that grouping. Our interpretations of larger regional dynamics and histories need to carefully tack between using the
data from the Tsaghkahovit Plain to stand in for the region as
a whole—because of the available detail and the clear material
links between sites across Armenia and Georgia—and thinking
about the accumulating archaeological traces that highlight the
ways in which the Tsaghkahovit Plain was different from other
contemporaneous places.

The people who lived at Gegharot and Tsaghkahovit were
connected to a wider network of people with whom they had
certain things in common. They made black-burnished pottery
and produced metal objects using openwork and lost wax casting processes that were recognizably similar to those produced at
other sites across Georgia and Armenia, built walled sites on the
tops of foothills, and buried their dead in kurgans and cromlechs.
As producers of fine bronze metalwork, they were part of the
larger regional patterns of innovations in metallurgy and a massive increase in the production of metal objects in the latter half of
the second millennium BCE. Chernykh (1992) called this shared
technological and stylistic tradition the Caucasian Metallurgical
Province. Within the bounds of this metallurgical ecumene, local ceramic and mortuary traditions were more fragmented than
in early periods, as different styles and burial practices proliferated.[1] This material culture horizon is long-lived, continuing
into the mid-first millennium BCE, and thus extending across
the boundary between the Late Bronze Age and Early Iron Age
periodization.

The shared similarities in material culture, which define the
material culture horizon, suggest that people living in the Tsaghkahovit Plain were connected to the wider world outside, even if
those connections are not always directly evident in the material
traces recovered from excavations. It is quite possible that during
the Late Bronze Age, people traveled around the region without
leaving durable traces, either because they traveled for reasons
other than trade or because they were primarily exchanging or
gifting material items like honey, wool, felt, leather, grapes, and

millet, whose perishability resulted in fewer traces for archaeologists to find thousands of years later. Small finds, such as Mitannian common-style cylinder seals and obsidian tools and fragments made from nonlocal obsidian sources, hint at the links between people living in plain and elsewhere in the region and beyond.

At the same time, however, excavations also show that people living in the Tsaghkahovit Plain did other things differently from people living elsewhere in the region. While architecture is not destiny, the diverse kinds of buildings and spaces found across the region suggest differences in the everyday lives of people in the South Caucasus in the second millennium BCE. There is considerable variation in the construction of walls, the size of the enclosed area, and the relationship between architecture within and outside the walls of these sites. More broadly, across the region, there is evidence of people living within the walls at some fortress sites and outside the walls in associated settlements at others, and there are some Late Bronze Age sites that lack fortifications entirely.

What we know about the basics of life at Sabechdavi, a large walled in Georgia, hints at differences in ways of life from those in the Tsaghkahovit Plain (Sagona 2018, 385; Narimanishvili and Amiranashvili 2010; Shanshashvili and Narimanishvili 2012). Within the walls of the sites, inhabitants constructed thirty single-room structures, each with a circular hearth at the center. Outside the walls, people and animals appear to have lived and worked together in a group of approximately forty larger, two-room buildings. In one building, one room had a plaster floor with a hearth and a second room was paved with flagstones, suggesting that livestock might have been kept within the building's walls. This close cohabitation is also suggested by the fragments of ceramic vessels that excavators believe might have been churns, evidence of household dairying.[2] At Sagoje, another site in Georgia occupied during the early to mid-second millennium BCE, people lived in pit houses, with an outdoor cooking area found between two of the buildings at the site (M. Abramishvili and Orthmann 2008; Sagona 2018, 386). Around 1300 BCE, the site was burned. Unlike the conflagration at Gegharot, it appears the inhabitants of the site may have gathered up and removed their belongings before the fire. Archaeologists have also excavated a handful of

intriguing ritual spaces in Georgia, which are unlike anything
found in the plain (reviewed by Sagona 2018, 413–16).

1. Different archaeological cultures were established during this period
in Colchis (western Georgia) and in southeastern Azerbaijan and northern
Iran (Talish culture; see Sagona 2018, 380). The Koban archaeological culture was established in the western and central Caucasus during this time.
2. The identification is due to unstated assumptions about vessel form
and has not been confirmed by residue analysis.

RETHINKING WHAT WE KNOW

While pastoralism has been a key concept shaping how archaeologists have
interpreted the archaeological traces of the Late Bronze Age in the South
Caucasus, very little specific attention has been paid to how humans and
herd animals lived together. But the large quantities of animal bones recovered from Gegharot and Tsaghkahovit, along with the other material
traces of actions and activity that archaeologists from Project ArAGATS
have analyzed, offer us a chance to think about how herd animals shaped
the contours of political and social life in the past. In them, I see an opportunity to consider the plastic potential of human-animal relations, moving
away from seeing herd animals as merely hindrances to so-called normal
political processes or things to be accumulated to gain power.

During the second half of the second millennium BCE, the archaeological landscapes of the Tsaghkahovit Plain, and the South Caucasus
more broadly, were dominated by the walled sites and fields of kurgans
and cromlechs. Our understanding of these archaeological traces and the
relationships between them tacks between the questions provoked by their
presence—*Why were they built? What went on inside the walls? How did
it impact people's lives?*—and the habits of interpretation that have sedimented around them in the archaeological literature. The most durable
habit of interpretation is to read the paucity of Middle Bronze Age sites as
evidence of nomadic pastoralism and the appearance of walled sites in the
Late Bronze Age as an abandonment of pastoral mobility and resumption
of sedentary life (as well as sedentary political organization). Woven into
this story is a subplot about inequality, read primarily from mortuary practices and how they shift through time (box 4.2).

In these stories, Late Bronze Age walled sites are interpreted as indexical or even iconic evidence for new kinds of political organization. The
replacement of the massive, treasure-rich kurgans of the Middle Bronze

Age by greater numbers of smaller and less ostentatious burials fills out the narrative of political transformations across the second millennium BCE: "The social inequalities visible in the kurgans of the early second millennium appear to have been formalized into a tightly integrated sociopolitical apparatus where critical controls over resources—economic, social, sacred—were concentrated within the cyclopean stone masonry walls of powerful new centers" (Adam T. Smith, Badalyan, and Avetisyan 2009, 30). Herd animals (and their relations with humans) are assigned a limited role in this sociopolitical apparatus, reduced to the external cause of human mobility or the stuff of human political life (part of tribute or feasting), if they appear at all (Lindsay and Greene 2013; Adam T. Smith 2015).[14]

Box 4.2 How Unequal? What Kind of Power?

Current interpretations of political life in the Late Bronze Age in the South Caucasus tie walled sites and tombs together further, reading the differences between Middle and Late Bronze Age mortuary practices as evidence of a shift in the arena of political authority—away from mortuary practices (reflecting the authority of individual leaders) toward new forms of architecture for the living. Seeing the lavish burials of the Middle Bronze Age as a "material apparatus of political violence dedicated to the manufacture of social distinction" (Adam T. Smith 2015, 136) focuses on the massive amounts of labor required to construct them—an estimated twenty-three thousand days of labor for Tsnori Kurgan 1 (Chernykh 1992, 101)—and the vast inventories of precious items contained within them. In contrast, the amount of coordinated labor needed to construct Late Bronze Age walled sites is thought to testify to the existence of centralized institutions of political authority, rather than the personal charisma of individual leaders (Badalyan et al. 2008). This line of thinking sees evidence of individualized, personal power in the construction of Middle Bronze Age tombs and centralized, nonpersonal forms of power in the construction of Late Bronze Age walls.

But there are other ways we could interpret the shift in large, collective labor projects from mortuary monuments to walled sites. To start, we might ask how that shift was connected to the expansion of burial monuments to a wider segment of the population. One possibility is that the changes in mortuary practices represent a diminution or attenuation of certain relations of authorization-subjection and affiliation-distinction, rather than their consolidation and entrenchment elsewhere. Recently, Erb-Satullo (2021) suggested that the sharp drop in gold objects in Late Bronze Age assemblages in the Middle Kura zone (between the Greater and Lesser Caucasus) was the result of the rejection of extreme social hierarchy of the preceding Middle Bronze Age. Yet there was no drop in the prevalence of gold in the Middle Araxes Zone (including the Ararat Valley and the southern highlands of the lesser Caucasus), where the Tsaghkahovit Plain is located. This suggestion raises further questions about the possible interconnections between the expansion of bronze and iron metallurgy (and the continued inclusion of bronze and iron objects in grave assemblages) and political life in the Late Bronze Age. Is the continuity of goldwork in the Middle Araxes Zone evidence of greater continuities in political authority? Or is it a minor component of an otherwise shared regional shift toward communities with more muted (or fluid) forms of social inequality?

Focusing on the Tsaghkahovit Plain, the obvious discrepancies in tomb construction and the kinds and amounts of items accompanying the dead between the Gegharot kurgans and Tsaghkahovit cromlechs is typically taken as evidence of the persistence of social inequalities. However, even the richest kurgan at Gegharot appears moderate when compared to the much more lavish burials at sites such as Tsitelgori, Lori-Berd, Shirakavan, and Lchashen (R. Abramishvili and Abramishvili 2008; Devejyan 1981, 2006; Torosyan, Khnkikyan, and Petrosyan 2002; Mnatsakanian 1965), let alone the even more spectacular Middle Bronze Age kurgans found across the region. The expansion in the number of burials and ways in which people buried their dead suggests that mortuary practices may have created smaller-scale (and potentially less hierarchical) relations of affiliation-distinction. The spatial proximity of many walled sites and cemeteries suggests that felicitous authority was probably not exclusively associated with walled sites—either as construction projects or as containers for other activities. The inclusion of a wide variety of items within tombs—metalwork, ceramics, but animal remains as well—also needs to be part of how archaeologists interpret the relations between mortuary practices and other practices elsewhere, and how that shaped felicitous authority and the creation of political communities.

Despite the similarity assumed in the shared practice of building sites enclosed by walls, the diversity of what archaeologists find at the small number of sites with more substantial investigations suggests there was variation in the use of space. How does thinking about the diversity of the organization of space within and beyond the walls of Late Bronze Age sites challenge current habits of interpretation? It hints that these spaces, through their construction and ongoing maintenance and occupation, played different roles in establishing, maintaining, or contesting relations of affiliation-distinction and authorization-subjection—or that the interweaving of the warp and weft of affiliation-distinction and authorization-subjection varied too. The large numbers of similar rooms and buildings at Sabechdavi evoke different activities and experiences than the traces of more varied architecture (and its reconstruction) excavated at Tsaghkahovit and Gegharot. This calls into question the interpretive habits that treat the walled sites as necessarily emblematic of centralized authority or the reification of sovereignty in material assemblages (cf. Adam T. Smith, Badalyan, and Avetisyan 2009; Adam T. Smith 2015, 157).

My focus on human-animal relations and my performative approach to understanding political life in the past interrupts the typical interpretations of the archaeological evidence from the Late Bronze Age South Caucasus in two different ways. First, at the level of long-term and regional-scale interpretations of the ancient South Caucasus, we should begin to read the persistent differences between the ancient history of South Caucasus and the ancient histories of Mesopotamia, Anatolia, and Persia on the one hand, and the Eurasian steppes to the north on the other, as evidence of different postdomestication, premodern histories of human–herd animal relations. Domesticated herd animals have had an important role in the histories of all three regions, but the differences in *how* humans and herd animals lived together in the ancient South Caucasus, Southwest Asia, and the steppes highlight the plastic potential of human–herd animal relations in the deeper past.

In the chapters that follow, I use the archaeological data from the Tsaghkahovit Plain to examine the ways in which herd animals were active participants in political and social life. Focusing on the performativity of politics and examining relations of affiliation-distinction and authorization-subjection brings new questions and themes to the center of my analysis.

Rather than focusing on mobility as a political problem (e.g., Kradin 2002; Salzman 2004) or as the foundation of nonnormative "pastoralist politics" (cf. Frachetti 2012; Honeychurch 2015), I examine how more-than-human labor shaped political life in fundamental ways, twining together the reproduction of herds and humans. Instead of seeking evidence of the accumulation of herds as signs of durable hierarchy and political inequality, I investigate how herd animals shaped political life in the plain through their intertwining roles as both objects and producers of value.

The other intervention I am making is at a much smaller scale: interrupting the emerging interpretation of some of the archaeological traces from Gegharot, which have begun to sediment into a new narrative about political power and authority in the Late Bronze Age. My own focus on human-animal relations and on the zooarchaeological assemblages from Gegharot led me into a reanalysis of a specific set of material traces—a small group of rooms and their contents—which, in turn, led me to a new interpretation of the data and a new vision of political life in the Late Bronze Age Tsaghkahovit Plain.

During the excavations at Gegharot, archaeologists encountered a few unusually well-preserved rooms. These rooms share a similar set of architectural features and inventories (Adam T. Smith, Badalyan, and Avetisyan 2004; Badalyan et al. 2008, 2014; Adam T. Smith and Leon 2014). Broadly speaking, they have a clay basin (sometimes referred to as an "altar") along one wall and a large inventory of in situ small and medium ceramic vessels in an array of forms and sizes, along with other variable features (such as pits or grinding installations) and artifacts (see box 4.3).[15] These traces stood out from the rest of the site, within the experiential encounter between archaeologists and sites and artifacts. As it unfolded, this encounter initiated a new habit of interpretation. As they were excavated and analyzed, these rooms acquired the label of "shrines"—an evolving act of classification and interpretation that has been taken up in recent accounts of political life in the Late Bronze Age (Adam T. Smith 2015; Erb-Satullo and Jachvliani 2022).

Box 4.3 The "Shrines" at Gegharot

The first room identified as a shrine is located in the middle of a series of walls and rooms on the western side of the citadel (Badalyan et al. 2014). It is a single room with a preserved clay floor. On the floor, in the southeastern corner of the room, was a kidney-shaped basin ("altar") made of baked clay. In the northern part of the basin, there was a stationary hearth made of ceramic. Inside the chamber of the hearth was a hollow ceramic object known as a *manghal*.[1] Along with the hearth, there were seven whole vessels sitting in the basin (one large jar, some small jars, a bowl, and cups) and another *manghal*. Scattered around the base of the *manghal* were ceramic sherds, two obsidian tools and some flakes, and animal bones (both burned and unburned). The clay floor of the room was littered with in situ vessels and stone and bone tools. In the center of the room, to southwest of the basin, were a couple of multichambered pits.

Two similar rooms, part of the reoccupation of Gegharot, were found in other parts of the site—one on the southern end of the western terrace and another on the eastern citadel. The west terrace shrine consisted of a large room, which was built after the clearing of the destruction debris from the earlier occupation. Along the eastern side of the room, there was a clay basin with a stone stela set into it (possibly flanked by additional standing stones).[2] More than twelve large storage jars were found on the floor, along with bowls, cups, small jars, censers (found in the basin), and *manghals*. While excavating the room, the archaeologists found beads, numerous bone tools (including awls and spindle whorls), pieces of cut antler, a jewelry mold, a crucible, small metal objects (including a pin and a bracelet), and a clay stamp. This room was destroyed by fire during the second destruction event.

The third room is a rectangular stone building built on the northern end of the eastern citadel. Within the building, a stone platform was built atop of bedrock along the western wall. This platform was covered in clay and a clay basin was built on top. Within the basin, excavators found twelve vessels, small pots and jars, along with censers, pot stands, and a collection of colored pebbles. The packed clay and in situ artifacts were covered by a layer of destruction debris. Along the eastern wall, near the platform and basin, were a large quern and a small clay basin, possibly next to a stationary mortar. In the central space of the room, there was a large inventory (n = 45) of in situ vessels, ranging from large storage jars to small cups, along with censers and a *manghal*. There was also a pit in the southeastern corner of the room.[3] In addition, excavators recovered stone and bone tools (including a weaving comb), bronze arrowheads, a ceramic stamp,[4] scattered beads, and also animal remains. Pollen, phytolith, and macro-botanical analysis of the contents of these vessels provides evidence of wheat processing and storage as well as wine consumption (Adam T. Smith and Leon 2014, 554). In the doorway of the room, excavators uncovered a large scatter of animal bones, including large numbers of cattle and sheep/goat astragali (see chapter 7).

That the three rooms at Gegharot could have served similar purposes and hosted similar practices is reasonably clear. What is less clear to me is what those practices and purposes might have been. The two key features are: (1) the clay basins,[5] platforms, and hearths and (2) the array of in situ vessels, ranging from small cups, bowls, and jars to larger storage vessels. The proliferation of jars (and the range of sizes) suggests that the rooms may have been used to store a variety of things, including wine and both unprocessed and processed wheat. The presence of hearths, cen-sers, and *manghals* suggests that people may have been burning or heating things, with the further possibility that the clay basins might have been used to hold water or to isolate heated items.[6] The smaller items scattered among the features and in situ vessels are tools with a variety of uses (general-purpose stone tools, bone tools for textile crafts, metalworking) and items of personal adorn-ment. It is possible that stone tools and metal jewelry were man-ufactured within these rooms, and wheat was processed inside one of them.

1. *Manghals* are double-ended, ovoid ceramic objects found in the South Caucasus from the Middle Bronze to Iron I periods in settlements across the region. Although they are often interpreted as braziers or portable hearths, little is definitely known about their function or use. They are often associ-ated with oven installations or concentrations of charcoal and ash, and some *manghals* show evidence of severe burning. While some archeologists have grouped these artifacts with other artifacts identified as "censers," their rel-ative ubiquity at Gegharot, lack of decoration, and poor clay quality suggest a more quotidian use.

2. This standing stone may have functioned in some way to control or redirect airflow within the space, as with the "deflectors" found in kiva ar-chitecture in the southwestern United States. Unlike the basins in the citadel shrines, which abutted a wall or carved upslope bedrock, the basin in the western terrace shrine is set roughly one meter forward from the wall. Since

the room architecture and roofing are not well understood, it is not possible to pursue this possibility in more detail.

3. This pit contained a small assemblage (n = 88) of faunal remains and two pieces of groundstone.

4. Three of these stamps have been found at Gegharot, including one in a room that is not labeled a shrine (Badalyan et al. 2014, 182).

5. Clay basins found elsewhere in the site are not interpreted as having ritual functions. There are two other clay basins on the eastern citadel, south of the room labeled the shrine. The first basin was in a small room just to the south of the room labelled the shrine, and didn't contain any artifacts. The second basin was found further to south in the same trench. This basin contained seven complete vessels, an assortment of tools, sherds from a large pithos, and an assemblage of faunal remains. The bones were quite fragmented and quite a few were gnawed, suggesting that they been left exposed for some time before being buried. There were bones from cattle, sheep, and goat, along with other species and all anatomical regions were represented. The assemblage had seven astragali: one cattle (left), four sheep (2 right, 2 left), one goat (left) and one sheep/goat (right). The sheep/goat astragali was worked.

6. The loci coded as "Special Features," consisting mainly of the clay basins, have a higher proportion of sheep/goat bones than the overall assemblages.

The interpretation of these rooms as shrines emerged from the excavators' sense that the features and contents of the rooms were unusual and the similarity they perceived between the shallow clay basins and the more elaborate basins found at the later (Iron I period, 11th–9th centuries BCE) site of Metsamor (Adam T. Smith, Badalyan, and Avetisyan 2004, 29).[16] The initial diagnosis led excavators to interpret the assemblages within the rooms through that lens. Rather than workaday things in a quotidian space, the objects found in these rooms were presumed to be separate from everyday production and consumption. The large numbers of astragali were not butchery or consumption waste, but evidence for divination practices. Odd, rectangular clay objects might be abstract idols, not merely pot stands.[17]

Thinking about these rooms as sites of ritual practice and starting our interpretations of their assemblages from that assumption offers the promise of a specific and clear connection to political life in the Late Bronze Age—specifically, to relations of authorization-subjection. Adam T. Smith and Leon (2014, 533) suggest we might read these rooms as spaces that did not host public, mass rituals (that pull the body politic together through

shared participation in enacting a specific cosmography), but "more se-
cretive rites focused on managing risk by diagnosing present conditions
and prognosticating futures. The sequestering of technologies of divination within the fortified citadel—itself the critical new technology of Late
Bronze Age sovereignty—suggests that esoteric ritual was fundamental to
the emergent South Caucasian political tradition." Within this interpre-
tative framework, they pointed to artifacts they interpreted as evidence
of three forms of divinatory practices: astragalomancy (using astragali),
lithomancy (using stones), and aleuromancy (using flour).[18]

This interpretation draws on the inventory of items found only in one
of these rooms: a large number of astragali, a collection of colored pebbles,
and a grinding installation and clay stamps. At the time of excavation and
the initial analysis, the large number of astragali, both worked and unworked, struck excavators as unusual—which, in some ways, it was. Early
analyses (with coarse spatial resolution) suggested there were caches of astragali associated with the other shrines (Adam T. Smith and Leon 2014),
but when I examined the matter more closely, the data show that only the
east citadel shrine has a large collection of astragali—and there is no meaningful patterning in the number of left and right astragali as was thought
initially.

Also unaccounted for in early analyses is the fact that the astragali in
that room are actually one part of a much larger pattern of unusually large
numbers of cattle and sheep/goat astragali across a wide range of contexts
at Gegharot, not just the shrines. Labeling the rooms as shrines proposes
that what took place within their walls were *rituals*, rather than quotidian
tasks like preparing or storing food, making tools and craft items, sleeping,
gossiping, and so forth. In chapter 7, I question this interpretation by asking what becomes possible if we carefully investigate the material traces of
activities that took place there. Rather than categorizing these spaces and
their contents through the binary of "quotidian" or "ritual" (cf. Fowles
2012; Brück 1999), what might we learn about the kinds of object itineraries and social action that threaded through these spaces, gathering and
dispersing people and things?

Our current understandings of political life in the Late Bronze Age Tsaghkahovit Plain—how relations of affiliation-distinction and authorization-
subjection were woven together through richly performative practices that
tied together the living and the dead and activities within and beyond the
walls of sites—are caught in the tension between the questions provoked
by material traces and our habits of interpreting them. The expansion of
burials to a wider proportion of the population suggests that mortuary ritu-

als created a more encompassing form of relations of affiliation-distinction. What is less clear is whether this change was because this form of felicitous authority expanded, becoming accessible for a wider range of people, or because elites were no longer able to maintain its exclusivity (robbing it of its performative capacities for authorization). Over time, elites may have found that displays of extreme differentiation (on the basis of material goods) were no longer able to generate felicitous authority.

The presence of both walled sites and fields of tombs—and the memories of past actions and imaginings of future ones that they provoked—would have shaped the experiences of herders and herds as they moved through these landscapes daily. What is harder to know is how the practices that took place within and beyond the site walls contributed to the formation of relations of affiliation-distinction and how they were involved in the production of felicitous forms of authority (and to what ends). What we do know from the analysis of bones and ceramics points to active interrelations between activities taking place within and around walled sites and those that were part of mortuary practices. Similarly, the traces we've recovered of the tasks of everyday life indicate that quotidian activities were deeply connected to, not isolated within or excluded from, the spaces bounded by the site walls. Thus it would be productive to ask whether we might interpret the changes in the built environment in the Late Bronze Age as something other than symbols of increasing sedentarization and normative political authority or spaces containing the machinery that materialized politics.

In what follows, I dig more deeply into the unexpected patterns that emerged from the zooarchaeological and isotopic analyses I conducted—patterns that unsettled my own habits of interpretation. Some of this unsettling is a result of thinking about the political importance of human–herd animal relations in a way that draws our attention to how political life moves across scales, transcending distinctions between domestic or everyday contexts and the more spectacular forms of macroscale political life. The importance of walled sites and the fields of tombs in the Tsaghkahovit Plain transforms if we view them as a node in the interconnected itineraries of animals pre- and postmortem (along with ceramics, metals, and many other items). Mapping those itineraries opens a space to develop new questions about how human and herd animals lived and worked together and how political life was actively brought into being within and beyond the walled sites of Gegharot and Tsaghkahovit.

· 5 ·

MAKING MILK
Human and Animal Labor

This chapter deals with a surprising discovery—one that led to an archaeological mystery. The mystery I try to solve in the following pages is, admittedly, a peculiarly archaeological problem. One where humble materials like bone, stone, and dirt crash in and shatter the delicate apparatus through which archaeologists are busy distilling stories about the past. But, in contrast to the romantic image of archaeology, this surprise—and the mystery it uncovered—was not revealed while hiking across the countryside, discovering lost cities, or finding meaningful patterns in the rocks scattered along the hillsides or hidden in remote valleys. Nor was I digging into the earth and slowly . . . carefully . . . painstakingly . . . brushing away the last few millimeters of dirt covering an ancient object.

Instead, I was sitting in front of my laptop in Chicago, on a cold January afternoon. The last few rays of weak sunlight were filtering in through the windows and a cup of coffee sat cooling on the desk. I was slumped in an uncomfortable office chair, surrounded by messy piles of books and papers covering both the desk and the floor. Everything was finally ready. The code to run the analysis of the data had been debugged, the data cleaned, and finally, after a series of frustrations and setbacks, I could get the computer to do what I wanted. All this effort was required to generate a deceptively simple graph. This figure would visualize a set of numbers, generated from the analysis of oxygen isotopes in the enamel of sheep's teeth—numbers that would reveal to me the time of year that these sheep, living over three thousand years earlier in the Tsaghkahovit Plain, had been born. But just a few keystrokes later, I was looking at something I had never expected to see: *sheep in the Late Bronze Age Tsaghkahovit Plain were born nearly year-round* (figure 5.1).

This finding surprised me because at first glance, it seemed strangely *modern*. The expansion of birth seasonality *feels* modern because year-round fluid milk production is depicted as a technological achievement—alongside refrigeration, pasteurization, and railroads—that was part of the development of industrial milk production in the nineteenth and twentieth centuries. From that perspective, there was no reason to expect it nearly three thousand years earlier. This sense of surprise turned the data into a mystery that needed to be solved. What was happening in the Tsagh-kahovit Plain during the Late Bronze Age? How might I explain the expansion of births across the calendar? Why did this expansion of birth seasonality happen millennia before it was *expected* to? As I puzzled over this expectation, I began to unravel the submerged connections between the role of intensified reproduction in industrialized agriculture and the tools zooarchaeologists use to study human–herd animal interactions in the deeper past. I realized that the homology between birth seasonality in the Late Bronze Age and in nineteenth and twentieth century industrial agriculture was only partial. Modern milk production for capitalist markets (and the technologies that enabled and emerged from it) is oriented

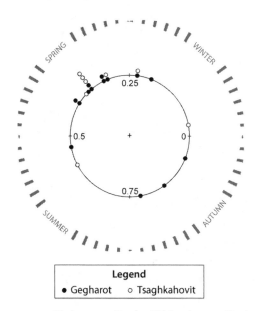

FIGURE 5.1 Birth seasonality (x_0/X) for sheep at Gegharot and Tsaghkahovit.

toward maximizing outputs and minimizing the cost of inputs. Looking at the organization of reproduction in the Late Bronze Age, I was struck by how laborious it must have been, yet without any great increase in the efficiency of production. Thus, the question was, Given that economistic logics of maximizing production didn't seem to be at work, where did that leave the interpretation of these data?

The sense that there is (or should be) a homology between the expansion of birth seasonality in the South Caucasus during the Late Bronze Age and the expansion of birth seasonality in the nineteenth and twentieth centuries comes from an entrenched genre of archaeological narrative. Bronze Age practices and technologies are often presented as either embryonic or precocious forms of the logics and practices of industrialization and modernity. But as I read more about the history of industrial milk, I realized that the stories linking milk in the present to milk in the past are composed from ingredients taken from the recent history of dairy production (cf. Armstrong Oma 2013b). The changes in the way people have produced, consumed, and thought about milk in the United States and Europe over the past two hundred years have been distilled into stories that seek evidence of increasing efficiency and technological progress in animal husbandry in the deeper past (cf. Porcher 2017b).

The history (and historiography) of industrial milk led me to a new line of investigation. Earlier histories of industrial milk had emphasized technological advances and industrial efficiencies, seeing mirrored revolutions in the more recent and deeper pasts (cf. DuPuis 2002; Sykes 2014). Newer histories of nineteenth- and twentieth-century dairy production have highlighted the social and political contexts shaping industrial practices *as well as* the impacts that industrialization had on human-animal relations and on animals themselves. What became clear to me is that the history of industrial milk production was a story about *labor*—both human and nonhuman. That led me to ask, What might be revealed if we examine human–herd animal relations in the Late Bronze Age as the site of *labor practices* rather than focusing on production?

When I look carefully at the transformations in human and animal labor that made the expansion of sheep births across the year in Tsaghkahovit Plain possible, efficiency and economistic logics are not what emerges. Attending to the textures of animal births, lives, and deaths in the Tsaghkahovit Plain reveals a critical terrain of *reproductive labor* that connects humans and herd animals. Examining this labor suggests some partial answers to the questions raised in the previous chapter about the nature of politics and authority in the Late Bronze Age. In the case of making milk and growing animals, human and animal labor together helped to shape relations of authorization-subjection and affiliation-distinction. Combining isotopic and zooarchaeological data reveals complicated systems of pastoralist production, which point to the possibility of multiple forms of felicitous authority emerging from human–herd animal relations in the Late Bronze Age Tsaghkahovit Plain.

HOW CAN YOU TELL WHEN SHEEP WERE BORN?

Archaeologists can identify birth seasonality in animals like sheep, goats, and cattle by taking advantage of what we know about the timing of tooth enamel formation and seasonal changes in the ratio of oxygen isotopes in precipitation. In temperate climates, the ratio of oxygen isotopes in precipitation varies seasonally. Essentially, this is because the heavier isotope of oxygen (oxygen-18) requires more energy to be evaporated, so as water cycles through evaporation and precipitation, its ratio of oxygen isotopes changes. As a result, summer and winter precipitation have noticeably different ratios of oxygen isotopes. Animals and plants take in water and incorporate it into the tissues of their bodies. In the case of tooth enamel, the enamel forms in layers (somewhat like tree rings) and isn't subsequently altered. So, within the enamel, there is a time series that records the ratio of oxygen isotopes in the water and food that the animal consumed as the enamel was forming.

Sheep, goats, and cattle have large teeth, which makes it easy to sample different sections of enamel that formed at different points in time. Archaeologists can drill samples from along the length of a tooth and measure the ratio of oxygen isotopes at each point (figure 5.2). While the details of this procedure are complex, in essence, sampling along the tooth produces a graph that represents the seasonal variation in oxygen isotopes.[1] The peak represents the warmer temperatures in summer and the trough represents the colder temperatures in winter. I analyzed second molars (M2s), which form during the first year of life in sheep, goats, and cattle. The enamel from an M2 gives us a record of what the animal was eating and drinking during the time when the enamel is forming, roughly the first year of life.[2] More useful still, the last part of the enamel to form is the part closest to the root, the cementum-enamel junction (CEJ). This gives us a fixed point to compare across individuals, even as the upper part of the tooth wears away over the animal's lifetime. Animals born at different times of the year will have a summer peak in oxygen isotope ratios either closer or further away from the CEJ, depending on how much time elapsed between the warm summer

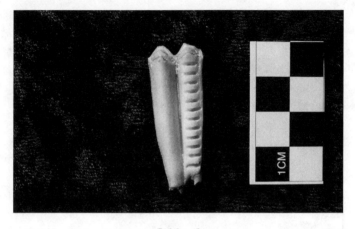

CAL-8

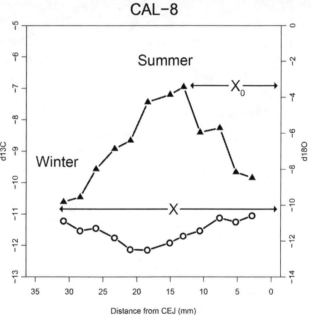

Distance from CEJ (mm)

FIGURE 5.2 Photo of a goat M2 incrementally sampled for isotopic analysis and plot of oxygen and carbon isotope ratios ($\delta^{18}O$ and $\delta^{13}C$) measured along the tooth. Filled triangles represent $\delta^{18}O$ values and open circles represent $\delta^{13}C$ values.

months and the end of the first year of life. To account for the fact that different individuals have differently sized teeth, the distances are normalized. The ratio of the distance of the peak from the CEJ (x_0) to the length of one annual cycle (X) is convenient and relatively intuitive numerical value (x_0/X) that expresses the season in which the animal was born.[3]

I analyzed teeth from sheep (n = 24), goats (n = 11), and cattle (n = 9) from large midden deposits at Gegharot and the Tsaghkahovit Residential Complex, as well as a small number of mandibles from graves and other special contexts (see Chazin 2021; Chazin, Gordon, and Knudson 2019; Chazin n.d.). For sheep whose birth seasonality could be successfully modeled (n = 22), those births covered 80% of the annual cycle (ca. 9.5 months; figure 5.3). Statistical testing indicates that the birth seasons from Gegharot and Tsaghkahovit come from the same distribution (Chazin 2021). The smaller samples from cattle and goats are harder to interpret especially since a number of the cattle had oxygen isotopes curves that didn't show the expected seasonal variation (Chazin, Gordon, and Knudson 2019; Chazin, 2023). Goats do appear to have an extended birth season, covering about 67% (ca. 8.0 months; figure 5.3). Cattle births cover about 37% of the annual cycle (ca. 4.4 months; figure 5.3). Summary statistics confirm the impression from the raw values, suggesting that both goats and cattle also had extended seasons of birth. For cattle, the expansion of reproductive seasonality is more subtle. The data suggest a main birth season of 4.4 months, which is slightly longer than the expected 3-month

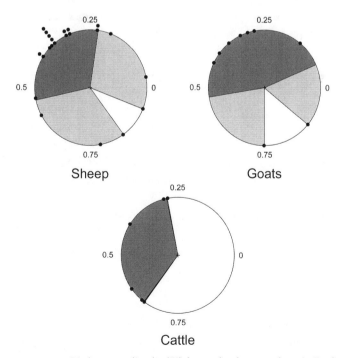

FIGURE 5.3 Birth seasonality (x_0/X) for cattle, sheep, and goats. Dark shading indicates the main season of births (see Chazin 2021).

period for seasonal reproduction in cattle (Balasse et al. 2021). It is not known how the unmodeled birth seasons would impact this measure.

Why Was This a Surprise?

The default scenario is that sheep and goats left to their own devices in temperate areas, will have a short (approximately 2-month) main season of birth at some point in the spring during which the majority of lambs and kids are born (Balasse and Tresset 2007; Dahl and Hjort 1976). There will also be a small number of lambs born "out of season." The data indicate that the main season of birth in the Tsaghkahovit Plain was much longer than would be expected (approximately 4–5 months versus approximately 2 months).[4] Wild and domesticated sheep and goats in temperate climates go into estrous during the late summer through early winter and give birth sometime between the late winter and early summer. The timing of the birth season varies with latitude and altitude. Places with shorter growing seasons have narrower seasons of birth. Physiologically, the timing of caprines' reproductive availability is governed by the amount of daylight (Chemineau et al. 1992), which helps to ensure that nursing females and young can take advantage of good grazing in the spring. Given the latitude (40°N) and high elevation of the Tsaghkahovit Plain, I had expected to find fairly strong seasonal constraints on sheep and goat birth seasonality.

Aseasonal reproduction in domesticated cattle is somewhat less difficult to achieve, as their reproductive availability depends on nutrition rather than daylight (Ezanno, Ickowicz, and Lancelot 2005; Hammond 1971). It is assumed that wild cattle had a seasonal pattern of reproduction, while at some point, domesticated cattle developed the physiological capacity for aseasonal breeding. Nevertheless, aseasonal reproduction in domesticated cattle still requires herders to manage both herd structure (mixing of sexes) and the availability of food (Balasse et al. 2021), especially in places with strong seasonal constraints on pasture quality and availability.[5]

Ethnographic studies and historical records make it clear that humans in the past took steps to alter the timing of birth seasonality for sheep and other herd animals (Balasse and Tresset 2007). Herders can constrain reproduction to shorten the birth season and avoid out-of-season births. Generally, tactics of this sort are meant to limit the amount of work associated with reproduction or ensure the animals will be strong enough to make the move to summer pastures. But herders can also intervene in sheep reproduction with the aim of having two separate birth seasons in one year.[6] The main advantage of this approach is that fresh milk (and other perishable dairy products) will be available for more of the year (Towers et al. 2017).

The data from the Tsaghkahovit Plain suggest human intervention into herd animal reproduction, which was meant to expand birth seasonality. Previously identified cases of expanded birth seasonality in the past were in climates that produced good pasture conditions in both the autumn and the spring, producing a bimodal pattern (Balasse et al. 2003; Hadjikoumis et al. 2019). But the distribution of births in the Tsaghkahovit Plain was not bimodal, and autumn would have been a time of poorer pasture conditions, not better ones.

In the context of industrial milk production in the nineteenth and twentieth centuries, the expansion of birth seasonality accompanied other interventions that greatly increased the amount of milk individual animals would produce and decreased the time interval between pregnancies. These interventions were woven together in a system that worked to increase overall production and also expand the seasonal availability of fluid milk. In the Late Bronze Age Tsaghkahovit Plain, milk was available nearly year-round—but I see no evidence that this shift in production practices would have resulted in more milk or more efficient production (cf. Towers et al. 2017).[7] In fact, the opposite seems much more likely.

Getting sheep, goats, and cattle to reproduce year-round is a lot of work! The simplest way for herders at Tsaghkahovit and Gegharot to override the system of biological control over reproductive timing (Balasse and Tresset 2007) was to feed them high-quality food at times of the year when natural pasture was unable to provide enough calories and nutrients. Another tactic would have been to wean young animals early while improving nutrition to reduce the anoestrous period after birth. Either way, supplemental feeding is critical to expanding birth seasonality. There is good archaeological evidence that Late Bronze Age herders did provide fodder to their herds (Chazin, Gordon, and Knudson 2019, Chazin n.d.). Foddering would have required cutting or collecting wild or cultivated plants and drying and storing them for later use. But the work didn't end there. Herders would have needed to care for pregnant ewes and newborn lambs throughout the year. Someone would need to do the daily work of milking and processing the milk nearly year-round, not just during the summer.

Extending birth seasonality wouldn't increase the total amount of milk being produced, since it is unlikely that individual animals would have given birth more than once a year.[8] Another point against arguing for the overall efficiency of production is that the Late Bronze Age herders didn't settle for the compromise position of two seasons of birth. Having flocks give birth twice a year (separated by roughly six months) would extend the seasonal availability of milk and young lambs while also reducing the labor associated with reproduction and lactation. Moreover, the age at death data from the Tsaghkahovit Plain doesn't match the ideal-typical models that zooarchaeologists usually use to identify intensified production in the past. Thus, the situation in the Tsaghkahovit Plain is one where considerable effort was expended to change the seasonality of reproduction, but unlike modern industrialized production, herders weren't maximizing outputs or minimizing labor inputs. To make sense of this labor—which was neither straightforward intensification to produce a surplus nor business-as-usual subsistence production—it is necessary to rethink what we know about the history of modern milk and the connections drawn between the present and the past.

MODERN MILK AND THE SECONDARY PRODUCTS REVOLUTION

The pattern I saw *felt* modern because the production of fluid milk year-round is generally understood as a product of modern technologies. Prior to the industrialization of milk production, in temperate regions, foods such as milk and other fresh dairy products were typically seasonally limited (DuPuis 2002, 28).[9] This was a natural consequence of the seasonality of dairy animal reproduction and the perishability of milk. Moreover, drinking fluid milk was not necessarily the most common way of consuming dairy products (DuPuis 2002, 29; Lysaght 1994; Wiley 2011, 44). But as fluid milk became seen as a necessary food for feeding human infants year-round, the seasonal availability of milk became a problem that needed to be solved (along with the problems of preservation and transportation).[10] Pasteurization, refrigeration, railroads, and the extension of birth seasonality (through improved nutrition and, later on, artificial insemination) were the modern technological solutions that made the availability of year-round fluid milk possible.

For the past 150 years, the story of milk in the United States and elsewhere—its expanding availability and the idea that it was a necessary food—is usually told as a thoroughly modern story of progress (see Du-Puis 2002). Advances were made possible through technology (railroads, refrigeration, pasteurization) and scientific research (in the fields of nutrition, microbiology, and veterinary science). The story goes something like this: as scientists discovered the natural goodness of milk as a food (by identifying the nutrients contained within it), science and technology made milk safe and available year-round. This version of the history of industrial milk tells us how as time went on, technological progress made it possible to produce more efficiently, as farmers began to produce more milk per cow per year. This, not coincidentally, is also the story that the Secondary Products Revolution (SPR) tells us about the origins of dairy production in the deeper past.

Secondary products are substances like milk, wool, traction power, dung, and blood that can be harvested from a living animal, in contrast to meat, hides, sinews, and bones, which require slaughtering the animal (Bökönyi 1974). The SPR, in its original form (Sherratt 1981), argues that the exploitation of milk and other secondary products was a later stage in animal domestication—a technological or economic innovation with important consequences. It presents the Secondary Products Revolution as an intermediate and consequential step between the Neolithic revolution and the industrial (or agricultural) revolution, giving milk a starring role in the origins of modernity.[11]

The specifics of the narrative Sherratt offered—as an interpretation of the available archaeological evidence from Europe and Southwest Asia—are as follows: increasing population and territorial expansion led to a shift from exploiting domesticated herd animals for meat toward exploiting their milk, wool, and traction power. Sherratt argues that these three secondary products increased the efficiency and output of economic activity in different ways. The widespread exploitation of milk as a food for humans made it possible to support a larger population, as he calculated that milk could provide more calories per animal. Moreover, herds could turn a caloric "profit" out of lands that weren't suitable for plant agriculture. Wool provided an easily transportable trade good. And animal traction, in combination with the plow, opened up new land to cultivation and increased the productivity of land already in use. Taking his model one step further, Sherratt suggests that increasing reliance on traction, milk, and wool, concomitant with the expansion and intensification of plant agriculture and pastoralism, may have led to substantial changes in gender roles and the transmission of property.

The connection drawn between modernity and the Secondary Products Revolution emerges from the way the argument established transformations identified in the deeper past as the origins or prototype of later developments. This link was explicit in Sherratt's (1981, 301) original presentation of the SPR. He argued that using secondary products *to expand production and increase efficiency* was the intermediate step between domestication and the industrial revolution, writing that "the secondary products revolution . . . created many of the basic features of the modern world."

Lives (and Afterlives) of the Secondary Products Revolution

Sherratt's model occasioned much debate within archaeology, and he revisited the archaeological evidence twice more in the following two decades (Sherratt 1983, 1997).[12] For both traction and wool, the accumulation of data since Sherratt wrote continues to support the basic claim that plowing, wheeled vehicles, and woolen textiles developed after the initial domestication of cattle and sheep (Greenfield 2010; Sykes 2014). In contrast, for dairy products, the introduction of new molecular and genetic methods has dramatically transformed the terrain of the discussion about the SPR. These technologies have made it possible to identify and track the genes for lactase persistence and the molecular residues of milk and other dairy products (first in the fabric of ceramic vessels and later on in the dental calculus from human teeth).

It is now clear that, contrary to Sherratt's original argument, early farmers were collecting and consuming milk from cattle, sheep, and goats. Studies of ceramics revealed extensive and early milk consumption in archaeological sites around the Sea of Marmara in the seventh millennium BCE (Evershed et al. 2008), in early farming sites along the northern Mediterranean (Debono Spiteri et al. 2016), and in the early Neolithic in the United Kingdom (Cramp et al. 2014; Richards, Schulting, and Hedges 2003). Dental calculus studies have provided direct evidence of human dairy consumption in samples dating to between the third and fifth millennium BCE in Europe, the Caucasus, and the Eurasian steppes (Warinner et al. 2014; A. Scott et al. 2022).

For some archaeologists, the mounting evidence that milk was exploited from shortly after herd animals were domesticated invalidates Sherratt's arguments (see, e.g., Vigne and Helmer 2007). To their minds, the fact that milking was an early part of domestication suggested that the use of secondary products would not have had a transformative effect in later periods because it was not novel. However, other archaeologists—rightly to my mind—argue that the SPR was not fundamentally an argument about the *earliest use* but rather *"when the scale of exploitation changed"* (Greenfield 2010, 43). Scholars in this camp emphasize that the SPR is a model for, and an argument about, the intensification of production (Greenfield 2010;

Greenfield and Arnold 2015; Marciniak 2011; see also Allentuck 2015). Despite these ongoing debates over how to investigate and interpret the new evidence of human–herd animal interactions in the deeper past, the other half of the SPR—the idea that the origins of the modern world can be found in animal exploitation in the deeper past—continues to circulate within archaeology and beyond, having been enshrined in how we talk about the history of milk.

One common zooarchaeological tool, the survivorship curve, illustrates the larger issues at stake. Survivorship curves track the age at which animals are slaughtered, usually based on age at death as determined by the relative wear of the mandibular teeth.[13] They are based on calculations of animal mortality, and they provide a convenient means of visualizing what porportions of the animals were killed at different ages. Payne (1973) developed a set of ideal-typical models for the efficient production of meat, milk, and wool that specified culling decisions based on age and sex (see Grant 1975 for similar models for cattle), which were presented visually as survivorship curves (figure 5.4). In the meat-maximizing model, young males, and potentially some females, are slaughtered once they reached full size (at between 18 and 30 months). This avoids wasting pasture or fodder on animals that won't grow any larger. Enough females are retained to reproduce the herd. In the milk model, males are slaughtered very young to prevent them from competing with humans for milk (or wasting pasture or fodder). Females are only slaughtered once they are no longer capable of reproducing. In the wool/traction model, males and females are kept into adulthood and only slaughtered once they can't provide traction or the quality of their coat decreases. These models are ideal-typical inasmuch as they represent the logical endpoints of the efficient production and exploitation of *one* product (either meat, milk, or wool or traction). These extremes are contrasted against more conservative subsistence practices whereby herders prioritize stable herd demographics in the face of risk and consistent, if inefficient, production (cf. Marom and Bar-Oz 2009).

Survivorship curves have played a key role in debates about ancient dairying, largely because Payne's models offer the promise of identifying the kind of intensification imagined in the SPR. Their economistic logics establish a connection between herds and herders in the deeper past and the later histories of industrialized agricultural production. But the use of survivorship curves has not been limited to assessing the SPR model (e.g., Crabtree 1990; deFrance 2009). They are well established in zooarchaeological practice because they enable zooarchaeologists to contribute to the wider archaeological conversations on surplus. Survivorship curves are

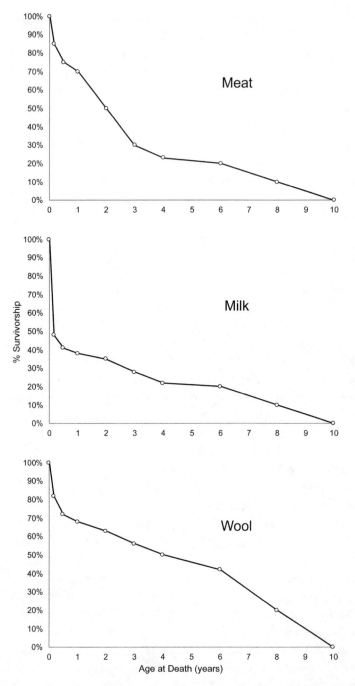

FIGURE 5.4 Payne's models, showing culling patterns based on age (Payne 1973).

one of a wider set of analytical tools in archaeology that rely on, and also entrench, the idea of surplus production as the key factor linking economic and political life in the past.[14] There is a deep-rooted recursion between the sense that surplus makes in archaeological theories and the abilities of survivorship curves to reveal surplus in the archaeological record.[15] The result is twofold: (1) it lodges economistic logics within taken-for-granted aspects of archaeological practice and (2) it entrenches the sense that the political role of herd animals is as the stuff of politics—merely a resource for human political projects.

What *has* changed in recent decades is the role of the genetics of lactase persistence in finding the origins of the present in the past. Rather than the increasingly efficient exploitation of herd animals for calories and cash, these narratives rely on tracing genes. In a recent review, Roffet-Salque and colleagues (2018, 127) use genetics to claim a link between the present and deep past: "The multi-billion Euro modern dairy economy is the direct consequence of both humans' ability to tame ruminant species and their genetic adaptation to animal's milk, namely lactase persistence (LP), with most people in Europe being tolerant to lactose." Narratives about the relationship between the genes linked to lactase persistence and ideas about European history and identities circulate widely beyond technical discussions of animal husbandry and ancient genomics in prehistory. An article in the *Economist* publicized the results of a study by an economist testing the theory that "people who could digest milk, . . . used resources more efficiently than those who couldn't. They could extract liquid energy from livestock, in addition to the wool, fertilizer, ploughing power, and meat for which others raised them" ("No Use Crying" 2015). The appearance of this line of thought outside anthropology can, in part, be traced back to Jared Diamond's use of Sherratt's arguments about the SPR (see Cook 2014; Diamond 1997, 449).[16]

Nevertheless, we should acknowledge that these narratives persist for reasons beyond the specific arguments about the SPR or even the weight of the archaeological evidence. This reflects the ease with which we can accept one or both of the following propositions: (1) milk is an important and transformative food and (2) intensification of production in the past is the origin story of industrialization or political complexity. If these ideas appear simple and intuitive, it is because they were deeply shaped by the history of industrialization of milk production in the United States and Europe. The continued appeal of linking the history of capitalism and colonialism to ancient dairying in Europe and the Near East is perhaps less than surprising, as whiteness and milk drinking were equated with one another long before the development of next-generation genomic science and archaeological discoveries of early milking. The connection between European or White "superiority" and milk emerged at the beginning of industrialized production of milk and the scientific discovery of its macronutrients in the nineteenth and twentieth centuries (DuPuis 2002, 11; Wiley 2011, 37; 2014, 108–10, 159), which produced a commonsense understanding of milk's importance.[17]

Moreover, the SPR and industrial milk production appear to form a simultaneously logical and historical sequence. When combined, they plot out increasing technological intervention into the bodies and lives of herd animals, over the centuries and millennia, in the pursuit of more efficient extraction. The timeline begins with domestication, continues through the manipulation of herd demographics through strategies of culling on the basis of sex and age and then to intensive and intentional selective breeding, and culminates in industrial control over of the bodies of cows and the molecules of milk. The SPR, especially in its original form, exemplifies what Jocelyne Porcher (2017b) calls *zootechnics*. Zootechnics narrowly focus analyses of human-livestock relations through logics that are industrial, utilitarian, and productivist—what Graeber (2001, 263n5) calls economistic logics. In the SPR model, these narrowly focused logics of intensification are what establish the connection between the deeper past and present.

But economistic logics are not the only way to bridge between the present and the deeper past. When reading recent scholarship on the history of industrialization in milk production, I noticed that multiple historians had written about the changes in dairy production as changes in the *labor* of cows. I was struck by this narrative, which told the history of industrialization as a series of changes in the working conditions for herd animals. It led me to pay close attention to the transformations in human and animal labor in the Late Bronze Age Tsaghkahovit Plain, not to present them as embryonic forms of what would come later, but as part of a wider acknowledgment of the necessary interrelationship between labor and reproduction in humans' relationship to domesticated herd animals.

Retelling the History of Industrial Milk

"Got milk?" is the iconic exhortation of the US dairy lobby in its long-running ad campaign to encourage people to drink fluid milk every day. It nicely encapsulates the tension between the ubiquity of fluid milk in the

modern United States and the work needed to create and maintain that
ubiquity. Advocates of fluid milk consumption argue that milk is a natural
and "nutritionally complete" food. This stance subtly suggests that people
in the past would have taken advantage of the goodness of milk had they
been able to overcome the technical problems of storage and the seasonality of reproduction.[18] But as Melanie DuPuis (2002) details, both the idea
of the "natural" goodness of milk and the industrialization of its production
in the United States came out of a fraught history of struggle over science,
gender, reproduction (both human and animal), religion, and politics.

This history was, most definitely, not a natural and unremarkable con-
tinuation of earlier agrarian foodways, where milk was processed into a
variety of products and either consumed within the household or sold at
market. Instead, the widespread naturalization and expansion of fluid milk
consumption began with the larger-scale substitution of cow's milk for human breast milk in the nineteenth century in the United States and Europe
(DuPuis 2002). Supplementing or replacing human breast milk with milk
from domesticated herd animals was only an occasional practice prior to
this point, albeit one with a long history (Dunne et al. 2019). But in the
nineteenth century, changes in how labor was organized collided with
then-current ideas about women's proper roles as mothers. In the after-
math, feeding infants on cow's milk, once an ad hoc solution to individual
problems with breastfeeding, became a normal choice for many mothers.

Previously, especially in rural settings, breastfeeding was a part of
women's informal collective labor arrangements. But in the cities, breastfeeding became an individual activity. Poor, middle-class, and elite women
in cities felt the pressure of these changes in different ways. Poor women, especially single mothers, were caught between the need to breastfeed and the
need to earn wages through work outside the home. Middle-class women's
relationships to breastfeeding were remodeled by their increasing isolation
in the urban domestic space, which disrupted their networks of labor and
support (DuPuis 2002, 62). For upper-class women, paying for a wet nurse
was a possibility but one that was increasingly fraught. Wet nurses tended
to be poor women from the urban slums, and fears of moral and physical
contagion through their bodies made this practice unappealing to upper-
class families in the United States.[19] These different trends converged to
dramatically increase the use of cow's milk as the primary food for infants
in cities in the nineteenth century (see also Smith-Howard 2014).

As cow's milk became a standard food for urban infants, drinking milk
transformed from a seasonal (and primarily rural) practice into a year-
round, urban one. The new demand for fluid milk in all seasons was met

by early attempts to industrialize milk production. Cows were kept in close quarters and fed on the leftover grain from breweries in "swill dairies," located at the edge of the cities they supplied. In addition to problems of microbial contamination, the rush to supply milk also encouraged swindlers to adulterate the urban milk supply in appalling ways (Atkins 2010). As women in cities fed infants cow's milk, there was a shocking increase in infant mortality. Once the connection was made between cow's milk and infants' deaths, reformers were able to articulate "dirty milk" as a social problem. Even though milk from swill dairies was known to be dangerous, reformers in the United States did not advocate a return to breastfeeding as the solution. Breastfeeding was rejected because experts feared that women's bodies were also contaminating.[20] Women whose bodies were marked by "physical feebleness or moral degeneration, both of which were the result of city life" (DuPuis 2002, 64), could not safely breastfeed their children.

The solution to the presumed dangers of breastmilk from hysterical women and slum-dwelling wet nurses as well as those of the pathogen-laced, adulterated milk from swill dairies was wholesome milk from rural cows. The idea that cow's milk could be better than human breastmilk drew strength from both religion and science. During the Great Awakening, reformers, citing biblical allusions to milk and honey, promoted milk as a whole or perfect food (and a solution to the plight of the urban poor). This biblical justification was later reinforced when early nutritional scientists discovered that milk contained a panoply of new biomolecules, like Vitamin A.[21] For urban reformers, the appropriate source of this milk was initially rural farms and pasture-raised cows (in contrast to the notorious swill dairies). Over time, this evolved into a contrast between scientifically organized and hygienic industrial production on modern farms and the backward and unsanitary practices of traditional farming.

The demand for milk year-round led to drastic changes in the interactions between dairy farmers and their cows. To produce milk in all seasons, farmers had to improve the nutrition of their stock override the natural seasonal tempo of their reproductive cycle.[22] Rather than being turned out into pastures to graze, cows were increasingly being fed special fodder crops grown exclusively to feed dairy cows. DuPuis (2003, 133) gives an interesting gloss on this transformation: "The increasing specialization in dairying was, for farmers, a taking on of the work previously done by the cow. The cow no longer provided the work of her own self-management" (see also Smith-Howard 2014, 114). The shift to foddering was the first step in an evolving process of intensification driven by the desire to increase milk output. Over time, agricultural and biological scientists developed a panoply of techniques and interventions that increased the year-round reproductive availability of dairy cattle and the amount of milk produced per cow. Eventually, these techniques expanded to include specialized breeding of dairy cows, artificial insemination, and increasingly targeted dietary regimens (Smith-Howard 2014; Wilmot 2007).

There are two important insights to be gleaned from this version of the history of industrial milk. First, as DuPuis and others highlight, the demand for milk and the value of milk as a food are neither obvious nor preestablished. The traditional account of milk industrialization collapses the general caloric and nutritional value of milk with its potential as a substitute for human breast milk into a single idea of the "natural" goodness of milk. It also collapses the problem of seasonality and that of maximizing output into a single narrative of technological progress. This obscures the fact that the value of milk is not separate from the necessary relationship between fluid milk and other dairy products. This connection exists at two levels: the taste or desire for fluid milk versus other dairy products and the material reality that those products are produced from milk. On reexamining this history, what emerges is the complex relationship between the demand for milk and the seasonality of production. Not all needs, or desires, for milk lead to the need for year-round production.

The demand for fluid milk in all seasons in the nineteenth and twentieth centuries in the United States was not an example of a generalized model of intensification that seeks to increase overall output through efficiency. The initial factors that led to the industrialization of milk production were not solely aimed at increasing efficiency, but also at transforming cow reproduction in ways that better accorded with the politics of human reproduction and then-current ideas about class, gender, race, and health. It was only later, within that realignment of the relationships between cows' bodies and human bodies, that industrial interventions primarily sought to maximize output by intervening in the bodies of dairy cattle.

Thinking about industrial milk in this way also offers a second crucial insight that can be applied to the investigation of birth seasonality and milk production in the Late Bronze Age. DuPuis argues that foddering is an act in which the farmer takes on work previously done by the cow. This framing suggests that, rather than seeing the transformation of cows' diets as something the farmer (a *subject*) does to cows (as *objects*), the changes in what cows ate are actually a question of labor. Moreover, year-round milk production also tasks cows with a much heavier burden of reproductive labor. This reframing of the changes to human-animal relationships in industrialization of milk production inspired me to ask, What would change in the interpretation of the archaeological evidence of production if archaeologists approached it as a question of the organization of human and nonhuman labor instead of humans' use of raw materials or capital?[23]

ANIMAL LABOR: CONSEQUENCES FOR ARCHAEOLOGICAL PRACTICE

At a minimum, shifting from viewing herd animals as capital or resources to viewing them as beings that work argues for a social relationship between humans and herd animals.[24] Here the word *social* indexes the idea that both humans and herd animals belong to the category of subjects (see Battistoni 2017).[25] Although this is important, emphasizing labor or work goes beyond merely marking animals as subjects.[26] Thinking about animal work accommodates instrumental value (and relations) without allowing it to subsume or exclude other kinds of value and relations. Examining the work that herd animals do allows me to consider the instrumental aspects of humans' relationships to their herds without foreclosing the possibility for intimacy and relationships of care (Armstrong Oma 2010; B. Campbell 2005; Fijn 2011; Govindrajan 2018). It centers a sense of relationality that is ethically dense and ambiguous, encompassing humans' and herds' simultaneous interdependence and difference.

Not only is this an ontological claim—*these are subjects, not objects*—but it also declares that animals' labor is simultaneously "already-economic" and "also-political" (Battistoni 2017, 21). By allowing for the possibility of animal work, the expansion of herds and the production of things like meat, milk, wool, and other products become visible as the outcome of both human and animal labor and a site of politics. This derails the easy assumption that only the surplus produced through pastoralist production is relevant to understanding political life.[27] But it also provides a way to think about how the practices and actions that constitute and shape those relations of use form relations of affiliation-distinction and authorization-subjection.

What this entails, in terms of archaeological (and zooarchaeological) practice, is shifting away from using the logics of products (and surplus production) as the starting point or governing logic of our analyses. Moving away from the output of labor practices—and indeed, focusing on them as *labor practices* and not production practices—helps to root out economistic assumptions about efficiency and maximization. It avoids smoothing over differences in work practices that produce the same product. For herd animals, this is especially important for meat production, which can risk lumping together heterogenous labor relations under categories like subsistence production (Chazin 2023). It also makes it possible to integrate pastoralist mobility within the larger framework of labor. Foddering and mobility are different ways that humans and animals can work together to solve the issue of seasonal availability of pasture—and they have different impacts on other work tasks, like reproduction, lactation, and milking.

Thinking about animal work also helps us build from some of the important critiques of Payne's models and the use of survivorship curves in general. It offers a new perspective on one of the sticking points often highlighted by critics of Payne's dairy-maximizing model. Archaeologists have debated whether, in the deeper past, cattle and other herd animals had evolved the ability to let down milk in the absence of a calf or whether milkers would have used techniques (known ethnographically and historically) for encouraging milk letdown in the absence of the suckling infant (see Sherratt 1981; McCormick 1992; Halstead 1998; Balasse 2003a; Roffet-Salque et al. 2018). Critics argue, based on the historical record, that this ability evolved quite late—and even intensified dairy production in earlier eras would not have involved killing very young animals (McCormick 1992). Turning to labor shifts the terms of that debate into questions that must be explored archaeologically: Were calves key participants in the work activity of producing milk for human consumption? When and under what conditions were calves no longer required to participate?

Furthermore, one of the most problematic features of survivorship curves is that they collapse the bones recovered from excavations into a single unit of analysis—which, in the interpretations of the logics of culling and production, is then treated as a single herd (a demographic unit). For most cases, this necessarily glosses over the fact that faunal data are almost always aggregated—representing the accumulation of bones over time and likely from multiple, overlapping practices of production, circulation, and consumption. But nonetheless, we can salvage two things. First, is a curiosity about what we might learn about culling by looking at the age and sex patterns in zooarchaeological data. And second is allowing for interpretations that embrace the fundamental interrelationships of age, sex, eating and feeding, reproduction, lactation, and growing bodies that are the underlying cause of the "fuzziness" of zooarchaeological survivorship—forms of uncertainty that previously has been framed as a problem for modeling (e.g., Price, Wolfhagen, and Otárola-Castillo 2016; Greenfield and Arnold 2015; Marom and Bar-Oz 2009; Vigne and Helmer 2007). Rather than seeking to classify our data in terms of products, we can use it to pose questions about the interrelationship between human work and animal work (cf. Agbe-Davies 2015).

ANIMALS AT WORK IN THE TSAGHKAHOVIT PLAIN

It is perhaps all too easy to see the expansion of birth seasonality in herd animals as a form of increasing human control since control over reproduction has played such an outsized role in discussions of domestication and in industrial agriculture. However, if we shift to asking about labor, what becomes clear is that expanding reproductive seasonality so dramatically, especially for sheep, required a lot of labor on the part of people. But there's more. Thinking about labor highlights: (1) shifts in the balance of labor between humans and sheep, (2) the proliferation of labor, and (3) the role of labor in shaping relations between humans. Expanding birth seasonality required humans to take on portions of herd animals' labor. Rather than leaving to animals the responsibility for feeding themselves from pastures or fields, people in the Tsaghkahovit Plain stepped in by cultivating or collecting and storing food (Chazin, Gordon, and Knudson 2019).

To do so, people cut and collected plants, either wild grasses or cultivated plants like barley or millet, to supplement herd animals' diets (box 5.1). Winters in the plain, which is high in the mountains, would have been bitterly cold, and the inhabitants (human and animal alike) would have been snowbound for much of it. Herds would have found little to graze on even if they could break through the snow to get it, so humans had to work hard to provide enough pasture and fodder for the herds to keep them alive through the winter. The data show that some sheep, as well as cattle and goats, were fed fodder during the winter, but also at other points during the year. Approximately one fifth of the sheep and nearly two thirds of the goats analyzed showed direct evidence of foddering. Overall, the low levels of intratooth variation in the ratio of carbon isotopes offers more widespread, if somewhat tentative, evidence for foddering (as evidence of a more homogeneous diet than free-grazing in wild pasture; see Chazin, Gordon, and Knudson 2019, 63). The interpretation of isotopic results for cattle is complicated by the large number of individuals with atypical oxygen variation. These cattle were drinking from isotopically stable water (from unknown sources), which makes impossible to identify the seasonality of the carbon isotope variation (or their birth seasonality). Nevertheless, the overall picture that emerges from the isotopic data is that humans in the Tsaghkahovit Plain worked hard to supplement and shape what herd animals ate rather than leaving them to graze on natural pasture.

Box 5.1 Foddering

Isotopic analysis of sheep, cattle, and goat teeth from Gegharot and Tsaghkahovit reveals that foddering was not uncommon, nor was it limited to sheep or to animals born in the winter months (Chazin, Gordon, and Knudson 2019; Chazin n.d.). Isotopic analysis of carbon and oxygen isotopes reveals evidence of three different patterns (figure 5.5). These instances of foddering are archaeologically detectable because oxygen isotopes, varying with temperature, make it possible to identify the winter and summer seasons in the sequential samples along a tooth, creating a seasonal signal that can then be used to interpret changes in the ratio of carbon isotopes. Variation in carbon isotopes tracks two things: the balance between C_3 and C_4 plants, which varies both seasonally and between different biomes, and seasonal changes in plants' isotopic composition.[1]

Some animals were foddered over the winter (figure 5.5a). Normally, if an animal free-grazes on primarily C_3 plants, as we would expect in the Tsaghkahovit Plain, the peaks in the $\delta^{18}O$ and $\delta^{13}C$ values should occur at the same time. If animals are fed plants that were cut in the summer months during the winter, this inverts the two curves. One sheep I analyzed was fed a large amount of C_4 plants (either wild hay or cultivated millet) imported from elsewhere before being slaughtered between one and two years of age (figure 5.5b). The high $\delta^{13}C$ values indicate that during the winter, this sheep was fed a large amount of C_4 plants, which would not have been locally available as pasture. It is unlikely that the C_4 plants were grown in the plain itself. This suggests that individual animals may have received special attention within the larger context of routine, high-effort practices of care. The final pattern is more subtle (figure 5.5c). Many of the herd animals from the Tsaghkahovit Plain show very little variation in $\delta^{13}C$ values over an annual cycle. Yet even in a C_3 biome, there is seasonal variation in $\delta^{13}C$ values. This suggests some continual, and possibly substantial, human intervention in herd animals' diets.

1. C_3 and C_4 plants have a different process for photosynthesis, which produces a different ratio of carbon isotopes in their tissues.

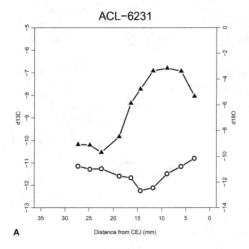

ACL-6231

A   Distance from CEJ (mm)

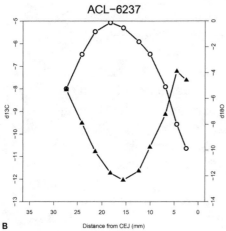

ACL-6237

B   Distance from CEJ (mm)

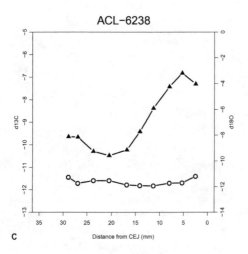

ACL-6238

C   Distance from CEJ (mm)

FIGURE 5.5 Examples of carbon and oxygen isotope data showing evidence of (a) winter foddering, (b) C_4 plant fodder, and (c) animals lacking expected seasonal variation in carbon isotopes. Filled triangles represent $\delta^{18}O$ values and open circles represent $\delta^{13}C$ values.

This shift in the work of feeding is one component of a larger prolifer-ation of labor. During the Late Bronze Age, everyone in the Tsaghkaho-vit Plain, humans and herd animals alike, was doing more work. While sheep, goats, and cattle didn't have to work as hard to keep themselves fed (especially in the winter), there was no such thing as a free lunch of hay. Collectively, herd animals at Tsaghkahovit and Gegharot—sheep most of all—were tasked with a proliferation of their reproductive labor across the seasons (Chazin 2023). Alongside this task, human labor proliferated even more markedly. Foddering required growing or collecting wild or cultivated plants, drying them, and then storing them, and in addition to the work of foddering, the expansion of birth seasonality would have transformed a number of other tasks from seasonally limited forms of work into year-round labor.

Someone would need to spend time taking care of pregnant animals and newborns all year long, not just during the spring. On top of that, someone would need to milk the lactating animals. Herders would probably have let the nursing animal suckle for a bit, then milked the mother, and finally re-turned the young animal for a last chance to suckle (cf. Fijn 2011). Milking requires keep track of individuals in the flock, monitoring their condition, and also establishing the intimate bodily rapport required to coax milk from an animal's udder. It is a labor practice that individual animals must be socialized into, and that socialization is another form of work (Mlekuž 2015, 279). It is likely that the schedules of the milkers revolved around the task for much of the year since it cannot be put off until convenient. After milking, the milk would need to be processed if it was not consumed immediately—another set of labor practices that was no longer confined to the summer season.[28]

This expansion and renegotiation of the distribution of labor between humans and herd animals may very well have deepened or intensified the social connections between species. People would spend more time during the year milking, and thus promoting the formation of interspecies social bonds. Moreover, Govindrajan's (2018) ethnographic work also indicates that the work of foddering, as an act of feeding and a form of care, can also create deep affective attachments. It is possible that as people developed a new repertoire of active participation in herd animal reproduction, this led to an increased sense of humans and herds as a joint social unit, tangling human and animal genealogies (chapter 6). This identification, or social in-corporation, could conceivably have been further structured, whether ex-plicitly or implicitly, by the knowledge that milk production joins humans

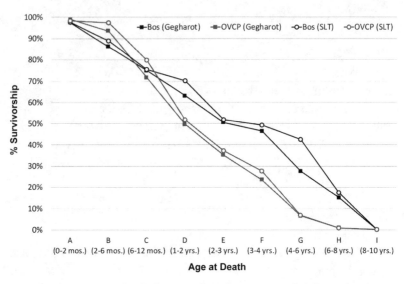

FIGURE 5.6 Cattle versus sheep/goat survivorship data.

and animals in the labor of (re)production but also in the consumption of herd animal milk to grow both herds and humans (Ingold 2011b).

Other lines of archaeological evidence reveal differences between the work of sheep, goats, and cattle. The survivorship curves for cattle, sheep, and goats in the Late Bronze Age Tsaghkahovit Plain show that on average, cattle lived to older ages than sheep and goats. Pairing birth seasonality with the survivorship data for sheep reveals at least two different sets of joint human-sheep labor practices (box 5.2). In the first practice, herders manipulated the timing of sheep's reproduction, restricting the season of birth and minimizing the labor involved. Doing so required keeping male and female sheep separate from each other to avoid reproduction out of season. This would result in a cohort of lambs born during a short season of birth in the spring, when they could take advantage of rich pastures. Some individuals from this cohort of lambs were slaughtered after reaching full meat weight but well before the end of their reproductive viability.

The second labor practice was labor-intensive, as sheep and people worked to extend births across the annual cycle. Herders would have supplemented the diet of ewes and allowed male and female sheep to intermix more often. As a result, some number of the ewes kept in this manner would become pregnant at different times of year, though herders likely took care to keep individual ewes from becoming pregnant too often. This produced a group of lambs that were born throughout the year. Some of these lambs were slaughtered in their second year of life (likely before reaching their full meat weight), while others were slaughtered between four and six years of age. This bimodal distribution of age at death may reflect the different life trajectories of male and female sheep. Because fewer males are needed to produce new lambs (as well as more milk), it is possible that primarily the male offspring were killed at a younger age. Unfortunately, there is no direct archaeological evidence available to test this surmise.

Box 5.2 Labor Practices

Archaeologically, the traces of these two labor practices emerge only when survivorship curves and the birth seasonality data are combined (figure 5.7; see also Chazin 2021). The survivorship curves for sheep in the Late Bronze Age Tsaghkahovit Plain show that 60% of sheep were slaughtered by two years of age (Age Class I) and 80% of sheep were slaughtered by four years (Age Class II). Taken by itself, this pattern is closer to Payne's meat-maximizing than his milk-maximizing model, but it is a poor fit either way. This may seem like a potential contradiction given all the work herders did to expand reproduction. What it actually indicates, however, is that herders in the Late Bronze Age Tsaghkahovit Plain did not respond to competing human and sheep claims on milk by slaughtering lambs at a very young age (to maximize the human share of sheep milk).

Instead, herders balanced human and sheep demands for milk and many sheep lived past weaning, if not to old age. Adding in the birth seasonality data gives a picture that is fuller and much more interesting. It shows two different groups of animals with two different life trajectories marked by both their births and their deaths. There is a group of sheep (Age Class II) that were born in the spring and slaughtered sometime between two and four years of age. In contrast, there is another group of sheep (Age Classes I and III) that were born throughout the year (including autumn and winter) and slaughtered in the second year of life or between four and six years of age. Other sheep, those slaughtered in the first year of life or after four years of age, have biographies that are unknown (due to the limitations of the faunal assemblages and the isotopic methods).

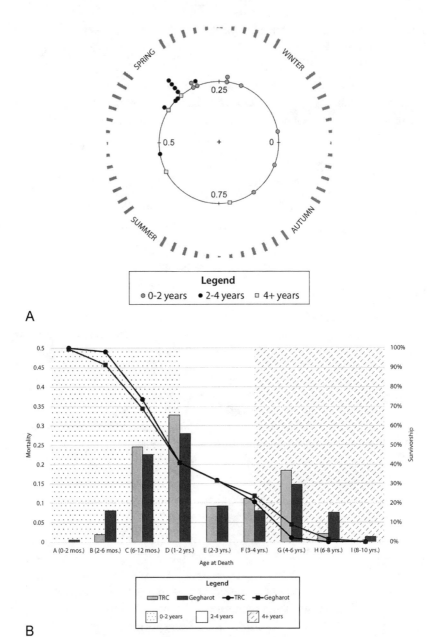

FIGURE 5.7 Sheep birth seasonality and age at death, divided by age class.

Given the smaller numbers of cattle and goats in the faunal assemblages, a one-to-one comparison isn't possible. But within the available data, there are indications that cattle and goats were herded differently from sheep. Cattle, on average, were slaughtered at older ages. Minimally, this indicates that the living animals had some sort of value, whether as a source of secondary products or as valuable in and of themselves (see chapter 6). Oxygen isotope analysis reveals different groups of cattle: those whose oxygen data indicate drinking from unknown, nonlocal water sources (and thus a different pattern of mobility) and those with oxygen data that show a moderately expanded season of birth and evidence of foddering. Goats have a similar aggregate survivorship pattern to sheep, but they don't show the same groups based on birth seasonality and age at death. Unlike sheep, goats slaughtered between two and four years (Age Class II) do not have a narrower birth season.

Taken together, these patterns indicate a complex set of activities spanning reproduction, feeding, seasonal movements, and culling. They varied across species and age classes, revealing multiple labor practices and coworking groups of humans and herd animals. Looking specifically at sheep, the picture that emerges out of this analysis is partial. Not only are we missing information about animals that were killed before one year of age, as I address fully in the next chapter, there are good reasons to think that the mandibles found on-site at Gegharot and Tsaghkahovit neither came from a singular "herd" nor constituted a single reproductive unit. Nevertheless, it is clear that the practice of extended birth seasonality channeled a wide variety of types of labor and altered their seasonality.

Minimally, this labor included haying, herding, caring for pregnant and young animals, and milking, but it may also have included tasks like cultivating specific fodder crops and processing milk into other dairy products. These changes would have necessarily impacted other kinds of agricultural labor, but the transformation of the seasonal patterns of herding could have also impacted the production of ceramics and metal. Changes in the labor connected to reproduction may have impacted work tasks connected to textile production, leather working, and other activities that used living animals or their products. Even though we don't know how work tasks were divided by age, gender, or other social statuses in the Late Bronze Age, it seems likely that this system would have impacted the work done by men and women (and people of other genders) of all ages. But at the same time, the complexity of the arrangements indicates that these changes would not have impacted all people within those social categories in the same way. Laboring to make milk and grow sheep brought different people together, both by literally "working together" at specific tasks and also through shared goals that coordinated disparate activities.

The complex organization that is visible—even as its animating logics aren't fully known—points to several ways to connect animal labor to political life. First, the proliferation of labor and renegotiation of labor responsibilities across species lines (likely as forms of care) would have shaped the intimate connections between humans and herd animals. These practices of care would be part of establishing and maintaining relations of affiliation-distinction and authorization-subjection between species and also among humans. Furthermore, the proliferation of different tasks connected to different pastoralist strategies and to products and species was potentially fertile terrain for labor that created different kinds of people, along the lines of gender, age, and other social statuses. These strategies of production, and the differentiation of work and workers they created, are a space in which to look for relations of authorization-subjection.

What (and how) do the proliferation and differentiation of labor authorize? Who becomes authorized to act felicitously and to what ends? The proliferation in pastoralist labor—especially the two different labor practices of sheep-rearing—may have been linked in two different ways to the composition of felicitous authority. Milk, as both a product and process, has different affordances than either living animals or meat. The considerable effort put into making milk available across the seasons may have been in pursuit of the particular felicities that milk channeled more effectively than living animals or dead ones. Yet it doesn't appear that making milk replaced other pastoralist strategies for composing authority. This suggests that there were competing routes to authority rather than a stable and unified set of relations of authorization-subjection. In the following chapters, I return to the more typical domain of zooarchaeological inquiry—the value of herd animals and their products—to develop this hypothesis further through the analysis of the unusual patterns in the distribution of bones at Gegharot and Tsaghkahovit.

CODA: THE VALUE OF MILK

In this chapter, I have focused on recouping labor as a site of a more-than-human political life in the deeper past. My interpretation contends that the value of milk was not entirely reducible to the production of valuable stuff. This was in reaction to the sense, as inscribed by the Secondary Products Revolution and maintained by the reliance on survivorship curves as a tool, that the value of pastoralist production was in the production of wealth or capital. More milk was better because the stuff could be put to work in "doing politics."[29] This view of surplus obscures the political possibilities of labor itself. But it also makes it harder for archaeologists to build interpretations that incorporate nonutilitarian forms of value.

It is difficult to avoid the question Why? when thinking about the mystery of the year-round births. The activities I described in this chapter are equally distant from the default of business-as-usual subsistence production and from the ostensibly universal logics of utility (cf. Sahlins 1974; Graeber 2001). That leaves us to wonder about the particular cultural logics of value that undergirded all this hard work. Unfortunately, the Late Bronze Age South Caucasus is not an easy place for archaeologists to try and answer these questions. But in spite of the difficulty, I want to suggest two possibilities of worthwhile lines for further thought and investigation that struck me as I wrestled with the question, Why milk?

First, the material nature of milk itself—its qualities—has intriguing possibilities. Milk is a colloidal solution made up of a range of different kinds of substances: fats, sugars, macronutrients, and water. It can be disaggregated into a wide array of substances, each with its own specific qualities. Milk can be transformed into butter, curds, whey, yogurt, cream, skim milk, cheeses in nearly endless variety, and even alcohol (cf. Fijn 2011; Wiley 2014). At first glance, the importance of these material transformations is their ability to turn a highly perishable substance into products with a longer shelf life. But beyond preservation, these products also represent substances with different qualities. Perhaps the most potent aspect of this potential for transformation is the separation of the high-fat components of milk (like cream and curds) and lower-fat components (like skimmed milk or whey). This opens up the possibility for the consumption of these foods to enact relations of affiliation-distinction (see P. Manning 2012).

There are other powerful semiotic possibilities in milk, as a substance that forms bodies and that flows between bodies and between generations. Milk as a food draws attention to the power of all foods to forms bodies, which is heightened by its necessary connection to both sexual reproduction and bodily formation as well as its key role in nurturing offspring among mammals. The labor that went into enabling year-round births may have woven new connections between human labor and humans' and herd animals' biological and social reproduction. This semiotically rich terrain and the connections it forged likely contextualized and shaped how milk was processed, circulated, and consumed. As archaeologists discover more about consumption practices as well as age- and gender-related social roles in the period, hopefully these become questions we can investigate more fully.[30] Both these lines of speculation highlight the need for archaeologists to develop tools to investigate the contours of value in the past. It is not enough to assume that the value of herd animals is limited to their role as a source of calories or cash. In the next chapter, I take up the question of value more directly as I continue to build a way to account for herd animals not just as *objects of value*, but as *producers of value* themselves.

· 6 ·

LIVESTOCK AND DEAD THINGS

Pre- and Postmortem Value

One archaeological mystery was more than enough. Nevertheless, the data from the Tsaghkahovit Plain were not done with surprising me. This new surprise, like the unexpected discovery of year-round birth seasonality, jumped out from the colorful lines and numbers on the computer screen. Rather than the singular jolt of figure 5.1, this mystery emerged across a series of counts and calculations rendered visually as bar graphs, each of which added to my sense of puzzlement. As part of more or less standard practice, I was digging around in the data, trying to get a sense of what parts of the body were present in the faunal remains recovered from Tsaghkahovit and Gegharot. Did the bones from these sites come, in aggregate, from the entire skeleton? Or were bones missing, and if so, could I hazard a guess as to why? Was it the result of the hard conditions bones suffer after deposition, ravaged by freezing and thawing, water trickling and rushing, inhospitable soils and hungry microorganisms reducing them to nothingness? Or was it a trace of what happened to animals' bodies after death during the Late Bronze Age?

Bones were definitely missing. But the missing bones weren't the small, delicate bones that are most likely to be ravaged by time. Plenty of sturdy bones capable of withstanding the rigors of deposition for millennia were also missing (box 6.1). That led me to ask, Was it not so much that certain bones were missing, but that there were too many of the other ones? Looking at the data, what became evident was that there were far more jaw bones (mandibles) and ankle bones (tarsals) than would normally be expected (figures 6.1–6.3). Why was this unexpected? Their presence in

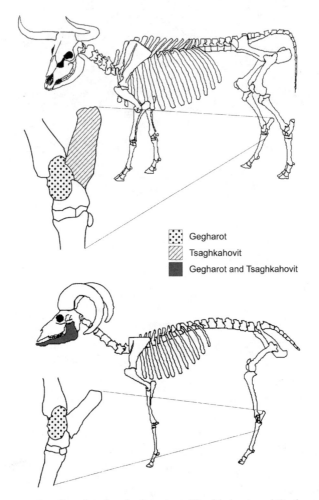

Gegharot
Tsaghkahovit
Gegharot and Tsaghkahovit

FIGURE 6.1 Overabundant body parts at Tsaghkahovit and Gegharot.

large numbers, pointing to the active selection of these bones over other body parts, didn't really fit zooarchaeological expectations for preferentially choosing meaty parts of the carcass to consume or what would be left over after removing the choicer bits of the carcasses, the remains of less meaty parts of the skeleton often referred to as butchery waste.

Those expectations are grounded in a paradigm focusing on the value of the dead animal, while often failing to consider the value of living animals (Russell 2012, 297). This oversight emerges from two aspects of zooarchaeological practice: (1) we start from the material remains of dead animals, and (2) we have a deeply embedded tendency to see animals as the source of calories and proteins or raw materials. Yet Africanist anthropology offers us a competing paradigm, one that stresses the value of living herd animals and is explicitly articulated through its difference from economistic and zootechnic paradigms of value (Porcher 2017b). Anthropological accounts of African cattle pastoralism stress that cattle are valued for the way they weave together society, becoming the ultimate source and figure of value itself (e.g., Herskovits 1926; E. E. Evans-Pritchard 1940a; Hakansson 1994; Comaroff and Comaroff 1990). This turn to the value of the living animal is an important corrective to zooarchaeology's history of reducing animals to calories, protein, and raw materials for production. Nevertheless, neither model alone—neither the utilitarian logics of calories and material production nor the value of living animals in creating and maintaining social relations—could explain the patterns I found in the faunal remains at Gegharot and Tsaghkahovit.

Models that seek evidence of utilitarian, maximizing, or productivist logics in human's use of animals in the past create an analytical bridge between the present and the deeper past. These zootechnical approaches to reckoning herd animals' value mirror how we think about their value in industrial agriculture. They assume that the difference between industrial agriculture and pre- and nonindustrial contexts is the extreme ends to which, as well as the means by which, the industry pursues efficiencies and monetary profit. Only in modernity is it truly possible to derive this kind of value from every part of the animal but the "squeal."[1] It is tempting to see the difference between models that are based in the value of living animals and those that assume their value as commodities or raw materials as the distinction between different kinds of human-animal relations: one in which the order of human life is integrated with (and perhaps even in service to) the lives of herd animals and one in which animal life is objectified and subjugated to human desires and needs. This stance resonates with critiques of industrial agriculture, linking the utilitarian value of animal bodies to instrumental relationships between humans and animals—all driven by the sense of human mastery over the nonhuman world.

However, Alex Blanchette's (2015, 2020) recent ethnographic work on industrial pig farming in the US Great Plains region suggests that this simple division obscures more than it enlightens. He describes how the endless pursuit of novel forms of postmortem value, driven by twentieth-century industrial imaginaries, has actively reshaped not only the bodies and genetics of pigs but also human labor, bodies, and social lives in the large region where this vertically integrated form of intensive pig farming takes place. Fragile porcine bodies, overengineered in the endless pursuit of standardization and maximal efficiency, create precarious forms of life that require a massive effort on the part of people to sustain. These superhuman efforts have impacts and ramifications that extend far beyond the barns and slaughterhouse floor, reaching into local microbiomes, the battered bodies of slaughterhouse workers, and the routine forms of sociality and care of the people whose labor supports these fragile pigs.

Blanchette (2020) details how the quest for profit is driven, not by meat production (in an era of impossibly cheap meat for domestic consumption), but by the transformation of other parts of hogs' bodies into raw materials that permeate our world and our bodies (even if we never eat pork). His book *Porkopolis* gives us an unfamiliar glimpse of our own world, one where we are caught up in porcine lives in a way that rivals the impact of cattle in African Cattle Complex societies. However, while it is readily apparent that cattle shape the worlds of pastoralists like the Nuer, it appears nearly impossible to trace all the porcine filaments weaving our world together. Our tropic mapping of industrial agriculture onto human dominance obscures the reshaping of our worlds—certainly driven by profit and instrumental views of animals, but not fully accounted for by our idea of mastery.

Starting from bones—which bridge between life and death in complex ways—pulls our attention to actions that create social worlds and form social identities in ways that are less noticeable in the flow in everyday life (both today and in the past). The data from the Tsaghkahovit Plain compelled me to think about value in a different way. I don't abandon the basic insight of the anthropology of value—that there are meaningful and important differences between capitalist and noncapitalist forms of value. That would be to make the mistake of zootechnics and assume that the value of animals was the same in the past as it is in contemporary industrialized agriculture. But where herd animals are concerned, that difference is not simply the difference between valuing the living animal (as a dense node of social relations) and valuing dead animals (as commodities or raw materials for production).

Rather, the way forward is to consider value in both instances as a complex social practice that emerges from *action*. Both the economistic values of capitalism and industrial agriculture and the value of living animals for sustaining "wealth-in-people" in African polities are shaped by the structuring, but nondeterminative, differences in the possibilities for social action afforded by living and dead animals. The value of living animals emerges from the possibilities of future reproductive labor, which can effect a variety of forms of spatiotemporal transformations. The value of dead animals is also complex, as it braids together the semiotic possibilities of wholeness and difference and the power of consumption as a practice that shapes subjectivities and has complex temporal rhythms and unstable futurities.

THE PROVOCATION OF ISOLATED ELEMENTS

Zooarchaeologists examine the kinds of bones found in various locations in archaeological sites, with an eye to teasing apart what happens to animals' bodies after slaughter—tracing the movement of different parts of the body through activities of butchery, food preparation and consumption; the manufacture of a wide array of objects from different bodily materials and substances; and the deposition of those materials at the end of their various itineraries. These analyses present a picture of the everyday repetition of activities connected to the most basic pieces of social life—the daily tasks of many different people across different seasons. Out of that repetition, we often get a glimpse of how people and things moved through the spaces of a site and how the rhythms of daily life may have shifted over time. What is interesting about the assemblages from Tsaghkahovit and Gegharot is the uniformity of patterning in body parts across different contexts of deposition, including middens, pits, destruction debris, and so on.[2] In all these contexts, what the data show is that against the background of fairly even proportions and low numbers of most parts of the skeleton from cattle, sheep, and goats, a couple of skeletal elements are noticeably overrepresented (see figures 6.2 and 6.3 and box 6.1). The practices that produced this patterning in the skeletal elements persisted across both periods of occupation at Gegharot during the Late Bronze Age.

Box 6.1 Taphonomy and Counting Body Parts

Taphonomic analysis of the faunal assemblages at Gegharot and Tsaghkahovit indicate that density-mediated attrition had minimal impact.[1] Plotting element density[2] against Minimum Number of Elements (MNE) shows no relationship between the density of elements and their MNE for either site nor for cattle and sheep/goats.[3] Calculating the humerus index, which measures the ratio

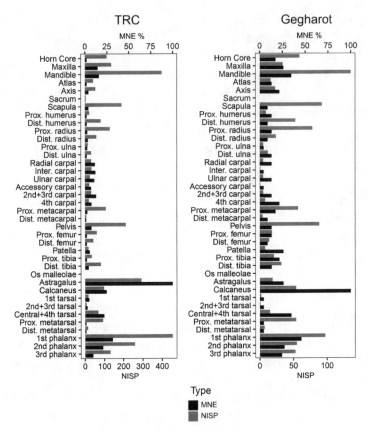

FIGURE 6.2 Cattle body parts. The gray bars represent the number of identified specimens (NISP) for each body part and the black bars presents the body part's minimum number of elements (MNE) as a percentage of the body part with the highest MNE.

of proximal humerus fragments (a low-density element) to distal humerus fragments (a higher-density element), offers another means to assess the level of density-mediated attrition. The humerus index was 29% for cow-sized remains at Gegharot and 27% for sheep-sized remains.[4] At the Tsaghkahovit Residential Complex (TRC), the indexes were lower—19% for cow-sized remains and 16% for sheep-sized remains. These values are higher than those recorded from a number of Anatolian assemblages (Arbuckle, Oztan, and Gulcur 2009, 146). Furthermore, other elements where the distal and proximal ends vary in density, like the femur and tibia, have much more even ratios (see figures 6.2 and 6.3), suggesting that there may have been attritional processes

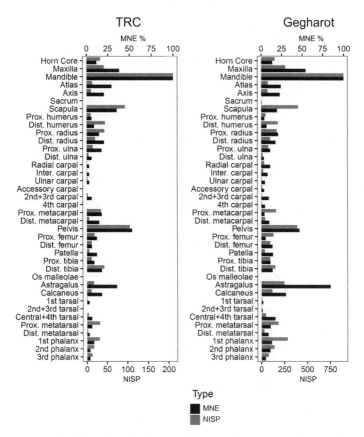

FIGURE 6.3 Sheep/goat body parts. The gray bars represent the number of identified specimens (NISP) for each body part and the black bars presents the body part's minimum number of elements (MNE) as a percentage of the body part with the highest MNE.

specific to the humerus, perhaps relating to butchery or cooking. Calculating a modified form of Marean's completeness index (cf. Arbuckle, Oztan, and Gulcur 2009; Russell and Martin 2005, 90) for cow-sized and sheep-sized remains from different contexts of deposition at both sites gives values ranging from 70% to 92% (and values for the site-sector assemblages ranged from 77% to 87%). This suggests that postdepositional factors were limited and that much of the fragmentation of bones was likely the result of human action (cf. Russell and Martin 2005, 90). Altogether, this indicates that the patterns in the data reflect human action in the Late Bronze Age, not the uneven destruction of bones postdeposition.

Digging more deeply into the data reveals that different body parts are overly abundant at the two sites and that the patterns vary between cattle and sheep/goats (figures 6.2 and 6.3). Cattle astragali are overrepresented at Gegharot and cattle calcanei are overabundant at the Tsaghkahovit Residential Complex. For sheep/goats, astragali and mandibles are overrepresented at Gegharot—and at the TRC, there is an overabundance of mandibles. The overrepresentation of mandibles is especially surprising since the method used to calculate the MNE for mandibles is conservative and likely an undercount. The method used to calculate MNE is shaped in part by how the assemblage is divided into different groups. When different contexts of deposition are analyzed separately, the general pattern seen in the site assemblages—one or two overabundant elements alongside a relatively even representation of the rest of the skeleton (in much fewer numbers)—remains. Doing the analysis at the level of depositional context type reveals one further aspect of the data. At Gegharot, cattle astragali are outliers in all contexts of deposition. But the faunal remains from midden contexts also show higher numbers of calcanei and central fourth tarsals, the two other main elements of the hind ankle joint. At the TRC, the overall pattern of abundant cattle calcanei and sheep/goat mandibles is present across the main depositional context types.[5]

MNE is limited as a method of quantification because it can only be calculated for skeletal elements that are easily identifiable to genus or species when fragmented and it is sensitive to the level of aggregation of the data. To assess what the analysis of MNE might have missed, I also compared the proportions of skeletal elements using weight (table 6.1). This approach allows for the inclusion of remains that can only be classed to body size and not species.[6] Elements identified as to body-size categories were divided into five anatomical regions (lower limb, upper limb, girdle, axial, and head). I compared the proportions of the weight of bones assigned to each region to the proportions of skeletal elements by weight from two type specimens. For cattle, analysis using weights shows more lower-limb bones than would be expected, which accords with the overrepresentation of astragali and calcanei in the MNE analysis. There are also fewer axial elements (ribs and vertebrae) than expected, which suggests off-site butchery. For sheep/goats, there are also fewer axial elements than expected. However, head and lower-limb bones don't appear overabundant. This suggests that sheep/goat mandibles and astragali were separated from the cranium and the other bones of the lower limb, respectively. This is confirmed by a finer-grained analysis by weight within anatomical regions (see table 6.1).

1. Screening also had a negligible overall effect on the percentage of remains identified to genus and on the recovery of remains of animals of different body sizes (see Chazin 2016b for details).

2. Density values were those measured by Symmons (2002), following recommendations in Orton (2010a).

3. The lack of relationship between element density and MNE holds true even when astragali are excluded from the data at Gegharot.

4. Cow-sized and sheep-sized remains refers to bone fragments identified to the genus-level plus those remains that could be classed to mammalian body size categories but not a more specific taxonomic identification (e.g., long bone fragments, rib fragments, etc.).

5. For some contexts of deposition, most notably the middens at Gegharot and the majority of contexts at the Tsaghkahovit Residential Complex, cattle mandibles are overabundant when calculated by NISP but not when calculated using MNE (based on teeth in toothrows for mandibles). This is not the case for sheep/goat remains, where the patterns in NISP and MNE are in alignment. This suggests that cattle mandibles are being more heavily fragmented than sheep/goat mandibles and more teeth are missing, despite their larger size and robusticity. It is not clear what practices would produce this pattern.

6. While this does include some remains belonging to other taxa (including pigs, horses, and cervids), since domesticated bovids comprise 95% of the remains identifiable to genus, other taxa are unlikely to have a sizable impact on the overall pattern.

In short, there are more mandibles and tarsals than would be expected—from both cattle and sheep/goats at Gegharot and the Tsaghkahovit Residential Complex. These patterns in element distribution persist across both periods of occupation (Chazin 2016b, 317–18). But the details of that pattern differ within and between sites, as well as between large and small stock, which hints at a complex set of practices that broke down herd animals' bodies and circulated parts of the carcass and individual bones in different ways. What were those practices—and what kinds of value, or values, formed or were animated in these circulations of bones through space and time?

TABLE 6.1 Body part distributions by weight

Cow sized

WHOLE SKELETON

	Gegharot	Tsagh. Res. Complex	Ullerslev cow
Upper limb	23%	29%	26%
Lower limb	28%	22%	12%
Pelvic girdle	10%	15%	11%
Axial skeleton	17%	16%	32%
Head	22%	19%	20%

LOWER LIMBS

	Gegharot	Tsagh. Res. Complex	Ullerslev cow
Carpals	3%	1%	8%
Astragali	31%	4%	7%
Calcanei	9%	16%	10%
Tarsals	5%	3%	5%
Metapodials	21%	57%	42%
Phalanges	31%	19%	27%

HEADS

	Gegharot	Tsagh. Res. Complex	Ullerslev cow
Cranium	62%	58%	78%
Mandible	38%	42%	22%

Sheep sized

WHOLE SKELETON

	Gegharot	Tsagh. Res. Complex	Soay sheep
Upper limb	28%	31%	24%
Lower limb	13%	9%	15%
Pelvic girdle	10%	12%	8%
Axial skeleton	18%	15%	25%
Head	31%	32%	28%

LOWER LIMBS

	Gegharot	Tsagh. Res. Complex	Soay sheep
Carpals	2%	1%	7%
Astragali	28%	9%	6%
Calcanei	12%	4%	6%
Tarsals	3%	1%	5%
Metapodials	38%	74%	50%
Phalanges	18%	11%	26%

HEADS

	Gegharot	Tsagh. Res. Complex	Soay sheep
Cranium	54%	49%	67%
Mandible	46%	51%	33%

Valued Dead or Alive? The Failure
of Utilitarian Models

The appeal of utilitarian models in zooarchaeology, as elsewhere in archaeology, is that they take an identifiable, material characteristic of an archaeological object that is accessible to the archaeologist in the present and leverage that into an account of possible causality in the past. In a simple example, because we know that the upper-limb bones of a cow carry more meat than the lower-limb bones, it seems straightforward to argue that the presence of upper-limb bones in a specific archaeological context is related to the meat they once carried. These logics form the foundation for the models used to interpret skeletal element distribution analyses in "complex" societies. Zooarchaeologists have sought to use element distribution data to differentiate between subsistence production (aimed at meeting local needs for meat) and other products and patterns that suggest larger-scale practices of provisioning (either via a market or a centralized administration).[3] They also use these data to look for differences between elite and nonelite status as reflected in meat consumption (Crabtree 1990; deFrance 2009).

Provisioning could suggest one of two possibilities. First, in the case of the provisioning of whole animals on the hoof, we would expect to see a limited range of species and ages in the assemblages and evidence for animals being butchered on-site (Arbuckle 2012; Zeder 1988). In contrast, if sites were being provisioned with cuts of meat, we would expect to see an overabundance of elements from the meatier portions of the body and the absence of butchery waste. The patterning in the skeletal elements from the faunal assemblages in the Tsaghkahovit Plain don't meet the expectations for the implicit baseline of local subsistence, nor do they match the expectations of zooarchaeological models of provisioning.[4] The focus on sheep and cattle and the high numbers of young sheep and goats killed meet some of the criteria for on-the-hoof provisioning. Yet the low levels of on-site butchery argue against a system of provisioning live animals (which assumes a separation between meat consumers on-site and the herders who look after the flocks). Since there is no overabundance of meaty body parts, it also departs from models of the provisioning of butchered meat.

Elite consumption models don't help much either. Outside mortuary contexts, there is little evidence for mapping social hierarchy onto spatial divisions in the Tsaghkahovit Plain. While the Tsaghkahovit Residential Complex is extramural and the use of space seems to be potentially different from the use of space within the walls of Gegharot, the difference is not one that can be glossed as elite versus nonelite. In any event, the basic similarities in the zooarchaeological assemblages between Gegharot and the Tsaghkahovit Residential Complex belie any simple explanation of social hierarchy or distinction on the basis of access to meat or cooking practices.

Even though the typical models applied to complex societies don't fit the data, can their foundational logics still help? That is, can we account for the unusual pattern seen from Late Bronze Age sites in the Tsaghkahovit Plain in light of: (1) the value of meat obtained from that part of the carcass or (2) the utility of bones, sinews, and hides for the manufacture of other items? No, not really. The abundant mandibles and elements from the lower hindlimb are not particularly meaty portions of the carcass, nor is there any evidence that this pattern results from eating the marrow from the mandible or the metapodial (the bone directly above the ankle joint). The relatively smaller numbers of sheep/goat phalanges in the assemblage makes it unlikely that the astragali and calcanei came along with animal hides.[5] The data also suggest that some of the mandibles were not associated with a cranium or skull, given that there are far fewer skull fragments in most of the assemblages than would be expected.[6] Nor is there any evidence that mandibles, calcanei, and astragali were collected to manufacture bone tools.[7]

VALUE-IN-ACTION

Mere economic or caloric utility cannot explain the patterns in the skeletal element data from the Tsaghkahovit Plain. But as I discuss in more detail next, the data from the Tsaghkahovit Plain don't match the expectations of models of the value of living animals in historical and ethnographic examples from southern Africa. Instead, to understand the patterns I saw in my data, I needed to knit together ideas about the value of living and dead animals. Moving away from treating these models as tools of classification, I realized I required an analytical framework that allowed me to think about the value of living and dead animals at the same time, without presuming their essential difference. I needed to reconfigure zooarchaeology's tacit assumptions about value itself.

The division between the value of living animals and dead animals, as different *modes* of value, suggests that the primary difference is between: (1) situations where herd animals are objects of value that can be compared to a range of other objects, say X number of coats, Y yards of linen, or Z bushels of stored grain, and (2) those where the value of herd animals comes from their ability to cement human relationships. This binary is a

more specific form of the larger debate about the differences between gifts
and commodities. To summarize a complex literature in extremely broad
strokes, in response to classical and neoclassical economics' theories about
*the ways in which exchange establishes the equivalence between things (as com-
modities)*, anthropologists suspicious of the universality of those theories
offered up a theory of the gift that centered *exchange as a process that established relationships between people* (Gregory 2015, 13). As a result, when we
ask questions about the value of material things, there is a strong tendency
to distinguish between the "desirability of objects" and the "importance
of human relations" (Graeber 2001, 45). Within archaeology, this contrast
reinforces the discipline's epistemic pessimism about our ability to understand things like belief and meaning, not to mention the nonutilitarian
aspects of value in the past (Wylie 2000).

But the anthropology of value also offers a different way of thinking
about value, one that is more promising from an archaeological perspective
and certainly more suitable to my purposes here. The approach to value I
outline here is deeply shaped by Nancy Munn's (1992) work on value—
and is in conversation with, but ultimately differs from, David Graeber's
(2001, 2013) work on anthropological value theory. In place of a close discussion of the literature, I offer four postulates that shape how I think about
value in the rest of the book: (1) value emerges from action, (2) value-in-
action creates *social spacetimes*, (3) value is fundamentally political, and
(4) animals shape value in ways that matter but are not determinative.[8]

Value emerges from action. Thinking about value as something generated
through activity reframes our questions about value. It moves us away from
thinking about the value of objects—what is the value of a cow or a shell
necklace?—toward the value generated or transformed by action—what
kind of values come from slaughtering a calf? From tending a garden? From
trading a necklace for an armband? This shift in perspective creates a powerful alignment between how we think about value and the important role
of the *trace* in archaeological knowledge production (Joyce 2006, 2015b).
Actions that generate, transform, collect, and destroy value also create material traces that may be investigated by archaeologists. It is also, in essence,
a radically expanded labor theory of value (cf. Graeber 2001, 45–46). But
that is only if we use *labor* to mean the kinds of activities that produce people
as subjects of various kinds and that produce the world—encompassing
what we traditionally think of as work but extending well beyond to include
situations where what is being done doesn't look like productive activity.

Value-in-action creates social spacetimes. This postulate draws our attention to the ways in which actions like gardening, giving gifts, traveling, and

eating food create relations between people and things in time and space. Different types of action or practices *construct* different modes of space-time that people experience subjectively as the context for their actions (Munn 1992, 9–11). Crucially, as Munn argues, spacetimes are shaped by the "qualities or properties" of the various entities involved in the practices that shape different modes of social spacetime (see also Hamilakis 2014). Taken together, the first two postulates highlight the fact that this is essentially a performative approach to thinking about value.[9] But the approach I am advocating here goes one step further. A performative understanding of value-in-action offers the possibility of bridging the gap between thinking about labor-as-activity and about labor-as-domination, which I discussed in chapter 2.

Value is fundamentally political. Graeber made this point simply when he wrote that "the struggle to establish what value is," rather than merely to accumulate it, is the "ultimate stakes of politics" (2001, 88).[10] What this means is that rather than focusing on quantification—X cattle for Y bronze ingots or the number of sheep needed to produce 100 pounds of meat versus cheese—looking at value anthropologically means thinking about how the intended or imagined outcomes of actions are ranked or hierarchized. The political struggle over value is the social struggle over what kinds of actions and outcomes should be prioritized or enabled *and also* what ways of thinking about, reflecting on, or organizing action should be given precedence—and under what circumstances.

Politics is woven through value in two different ways. Munn (1992, 20) draws our attention to the fact that the positive or negative value of an act—whether it produces an increase or decrease in the desired outcomes—is necessarily defined in relation to the moral-political premises of social life and ideas about what constitutes the "appropriate and possible relations of power." Positive value produces the kind of world we desire to live in, and negative value threatens the success of collective projects of world-making. Different ideas about value, combined with different moral-political premises in regard to hierarchy, decision-making, cooperation, and competition, form different topologies for political and social life.[11]

If we examine the relation in reverse, struggles over relations of authorization-subjection and affiliation-distinction are worked out in the terrain of, and through the terms of, value-in-action. Value is a key component (or idiom) of authority because it mediates the tensions and contradictions of social relationships. In addition to this basic relation between value and politics, Graeber's (2013, 228) work on value draws our attention to the political stakes of the interactions between different kinds of value and different value projects. He emphasizes that the struggle to establish "what value is" involves "how different values (forms of 'honor,' 'capital,' etc.) dominate, encompass, or otherwise relate to one another."

Animals shape value in ways that matter but are not determinative. Animals matter to value because they are a fundamental part of how actions that generate, transform, or destroy value shape social spacetimes. For instance, the value of cooked food is shaped in part by the need to eat it before it rots. It has a limited temporal duration—especially when compared to something like a stone axe or a monumental building (Weiner 1992, 38; DeMarrais, Castillo, and Earle 1996). As such, cooked food has different implications for shaping spacetime than other materials. But it is important to remember that actions involving food can have a wide range of outcomes, and those outcomes are necessarily shaped by the context of culturally and historically specific value projects.

For instance, cooking food and eating it is a complex action in regard to its potential for generating social spacetimes. Eating is powerful (and sometimes fraught) because it involves sharing substances, and therefore the risks and rewards of becoming what you eat and belonging to those who feed you. Munn (1992) repeatedly notes Gawans' distaste for "excessive" eating because eating food forgoes the potential to use garden products to expand intersubjective spacetime in more valued ways. Nevertheless, in the example of familiarizing predation in Amazonia that I discussed in chapter 2, eating produces positive transformations in social spacetime—creating kin and forging other kinds of valuable relations (see Norton 2015; Fausto and Costa 2013).

Furthermore, the materiality of animals and of human bodies matters to the unfolding of value-in-action as a simultaneously material and semiotic practice. First, nonhumans of all kinds are key participants in how value-in-action creates social spacetimes and how individuals experience their own actions within those spacetimes. But in addition to that participation, nonhumans have an important role in shaping the political aspects of value-in-action. Munn notes how particular entities—bodies, shells, canoes—embody qualities (*qualisigns*) that signify the positive or negative value of the actions that produce or transform them.[12] In essence, they become iconic (in the Peircean sense) of those acts and the value they produce.[13] At the same time, these qualities can be embodied materially by different media, which permits disparate actions like giving someone a calf, brewing beer, and making a speech to be understood as part of the same overall project of creating or transforming value. The material qualities of animals (and of human bodies and actions) make it possible to make connections across different acts and actors and to move between different orders of meaning or different modes of social spacetime.[14]

Bodies and things have many different qualities, and the politics of value is shaped by the potential for any of these qualities to be used for different social ends. For instance, among the nineteenth-century Tshidi, cattle could be used to accumulate value (thanks to the appropriation of their reproduction) in order to claim power over other people in complex relations of authorization-subjection (see Comaroff and Comaroff 1990). At the same time, the differences in appearance between individual cattle and the similarities drawn between the qualities of people and cattle allowed cattle (as iconic of a wide range of actions) to naturalize inequality between people. Value produced through action sustains the frameworks that legitimizes authority.

At the same time, value-in-action also contains the possibility for contesting or reshaping authority—for the performative transformation of its own grounds, through the medium of values. The "bundling" of different material qualities in objects and bodies (Keane 2005) offers the potential for recontextualizations or reorderings that advance different claims about what kinds of actions produce positive value—and what constitutes positive value. This leaves space for challenges to the felicity of value-in-action and for the competition between, and encompassment of, different value projects through social action.

For the remainder of this chapter, I use these postulates to guide my exploration of the value of living and dead herd animals in order to get a purchase on the data from the Tsaghkahovit Plain. I rework and remix ethnographic and historical examples, paying close attention to how value shapes social spacetimes and political action. Applying these postulates to my archaeological data reveals that both living and dead animals were active participants in shaping social spacetimes in the Late Bronze Age, but in ways that complicate any easy division between the value of living animals as social subjects and dead animals as economic objects. In chapter 7, I push this analysis further, following the action I see in the archaeological traces and examining how choreographies of value involving living and dead animals shaped the interrelationships of authority and value in the Late Bronze Age.

CATTLE LIVES AND AFTERLIVES

The distinction between the value of animals before and after death is not a simple one. Industrial agriculture finds value in both living and dead animals. Importantly, the living animal is valued in the same way as the dead one: as part of the calculation of the relative cost of labor and other inputs versus the profit from selling products derived from the animals (living or dead). In contrast, anthropologists and archaeologists have suggested that outside capitalism's search for efficiencies and profits, living and dead animals have different values (e.g., Ingold 1988; Hall 1986; Comaroff and Comaroff 1990; Ray and Thomas 2003; Orton 2010a). I want to resist the temptation to assimilate the differences between the potential potencies of living and dead animals for different kinds of value transformations into the familiar, shopworn distinction between relationships between things and relationships between people. Instead, what I derive from the ethnographic and historical examples that populate these literatures is that living and dead animals offer different possibilities for the transformation of social spacetimes—in other words, particular aptitudes for different kinds of outcomes.

Some archaeologists writing about the origins of the African Cattle Complex distinguish between the use of cattle as *allocative* resources and as *authoritative* resources, a division imported from Giddens's (1984, 33) theory of structuration. Giddens defined resources as "forms of transformative capacity" that generate either "command over objects, goods or material phenomena" (allocative resources) or "command over persons or actors" (authoritative resources). He mapped this division in resource types onto two forms of domination: the economic and the political, respectively.[15] For scholars thinking about cattle pastoralism in Africa, this framework provided an explanation for the value of living cattle. To wit, cattle are valuable as authoritative resources—they enable some people to control the labor of others by creating social relationships between them (Hall 1986).[16]

The distinction between allocative and authoritative resources shares a family resemblance with the distinction drawn by scholars working on African history and archaeology between "wealth-in-people" and "wealth-in-things" (see Guyer 1995 for a detailed review). The term *wealth-in-people* was coined to better elucidate strategies of authority in African contexts that seemed at odds with Eurocentric models of power and the state, to serve as "a shorthand for many syndromes of inter-personal dependency and social network-building that clearly involve strategizing, investing, and otherwise cultivating interpersonal ties at the expense of personal wealth in material things" (Guyer and Belinga1995, 106). But as Guyer and Belinga note, the concept of wealth-in-people is weakened when it is simplified and reified into a distinction between people and things.

That simplification ignores the accumulated evidence that the relationships between people and things, especially in the realm of power and authority, are complex and nondualistic. Moreover, it leads to assumptions
about the role of accumulation—of both people and things. The strength
and appeal of Marxist accounts of accumulation lies in how they specify
the interrelationships between the gathering of things and the gathering of
power. Accumulation as "the simple arithmetical processes of addition and
compound interest" blunts the critical potential of this framework outside
capitalism (Guyer and Belinga 1995, 108). What falls through the cracks
is our ability to investigate the possibility of quantitative accumulation
that is outside capitalism or different from our utilitarian and maximizing
productivist logics.[17]

Despite its tendency to collapse into the division between people and
things, the distinction between allocative and authoritative resources contains a useful insight as it draws attention to the different affordances of the
bodies of herd animals of different ages and sexes. Archaeologists working
in southern Africa transformed Giddens's analytical distinction between
control over people and over things into a distinction between cattle as
a source of materials (hides, milk, and meat) and cattle as the objects of
transactions that create or maintain social relationships (Hall 1986; Reid
1996). Even more importantly, Reid (1996) linked the difference between
the two types to the different material potentialities of animals' bodies,
emphasizing the connection between the reproduction of the herd and the
value of herd animals.

Because fewer male animals are needed to reproduce the herd than females, young male cattle can be seen as allocative resources (distributed
after slaughter). In contrast, because of their future reproductive potential
(in calves and milk), which is often an explicit part of the relationships
transacted through the medium of cattle, female cattle are the authoritative resource *par excellence*.[18] The distinction drawn by Reid is based on,
and highlights, the different temporality (and spatiality) of the processes
of consumption and reproduction, as mediated by the differences in the
materiality of animals' bodies. This moves away from Giddens's original
distinction between people and things.[19] Both types of practices involve the
circulation of animals and their products, just as both also work to produce
relationships between people.

Reid's differentiation of the types and tempos of social relationships
built through the use of cattle as allocative and authoritative resources is
similar to Ingold's argument about the difference in the nature of property
(as a *social* relation) in meat versus dairy (or *milch*, in Ingold's terms) pasto-

ralism. Ingold (1988) argues that that when people primarily use herd animals as a source of meat (which can only be harvested from a dead animal), herd animals will be singly owned. In contrast, when herd animals are used for products like milk, blood, wool, or traction, animals will be enmeshed in bundles of overlapping claims of ownership (or rights). This bundling is the outcome of practices of gifting and loaning animals, with different shares of milk (or wool) and future offspring belonging to both parties.[20] Milch pastoralism weaves together different households, constituting simultaneously the differences and connections between different ages and genders through the ownership of animals, the labor of herding and milking, and the distribution of products and young animals. This form of action is a key part, not only of the circulation of necessary resources, but also of the production of relationships of authorization-subjection. In contrast, Ingold paints a picture of carnivorous pastoralism in which households use the accumulation of herds to loosen or cut ties with others so as to avoid the material and social entanglements that circulation creates.[21] But it is not difficult to imagine how the distribution of meat after an animal is slaughtered may also be a key part of creating and maintaining relationships.

What I take from these discussions is not that the difference between the allocative and authoritative modes is the difference between people and things. What they point to instead are the different topologies of social spacetime enabled by the circulation of animals pre- and postmortem. The reproductive capacity of herds—which covers both the production of milk and offspring—offers the potential to extend social relationships between people (and also animals) in time and space.[22] In other words, it is a model of a kind of *spatiotemporal transformation*. The potential for spatiotemporal transformation relies on the futurity of reproduction.[23] But the spacetime it creates is also shaped by the rhythms of the everyday, intimate, and seasonal labor of milking and the consumption of dairy, which accompany the desired expansion of social spacetimes through the reproduction of herd animals.

Sharing and distributing meat, in contrast, has other potentialities— thickening relations between people through the distribution or consumption of meat when animals are slaughtered or sacrificed.[24] Its semiotic logics draw on the simultaneous wholeness of the animal and the differentiation of its parts (as discussed later in the chapter). The rhythm of its temporality is often punctuated, shaped by the distinctions between everyday eating and marked occasions of commensality, like feasts. Its futurity is anchored in the necessity and pleasures of eating and the transformation of animal flesh into people's bodies.

Before I examine the differences between living and dead animals' ability to shape social spacetime in the Late Bronze Age Tsaghkahovit Plain, I want to emphasize how my reworking of the distinction between authoritative and allocative resources challenges the implicit division between modern and nonmodern and capitalist and noncapitalist forms of value. Capitalist and other more recent value projects also shape social spacetimes through the capacities of living animals—and not merely through the utilization of dead animals.

In the ethnographic and archaeological examples discussed earlier, the transformation of social spacetime is based on the generalized reproductive capacities of female herd animals. But the development of modern in-and-in breeding, most famously by Robert Bakewell in eighteenth-century Britain, generated a novel form of (capitalist) value from the same general reproductive potential (Ritvo 1994).[25] This new kind of breeding practice established what Harriet Ritvo (1994) calls "genetic capital," which figured the monetary (but not only monetary) value of certain sires of a particular breed by uniting individual reproductive capacity with the value of the line of the breed as a whole (see Franklin 1997).

It is interesting that this form of value emphasizes the importance of *male* reproductive capacity—in the form of a limited number of individual sires (see Rosenberg 2020)—rather than the more generic female reproductive capacity in models of authoritative resources and milch pastoralism. Sarah Franklin (1997) extends Ritvo's (1994) framework to the development of novel forms of reproductive technology, arguing that the cloning of Dolly created a new form of "breedwealth." Cloning is an intensification of the reproduction of the genetic value first established by in-and-in breeding, creating what Franklin (1997, 436) calls a "time compression." Cloning as a reproductive technology, in other words, attempted to accelerate the spatiotemporal transformations of "genetic capital."

For the Nuer in the early twentieth century, according to Evans-Pritchard's (1940a, 1956) accounts, clans had both human ancestors and ancestral herds. Not only did cows' reproductive potential form the basis for the matrilineal herd's extension through time, the cross-species consumption of cow's milk imbricated human and cattle genealogies though its production of consubstantiality.[26] Archaeologists studying the European Neolithic have argued that living animals shaped social spacetimes through the interlinkages between human and animal genealogies (Orton 2010b; Ray and Thomas 2003). In this scenario, the generalized futurity of herd animals' reproductivity capacity is "activated" or channeled through social logics of genealogy, which links the future of reproduction to the past of social relationships—in this case, both the social relationships of kinship and descent as well as property. Ray and Thomas (2003, 41) argue that cattle were simultaneously "a means of reckoning descent, and a means of constructing the very fabric of human genealogy."

The imbrication of animal and human genealogies is not limited the nonmodern. Harriet Ritvo (1987, 60) has shown the interwovenness of the projects of elite animal breeding and aristocratic values in eighteenth- and nineteenth-century Britain. She notes that "cattle portraits, the records of generations of celebrated stock, resembled a gallery of distinguished ancestors, and a collection of cattle pedigrees was like a family tree." She identifies in the practices of aristocratic livestock breeding both an image of the lord of manor as the patriarch of a transpecies extended rural family and the possibility that livestock breeding was both a model and a mirror for human practices.

Orton (2010a, 196) argues that cattle's social role in the Neolithic was shaped by the tension inherent in cattle's status as "sentient property": between "the accumulation of livestock as objects and their role in kinship relations as subjects." I am making a different claim. Tracing value-in-action requires attending to how the circulation of living animals—with an eye to their future reproductive capacity in both milk and offspring—has different capacities for the transformation of intersubjective or social spacetime from those of the circulation of animal bodies postmortem. The distinction is not between the connections among people and the circulation (or accumulation) of things or between use value and social or symbolic value (cf. Price and Makarewicz 2024). The distinction lies in the specific characteristics of the entwining of people and things together in space and time.[27] Whether they conform to the logics of accumulation, commodification, or the gift is a secondary set of questions, with potentially variable mappings across categories.

Living and Dying in the Tsaghkahovit Plain

How might I find traces of the potential differences between living and dead animals in the assemblages from Gegharot and Tsaghkahovit? The ethnographic and historical examples I discussed earlier suggest that in thinking about living and dead animals, archaeologists should attend to the differences between animals of different species, ages, and sexes and to the material possibilities of animal bodies—their ability to produce useful substances like milk, blood, and dung while alive and the material differences between flesh, sinew, meat, guts, and bones after slaughter. Luckily, zooarchaeology has developed methods for attempting to determine age, sex, and species and is already well primed to pay attention to the different material affordances of body parts.

The model of allocative forms of value from Africanist archaeology stress the differences between large and small stock and animals of different ages and sexes. The data I am working with are categorized by species and body size, but there are some additional complications in the data available to look at animals' ages and sexes. The bones from Gegharot and Tsaghkahovit are well enough preserved to determine age at death for many individuals (figure 5.6). But sex is much more difficult to distinguish for most of the bones found in abundance at the sites (box 6.2). The situation is also complicated by the two different itineraries for faunal remains deposited on-site as the result of butchery of whole animals (possibly off-site) and the bones that came in as isolated elements.

Box 6.2: Determining Sex and Age

Determining the sex of animals in the assemblages from Gegharot and Tsaghkahovit is complicated by the limitations of methods of analysis and the complexity of patterning in body parts. For the group of animals butchered and brought into the sites as carcass portions, I can use the pelvises that can be directly sexed to estimate the ratio of male to female animals. From the pelvises, it appears that for those animals, a higher proportion of male cattle were slaughtered at Gegharot than male sheep or goats at Gegharot or Tsaghkahovit (the data for cattle at Tsaghkahovit were too few to analyze—see Chazin 2016b). In contrast, using Log Size Index (LSI) analysis to estimate the proportion of males to females suggests that the numbers of smaller- and larger-bodied cattle were roughly equal but that there were more larger-bodied sheep.[1] This data may be evidence of different culling patterns for different ages of cattle. Since the pelvis fuses earlier than other bones, that data includes younger animals excluded from the LSI analysis of other body parts. This provides tentative evidence that some number of young male cattle were slaughtered at Gegharot, though not exclusively males since the LSI data show that female individuals (of unknown ages) were also slaughtered.

The data for the isolated skeletal elements are also patchy. Astragali can be metrically sexed, and analysis indicates that more of the cattle astragali at Gegharot came from smaller-bodied individuals than other skeletal elements. For sheep, the mean LSI value for astragali were smaller than for other skeletal elements, but the distribution was also more bimodal. Because astragali are a nonfusing element, the patterns in size reflect both age and sex, muddying the picture. But it is clear that the astragali came from a different group of animals than other skeletal elements in terms of sex or age. Mandibles, in contrast, provide excellent data about age at death but don't shed light on the sex of individual animals. The sheep and goat mandibles at both Tsaghkahovit and Gegharot come primarily from younger animals (nearly half are from individuals of two years of age or less at death), whereas the cattle mandibles included more older individuals.

Aging data based on skeletal fusion provide information about the age at death of animals slaughtered on-site or brought onto the site as large portions of a carcass. That evidence shows a roughly similar pattern to the one for the mandibles. Cattle are slaughtered, on average, at older ages than sheep or goats, though young animals from all three taxa are present in the assemblage. The patterns in age and sex data allow us to eliminate the possibility that either group of animals was the offtake of surplus young males from pastoralists' herds. Some of the cattle slaughtered on-site at Gegharot were young males, but they represent one subgroup in a larger population. There is, however, a real difference in the average age at which cattle are were slaughtered in comparison to sheep and goats, which is true for both groups of skeletal remains.

1. LSI analysis makes it possible to compare measurements from multiple body parts, expanding the sample size for analysis (Uerpmann and Uerpmann 1994). Unfused elements were excluded to minimize the impact of age-related size differences.

In the pastoralist models I discussed previously, large stock (such as cattle, horses, or buffalo) are seen as more stable forms of wealth (and thus of higher value) because of their relatively long lifespans, lower rates of reproduction, and greater production of milk (Dahl and Hjort 1976; Ingold 1988). These material qualities render large stock especially suitable for generating forms of value based in reproductive futurity. In contrast, smaller stock are generally understood as the "small change" of pastoralist wealth, being valued more for their ability to produce meat (cf. Hoag 2018). Their higher rates of reproduction in particular make it possible to extract meat readily through the offtake of reproductively "unnecessary" animals.[28]

This distinction has less to do with maximizing the production of meat, since cattle yield more meat at once, and more to do with the relative suitability of species in achieving different social ends. Similar to the distinction between male and female cattle, large stock are more suitable in certain ways than small stock for anchoring the circulation of animals between people and producing products such as milk and blood. Differences in reproductive capacities and body size shape the relative abilities of large and small stock to create value (and thus social relationships) in the transformation of social spacetimes through the futurity of reproduction and also through the distribution of body parts and products for use and consumption. If the longer lifespans of large stock were key to the value of their reproductive futurity and the higher reproductive rates of small stock were key to their value as a source of divisible, distributable material things in death in the Late Bronze Age Tsaghkahovit Plain, we might see traces of those kinds of value-in-action in different culling patterns between cattle and sheep/goats.

In fact, however, cattle in the Tsaghkahovit Plain were slaughtered at older ages than the sheep and goats—regardless of whether we look at mandibles or at postcranial remains. If we can conclude from this that the value of cattle was more strongly oriented toward the living animal, then we can potentially interpret the increased proportion of cattle during the second phase of occupation at Gegharot as a sign of increasing emphasis on the value of living cattle. Also suggestive, in light of the potential differences between pre- and postmortem value, are the practices of structured deposition seen in the kurgans near Gegharot and the cromlech burials at the cromlech cemetery near Tsaghkahovit (TsBC12). Burial 02 from TsBC12 included the complete skeletons of two sheep (one male, one female) and one goat (male). All three were less than a year old at death: the sheep were 2–6 months old and the goat was 6–12 months old. Similarly, both Kurgans 1 and 2 had very young caprines deposited in the satellite chamber. In contrast, the horse skulls included in the central chambers of Kurgans 1 and 3 were from older individuals. These mortuary practices seem to confirm that the value of herd animals in the plain was structured by a difference between large and small stock that is similar to ethnographic and historical examples.

This interpretation is complicated, or perhaps weakened, if we consider two other lines of evidence. First, the birth seasonality data discussed in chapter 5 show that at least in part, the small stock were valued for their ability to provide milk products. Herders went to greater efforts to expand the birth seasonality of sheep and goats than they did for cattle. This marks a difference from the ethnographic examples that needs to be accounted for. Furthermore, different sheep were involved in different labor practices, which may have been connected to different activities of value generation and transformation. Some sheep were slaughtered when they reached full size, as part of a process that streamlined the labor connected to reproduction. Other sheep were born year-round and either slaughtered when very young or lived to an older age, while reproducing and providing milk. It seems important that the differing organization of reproductive labor between the two groups of sheep is matched by different patterns of culling. This suggests that sheep and goats encompassed both potential forms of value, one that extended intersubjective spacetime through reproduction and the other that generated social relationships through the circulation of animals' bodies postmortem.

While the varying ability of animals of different species, ages, and sexes to expand social spacetime through reproductive futurity sheds some light on the differences in the biographies of cattle and sheep/goats, this difference doesn't immediately account for the circulation of isolated bones—the problem I started this chapter with. If we assume that their distribution is connected to practices that circulated meat to create social ties, it might explain why younger sheep and goats featured prominently. Nevertheless, the simple distinction between large and small stock doesn't explain why the circulation of elements postmortem included both cattle and sheep and goats. The circulation of isolated elements in question involved animals with different capacities for transforming intersocial spacetimes through future reproduction. Moreover, the division of animals' skeletons postmortem suggests that the postmortem itineraries of bones were a part of practices that took advantage of the partibility of bodies to generate and distribute value.

FROM NOSE TO TAIL: BREAKING DOWN BODIES

There is a danger in reducing the value of dead animals to the accumulation of either cash or calories. The value of a slaughtered animal is shaped through value-in-action and is not reducible to the accepted expectation in zooarchaeology that meat, milk, and wool are mere things that are subject to utilitarian logics or maximizing accumulation. Even in the hypercapitalist space of industrial hog production in the United States, the value of the dead pig emerges through a complex set of practices. Blanchette (2020, 211) details how the demand for cheap meat has led to the prolif- eration of the values extracted from porcine bodies, which have nothing to do with eating pork. Industrial pigs are turned into a wide variety of other things—there are over one thousand distinct product codes at one company—and for many of them, it is not immediately apparent that they originate from pigs at all. This process depends on the huge scale of in- dustrial slaughter and a wide variety of labor practices that "put people to work" on the bodies of living and dead pigs. In these processes, exec- utives attempt to enact the industrial vision of an industrial pig that can be, at least in theory, broken down seamlessly (and without waste) into thousands of different products. But in fact, as Blanchette stresses repeat- edly, this vision of the endlessly optimizable and standardizable pig—the fundamental moral-political premise of industrial value in hog farming—is threatened constantly by the unpredictable outcomes of its own processes.

So if the value of the industrialized and objectified dead pig is more complicated than mere accumulation, how might we rethink the value of the dead animal in noncapitalist times and places? The work of so- cial zooarchaeologists offers a springboard for thinking about the kinds of spatiotemporal transformations made possible by animals postmortem. The politics of commensality, discussed in the archaeological literature on feasting, remind us that the bodies of dead animals also have the power to shape relations of affiliation-distinction and authorization-subjection.[29] The butchery and distribution of a carcass is a potent way of generating many different kinds of social spacetimes—from the pointedly egalitarian logics of hunters sharing their prey to the hierarchical distribution of meat to lords and peasants at a public feast, or the "sharing out" of meat among meat pastoralists and the "shares in" individual animals among milch pas- toralists. Postmortem, the power of the allocative mode to generate and naturalize the simultaneous inclusion-exclusion of commensal distinction is grounded materially-semiotically in the unity, partibility, and differen- tiation of substances across herd animals' bodies.

The material nature of animals' bodies creates indexical, metaphoric, and metonymic possibilities. The relationships between the part and the whole, between cuts of meat and living beings, undergird a potent material metaphor for the unity and differentiation of the group. The material dif- ferences in the components of animals' bodies can be mapped and ranked according to criteria of value and distributed accordingly, materializing and realizing both the schema of values and the way in which people are fitted into them. These mappings have the potential to naturalize relationships between people, through the mapping of relations between material qualities and the ranking of people. Durable parts of the body, like horns, hides, and bones, have the potential to stand in metonymically for entire the animal, maintaining and materializing the memory of past actions such as feasts and sacrifices—but also the more quotidian aspects of humans' relationships with living herd animals.[30]

Large animals like cattle produce more fresh meat than a single household can consume before it spoils. This excess can be dealt with in two ways (absent refrigeration or canning). It can be preserved for future use by relying on cold weather or using large quantities of salt. The other option is to share the meat with others, either in feasting or in other practices of distribution (see McCormick 2002; Lokuruka 2006; Sykes 2010). In some instances, this kind of feast brings together elites and nonelites, creating relationships of affiliation. At the same time, the distribution of different parts of the body generates and stabilizes social distinctions, as mirrored in a hierarchy of value in the different parts of the body. While the amount and types of muscle and fat shape evaluations of the differential value of body parts, there is a lot of room for variation as well. Carcasses can be divided up in many different ways and cultural preferences will value different qualities in meat (such as lean or fatty, tender or tough, or with strong or subtle flavors).[31]

The distinction produced through the sharing of meat cannot simply be mapped to quantity, but rather involves the suturing of the qualities of people and those of body parts. But it is important to remember that the practices that enact this mapping were, for the people participating, embodied and affective experiences that shaped their understandings of themselves and the worlds they inhabited. They would have naturalized and routinized forms of inequality, simultaneously enveloping people in inclusion and exclusion, in authorization and subjection (cf. beer drinking among Moche elite as described in Weismantel 2021, 129–31).

Moreover, these practices would have changed through time as part of the process of contesting the relations of authorization-subjection and affiliation-distinction by challenging or changing the performative practices that generated them. Naomi Sykes (2010) traces changes in the skeletal elements found in elite and nonelite sites in Anglo-Saxon Britain, linking them to changes in political life. Her analyses revealed a shift in how portions of the carcass were valued over time. Elite sites from the Middle Anglo-Saxon period have lots of mandibles but few meat-bearing portions of the skeleton. Ecclesiastical sites have a large number of meaty forelimbs (but they are missing heads or hindlimbs), and rural settlements have mostly hindlimb and foot bones. In contrast, Late Anglo-Saxon elite sites, both secular and ecclesiastical, have a much more even representation of meat-bearing elements and foot bones from fore- and hindlimbs but very few mandibles, which are more common at rural sites.

In the earlier period, feasting in a noble's hall constituted the essential wholeness of the community (and individuals' membership in it) through sharing in the carcass, while also maintaining hierarchy through "cuts of different 'quality' being given to individuals as a meaty symbol of their status, gender, wealth or power" (Sykes 2010, 181). Heads appear to have been highly valued, hence the abundance of mandibles at elite sites. If feasting on hunted venison in the great hall in the Middle Anglo-Saxon period reflected the emphasis on the mutual duties and responsibilities of elites and their retainers, Sykes argues that the shift toward a more even skeletal part distribution of deer bones on elite sites in the later period reflects the "closure" of the hall, which moved the grounds of aristocratic authority away from connections to the king and toward individual control over property and resources. Part of this transformation involved the elite's monopolization of hunting and a waning of the custom of distributing hunted venison.[32] It may also mark the origin of the later medieval custom of gifting deer heads to the poor, which marked a distinct transformation in relations of authorization-subjection: away from mutually constituted rights and responsibilities, as based in hereditary authority, and toward charity based on socioeconomic inequality.

Meat-eating is not the only way in which the circulation of animal bodies postmortem is connected to value-in-action. Bones themselves can participate in value transformations and embody positive and negative qualities of value. Often individual bones are used because of their metonymic potential for representing individual animals and their biographies and taking advantage of the material durability of bone relative to flesh. Bones can be curated and displayed as trophies after hunting or to commemorate feasting events or sacrifices. Heads and visually impressive horns or antlers are often selected for this purpose (see the examples in Russell 2012). The display of animal bones as trophies overlaps with, and shades into, practices concerning the respectful treatment of slaughtered animals. Display would seem to be a key feature that marks the use of animals' bones as trophies or mementos of commensal events, even as the two aspects of bone curation cannot be entirely separated (Russell 2012, 59). Describing curated bones as trophies highlights their ability to act as metonymic mementos of past events, as well as potentially signifying qualities (such as prowess or generosity) of the people associated with the display. These bones are protected and maintained as part of the practice of maintaining the memory of past acts.

In contrast, the curation of isolated skeletal elements and their protection from damage is the primary orientation of practices concerned with the respectful treatment of animals after death. These practices are a key component of the maintenance of relationships of reciprocity between hunters and their prey (or with the spirit masters of those animals) or harmony with their herds. In some cases, part of this respectful treatment is keeping dogs away from specific body parts of certain species (see Russell 2012, 54–58). Mongolian herders protect the bones of domesticated livestock from dogs (Fijn 2011, 229). This practice is connected to the understanding that an animal's "spirit" or "energy" is retained within the bones after death.[33] Most of the bones are not curated but left to decompose back into the pasture. Herders in Inner Asia use curated bones in a number of ways, all of which draw on the metonymic potential of bones. Birtalan (2003, 42) describes how Buryat groups use a sheep astragalus to stand in for a sacrificial object in the ceremony for burying a child's placenta. Astragali are also used to tell fortunes (connected to childbearing) during these rituals. Other bones, such as the tibia, may be curated as part of other life-cycle ceremonies and events.[34] Bones, including astragali and vertebrae from wolves, are also used in charms to protect both animals and humans (Birtalan 2003; Fijn 2011). In addition, bones such as the skull and shoulder blade of certain, valued animals are placed on shrines (*oboos* or *ovoos*) as part of ritual practices to ensure the well-being of both humans and their herds.

Bones in Motion in the Late Bronze Age Tsaghkahovit Plain

What might we learn about the kinds of spacetime transformations that the circulation of isolated bones at Gegharot and the Tsaghkahovit Residential Complex enabled? Beyond the general partibility of carcasses postmortem, what characteristics might have taken on salience in the actions that circulated them? It seems very possible that these isolated elements drew on the metonymic potential of bones to stand in for individual animals, which were once living and now have been slaughtered and distributed. In contrast to skeletal elements like ribs and vertebrae, of which there are many within an individual skeleton, all the overabundant elements are only found once on each side of the body. There is a potential contrast between the metonymic potentials of mandibles and tarsals. Mandibles, being part of the head, may be more individualized, and processes of tooth wear visually reflect some aspects of individual biographies. In contrast, the tarsals do not reflect changes over the life of the individual.[35] But the casual nature of the deposition of these bones across the sites doesn't indicate that they were carefully curated, which may suggest they were somewhat interchangeable or replaceable.

Any metonymic use of the isolated skeletal elements that circulated in the sites of Tsaghkahovit and Gegharot in the Late Bronze Age would have been in addition to, and therefore likely in relation to, the other major metonymic use of bones at the time: the head and hoof burial. There are some interesting large-scale symmetries between these practices. Both involve bones from the head and the lower limbs. Likewise, both practices involved bones taken from the major domesticated taxa.[36] Yet within these similarities, there are potentially meaningful differences. The head and hoof burials deposit the skull and mandibles with the lower-limb bones (possibly including the hide as well) in one location. This practice clearly invokes the entirety of an animal through this minimal set of remains; in this case, the extremities of the body (head and feet). The isolated skeletal elements from the Gegharot and the Tsaghkahovit Residential Complex also come from the extremities but they are not deposited in a combination of heads and lower limbs. The isolated elements are also different because they only come from the hind limb, whereas head and hoof burials include both fore- and hindlimb bones. This raises the possibility that rather than sketching the whole through a minimally evocative set of parts, the isolated skeletal elements had a different role. Perhaps they functioned more like the astragali in Buryat rituals for placenta burial, in which a single element stands in for a whole animal, or represented or transmitted particular qualities from the body of the animal, making different kinds of people in the process.

The inclusion of heads and hooves in tombs in the Tsaghkahovit Plain was part of a wider set of practices—value-in-action—that involved herd animals. Alongside these evocative deposits, the dead were also buried with portions of carcasses and prepared food. From these traces, we can imagine that burying the dead involved slaughtering animals, dividing up their bodies, and cooking them. The drama of the slaughter and the apportioning of animal bodies—and possibly their consumption at graveside—would have been an embodied experience of the relations between the dead and the living as well as the relations among the living. But the felicity of these practices would have depended in large part on the ability of herd animals' bodies to naturalize those differences and inequalities, in part by mapping the qualities and potencies of their own bodies and others' bodies as well. The temporalities of eating—of the incorporation of bodily substances and the sensorial and affective memory of past meals—were linked to the other kinds of social spatiotemporal transformations enacted through mortuary rituals.

Thinking about the ways in which herd animals, pre- and postmortem, might have made possible certain kinds of transformations of intersubjective spacetime in the Late Bronze Age offers new interpretations for the zooarchaeological data from Gegharot and Tsaghkahovit. It indicates that the value of living and dead animals was at work, shaping the possibilities for political life in complex ways. Unlike in the ethnographic models from Africa, large and small stock both had a role in the connection between herds' reproductive futurity and value-in-action. But the distinction between herd animals' values in life and in death does not furnish a complete explanation for why mandibles and tarsals accumulated on-site in large numbers. What is missing is an account of how the relationships forged with living and dead animals, through the circulation of animal bodies pre- and postmortem, was one of many choreographies of value that created felicitous authority. Thus, in the next chapter, I explore how herd animals' bodies were broken down and put into motion, thereby transforming value and shaping political life.

· 7 ·

CHOREOGRAPHIES OF VALUE

During the Late Bronze Age, after slaughter, the bodies of herd animals were broken down, circulated, altered, and deposited in different ways and different places across the Tsaghkahovit Plain. Some of these postmortem itineraries appear quite mundane: evidence of the quotidian consumption of meat and the use of bones to manufacture tools and ornaments, and the deposition of the rest of the body alongside broken pots, used-up tools, and other detritus of everyday living.[1] Other itineraries, most notably the inclusion of animals (whole and partial) alongside the bodies of humans in tombs, seem to be dramatic evidence of the importance of animals in creating and sustaining the relations of social and political life. But the abundance of mandibles and tarsals at the sites of Tsaghkahovit and Gegharot are more puzzling. When compared to the quotidian uses of herd animals, these patterns stand out. These bones don't appear to have a practical use, and the patterns in the data suggest repeated and intentional actions of selection and circulation. Yet at the same time, they don't fit neatly into archaeologists' schema for identifying (and interpreting) the ritual or symbolic uses of animals either. They were not carefully treated, curated, or ritually deposited. They ended up deposited alongside everything else.

As I was struggling with how to interpret the unusual patterns I found in the animal bones from Gegharot and Tsaghkahovit, I looked into the widespread phenomenon of large caches of astragali at sites in ancient Mesopotamia, the Levant, and the Mediterranean. The patterns I found in my data were very different than those described for the astragali hoards.[2] While there are numerous astragali at Gegharot, the hoards of astragali described at sites like Meggido and Tell Ebla are much larger and more concentrated—684 astragali in a burial at Meggido, 200 in a temple at Tell eş-Şafi, and 406 in an amphora sitting on a platform at Tel Abel Beth Maacah (Susnow et al. 2021; Minniti and Peyronel 2005; Sasson 2007). Moreover, while many astragali in such hoards are worked, the actual patterns of alteration are quite different (higher levels of polish, different grinding and boring patterns, etc.).

But thinking about these astragali hoards and how they differed from what I was seeing in my own data revealed an important problem. Like the overabundant bones from the Tsaghkahovit Plain, astragali hoards require further interpretation because, when examined using zooarchaeological frameworks of analysis, they don't look like butchery or consumption waste. As Susnow et al. (2021, 75) note:

> Archaeologically retrieved astragali are generally interpreted, at least in part, by the context from which they were found. Those from temples, for example, were proposed to relate to divination. Those from burials have been explained as offerings or as amulets. Astragali from domestic contexts have been posited to be game pieces, dice, amulets or tools . . . astragali found in public storage and domestic spaces were interpreted as a form of currency. (2021, 75)

If they aren't butchery waste, then often archaeologists try to find the label for the context that will help us identify the kind of value (or meaning) of these bones. But the adequacy of this approach is worryingly dependent on our ability to identify "ritual," "domestic," or "public" spaces. It also tends to assume that contemporary (or historical, or ethnographic) understandings of these categories are meaningful and relevant to the time and place under discussion. More prosaically, this approach doesn't work when we consider the data from the Tsaghkahovit Plain. The ubiquity of the isolated elements and the interplay of similarity and difference across spatial scales upend this interpretive move.

To better account for the value generated and transformed through actions involving these bones in the Late Bronze Age Tsaghkahovit Plain, I examine the zooarchaeological data for traces of what I call *choreographies of value*—the performative participation of animals, people, things, and landscapes in the generation and management of social-material potencies. What emerges is the sense that these patterns, which confound any easy division between the everyday and the extraordinary or between economic and symbolic value, reveal a multiplicity of actions that drew together people, animals, things, and landscapes. If, as I argued in the preceding chapter, value emerges from action (rather than inhering in objects), then this multiplicity is key to understanding the value of the isolated mandibles and tarsals. The circulation of these bones was a part of choreographies that made material claims about how the world is and how it ought to be, thus contributing to the felicity of authority. But as I will detail, following these bones reveals forms of value-in-action that don't quite match the differences between the value of large and small stock, but instead either created a different kind of value or worked to synthesize the value of the futurity of reproduction instantiated in living animals and the social relations formed and strengthened through the consumption of dead animals.

Turning to traces of action and investigating choreographies of value interrupts the tendency within archaeology to typologize contexts as quotidian or ritual, secular or sacred, or public or private. This allows me to consider a different kind of context for the overabundant astragali in the Tsaghkahovit Plain. First, astragali and their movements can be contextualized by the abundance and circulation of other parts of herd animals' bodies. And second, context for any particular astragali or group of astragali is provided by the traces of choreographies of action they participated in, rather than their context of deposition.[3]

I use the term *choreography* to suggest an intentional coordination of different bodies in space and time.[4] This metaphor is capacious enough to admit the intentionality of human and nonhuman bodies and to leave open the possibility that the "dance" emerges from interactions between unruly bodies and spaces (and not the directions of some all-powerful choreographer). Tracing out the different possible choreographies of value that moved people, animals, and things through time and space in the past makes it easier to analyze activities that are set off from everyday life— while allowing their significance to emerge from an analysis of the broader patterns of social life in a specific historical context (R. Campbell 2012, 308; Brück 1999). Nevertheless, though I use *choreographies* to suggest an open-ended potential, the terrain of value is not an even playing field. It is necessary to consider how choreographies of value produce enduring inequalities and enable the felicity of authority.

CHOREOGRAPHIES OF VALUE AND POLITICS

Most of daily life is taken up with choreographies of value that we might think about as *implicit*. This encompasses much of the action, and the work, of everyday life: growing crops, raising animals, cooking food, eating, making everyday items of all sorts, gossiping, raising children, telling stories, and so forth. In these actions and activities, value is created and circulated but channeling or managing the metastructure of homogeneous potencies isn't the main focus of the action. Instead, these are directed toward the action's basic causal outcome: perhaps making a pot, milking a cow, or feeding a hungry child. Such choreographies of value produce the background of workaday, unremarkable practices of production, consumption, and circulation. It is against these relatively implicit choreographies of value that explicit choreographies stand out. Explicit choreographies of value produce material-semiotic narratives about how people, and animals, and things *should be*. The purpose of the action in these choreographies is to self-consciously attend to or direct the creation and distribution of value as homogenous social potential (though it may also entail certain outcomes that produce, transform, circulate, or consume materials). For explicit choreographies, I have in mind something akin to Severin Fowles's (2012, 151) description of Puebloan *doings* (rituals):

> Doings . . . do not necessarily integrate society. As I have emphasized, they are instead a kind of exegesis on worldly interconnection in which claims are made about the order of things, claims that may sometimes be designed to end quarrels but that are nevertheless always open to dispute, rejection, or revision. Doings, in other words, are explicit efforts to both mirror and assert structure, but they themselves are not structure. They are more accurately, a discourse about structure, which is why they are also a discourse of power.

The division between explicit and implicit is not a stark one, nor is it a binary distinction. Rather, it is better thought of as a gradient in regard to the explicitness of attention to the channeling of value. Moreover, both explicit and implicit choreographies of value are political—because both are involved in generating values and mediating the moral-political premises of social life.

Unreflective, everyday choreographies of value are not an apolitical background to practices of authority (see Dawdy 2020). They are, in fact, critical to authority. Through their unremarkableness—the way in which these things "go without saying"—implicit choreographies direct the actions and experiences of people without betraying, or even actively erasing, the origins or history of such activities and practices (cf. Pollock et al. 2020; see also Foucault 1990; Butler 2006). In contrast, explicit choreographies of value make claims about how the world should be: what kind of relations should exist between people, things, and animals and what kinds of people (and other beings) are authorized to maintain the order of the world. In doing so, they draw on their remarkableness—their capacity to be materially and semiotically persuasive and compelling, to function as a technique of power and mode of authority. Yet, like implicit choreographies, explicit choreographies draw their power from "what they hide and in what, by this process of obliteration, they allow to emerge" (Foucault 1994, 137).

Explicit choreographies of value work to establish the positive (or negative) value of transformations of social spacetimes and assert the relevant qualities that can be accumulated, generated, traced, translated, and transacted across bodies, objects, and actions. The explicit nature of the claims made by these choreographies of value also opens up the possibility of other material-semiotic practices that challenge them, potentially undermining the felicity of authority (cf. Dawdy 2020). Crucially, domesticated herd animals are well suited to participate in (and even combine) both these modes.

Herd Animals and Choreographies of Value

In pastoralist societies, herd animals are deeply woven into the fabric of everyday life through the quotidian tasks of animal care, the useful labor they provide, and their role in the daily nourishment of human bodies— not to mention the ubiquitous sights, smells, and sounds of herd animals. Of course, anthropologists and archaeologists have long been aware of the importance that domesticated herd animals play in less everyday, more extraordinary practices—and social zooarchaeologists have debated how we might find evidence of these things in the archaeological record. Thinking about value-in-action makes it easier to perceive how these two aspects of living with herds might interrelate by focusing our attention on the way that value is generated, transformed, and destroyed through both marked and unmarked choreographies of value.

I return once again to Radhika Govindrajan's (2018) work in contemporary Uttarakhand. Her moving account of animal sacrifice provides an illustrative example of this interrelation between the ordinary and the extraordinary. She describes a woman's sacrifice of eight goats to Ma Kalika, a Shakta goddess and patron of the local military regiment. For the woman making the sacrifice, it was fulfillment of a vow made years before, a recognition of the deity's successful intervention in the arc of her husband's military career and performance of her faithful devotion. At first glance, the offering of these *specific* goats may seem incidental to the religious practice and the relationship between individuals and deities it seeks to forge. Certainly that is the argument made by animal rights activists and by Hindu reformers, who label animal sacrifice a heterodox (and therefore repugnant) practice for devout Hindus. But Govindrajan (2018, 40) argues that the arduous, everyday labor of caring for these goats prior to their sacrifice—which she characterizes as "intimate relations of care and mutual subjection"—is at the center of what makes the ritual powerful for those who participate in it: "The death of an animal with whom people feel this embodied kinship creates a sense of loss and grief that is essential to making sacrifice truly a sacrifice" (37).

This is to say that the ritual of sacrifice Govindrajan describes can be understood as an explicit choreography of value that transforms the value generated through the implicit choreography of interspecies care and intimacy into devotion for the deity and the ongoing maintenance of peaceful relations between deities and multispecies communities in the mountains in Uttarakhand. The ritual of sacrifice discharges the devotee's debt, and collectively, the sacrifices offered by devotees maintain the community's good relations with the deities.[5] Moreover, she reveals how these explicit choreographies make other claims about the world and about power.

Key to the logic of animal sacrifice in Uttarakhand, and the controversies about it, is the material-semiotic argument that goats are an acceptable substitute for human children (the real desire of the gods) in a way objects like coconuts are not—both because goats are a sacrifice that really hurts but also because the goats themselves can be devotees of the goddess (Govindrajan 2018, 35).[6] Furthermore, devotees' insistence on the need for meaningful sacrificial relations with local deities and their continued practice of the ritual, in contravention of a recent court ban, is an explicit material-semiotic claim about the limits of the state's sovereignty and its ability to care for its citizens (57).

Contemporary controversies about sacrificial rituals in Uttarakhand highlight herd animals' capacities to be key participants in implicit and explicit choreographies of value, mediating the connections between them in critical ways. It also illustrates how explicit choreographies of value are sites for the generation of felicitous authority *and also* for the possibility of response, rejection, and transformation. For the people who participate, the power of the sacrifice is not the destruction of economic value (though it is, in fact, substantial). It is the sacrifice of a beloved relation to transform both the care and the loss into a peaceful relation with the deity. Critics, however, reject the material-semiotic argument at the heart of this explicit choreography of value. Many insist on a different, negative choreography:

that the killing of animals destroys the intrinsic value of a life without ben-
efiting the greater good. These positions reduce the moral value of the animals' death to the meat it provides, a position that is reflected in a recent
ruling banning sacrifices *qua* sacrifices inside temples (without outlawing
the slaughter of animals for food).[7] It marries a general principle of animal
welfare (that all animal deaths are a moral problem) to a specific logic of
good versus bad religion—a combination that, Govindrajan (2018, 54)
notes, is shaped by wider conflicts over Hindutva and exists within the
growing political violence against non-Hindus.

Centering value-in-action raises the thorny issue of how archaeologists can connect the patterns or traces they identify in the archaeological
record to interpretive accounts of past choreographies of value (particularly when there are no texts or oral histories to supplement archaeological data). Put simply, we need to keep in mind that explicit and implicit
choreographies of value might be closely interrelated in ways that matter
for our interpretations. This should alert us to how we might see the quotidian shaping the nonquotidian, and vice versa. But beyond this, it is also
important to keep an eye on how our assumptions and expectations shape
what strikes us as quotidian or nonquotidian.

This requires maintaining the distinction between anticipated or un-
anticipated patterns in the archaeological record and explicit or implicit
choreographies of value in the past. While an unusual finding may very
well be evidence of an explicit choreography of value, it may also *not*
be. Archaeologists tend to run aground when we try to ascertain what is
meaningful in the patterns we notice. *Meaningful* is an important term,
but the palimpsest of its different uses in the literature creates confusion.
Sometimes it means, Does this pattern or trace reflect symbolic meaning?
Sometimes archaeologists use it to convey something close to what I call
the explicit, namely, something that is a trace of nonquotidian practices.
A third possibility is that because of our expectations or assumptions, the
traces or patterns that stand out to archaeologists are only remarkable to
us. This may at first seem a pessimistic view of archaeologists' ability to
access choreographies of value in the deeper past. In actuality, the way forward is to follow Rosemary Joyce's (2015b, 184) call to treat archaeological
materials as "accumulated traces of action." In the same way one might
appreciate the melody or rhythm of a song in a foreign language without
understanding the words, archaeologists may be able to work out some of
the traces of choreographies of value, providing insight into value-in-action
without being able to map all its semiotic richness.

HEADS AND HOOVES

The zooarchaeological and isotopic data from the Tsaghkahovit Plain make it clear that herd animals led diverse lives in terms of diet, mobility, and interactions with humans and that their bodies traveled along multiple itineraries after death. In broad strokes, there appear to have been three main types of postmortem circulation. First, some herd animals were slaughtered and butchered off-site and large portions of the carcass were brought into Gegharot and the TRC. Second, isolated parts of heads and lower limbs from animals slaughtered off-site were brought to both sites. Third, the bodies of herd animals were incorporated into tombs in a variety of ways, echoing both forms of nonmortuary circulation.

Dismemberment

Looking at the patterning in body-part representation provides some clues about what happened to animal bodies after slaughter. It reveals traces of the actions that broke down carcasses, sending different parts of the body moving along different paths. The relative absence of vertebrae and ribs on-site suggests that the initial slaughter and butchery took place off-site, leaving parts of the carcass behind and bringing meat into the sites as butchered portions of the carcass. Yet layered over the traces of this pattern of circulation is another pattern. In short, whether we count by Minimum Number of Elements or measure by weight, mandibles and tarsals from slaughtered animals are found in larger amounts than any other part of the carcass. The particular bones that are overrepresented varies by species and between sites (chapter 6). Sheep/goat mandibles are overabundant at both sites, and sheep/goat astragali are overabundant at Gegharot. Cattle astragali are overabundant at Gegharot and cattle calcanei are overabundant at the TRC.

The selection and circulation of the bones of the ankle (astragali and calcanei) may be related to the process of skinning and dismembering the bodies of the herd animals. Skinning an animal may begin with cutting around the ankle, near the astragalus—and it is not uncommon to see small skinning cut marks on an astragalus from the Tsaghkahovit Plain. Moreover, these bones can be the point at which the lower leg is disarticulated from the rest of the hind leg. Similarly, skinning can also involve making cuts around the mandible. But the selection of sheep and goat mandibles might have involved a different, or multiple, logics. Mandibles, as part of the head, may metonymically represent individual animals. Mandibles, calcanei, and astragali are all bones found once on each side of the body, which allows for the conceptual pairing and separate circulation of right and left. However, unlike the ankle bones, the right and left mandibles are joined together in the skeleton and can be split apart. If the choreographies of value took advantage of the pairing of right and left, they circulated these bones in patterns that deposited roughly equal numbers of right and left mandibles, astragali, and calcanei at both sites. An analysis of body size suggests the overabundant cattle and sheep astragali are from a different group of animals than other bones from the middens at Gegharot (Chazin n.d.). This difference suggests there was intentional selection of astragali from a subset of slaughtered animals on the basis of age, sex, or some other characteristic.[8]

Divergence

After slaughter and butchery, the trajectories of cattle and sheep and of heads and hind legs begin to diverge. The data indicate that cattle astragali and calcanei were either collected through a different process or treated differently (in terms of curation and storage) from sheep/goat mandibles and astragali. The clearest evidence of this divergence comes from the high rate of gnaw marks on cattle astragali and calcanei. At the TRC, cattle astragali and calcanei have much higher levels of gnawing than the rest of the assemblage (calcanei: 28%, astragali: 32%, total assemblage: ~5%).[9] Likewise, at Gegharot, many cattle calcanei and astragali were also gnawed (calcanei: 27%, astragali: ~11%, total assemblage: ~5%).[10] In contrast, sheep/goat astragali and mandibles don't show higher rates of gnawing. This pattern suggests a couple of possibilities. The calcanei and astragali from cattle may have first been left off-site along with the other parts of the skeleton, like ribs and vertebrae, having been discarded as butchery waste—thus leaving them vulnerable to being gnawed by dogs or wild animals. Or, although perhaps less likely, these bones may have been brought into the sites but stored or deposited in a place where dogs or rodents could access them (separately from other where other parts of the carcasses were stored or deposited).

Regardless of how it occurred, however, gnawing does not appear to have prevented these bones from moving through further steps in these choreographies. The divergence in itineraries may result from differences in how often cattle and sheep/goats were slaughtered. Because they are much larger animals, slaughtering a cow produces a much greater quantity of meat (which risks spoiling if not consumed). Cattle are less common in the assemblage overall and they were killed at older ages on average, suggesting they were slaughtered less frequently than sheep or goats. The higher rates of gnawing may reflect the longer temporal gap between slaughter and the collection or use of the astragali and calcanei.

Another point of divergence in the paths of isolated elements is the alterations of some of the astragali from both cattle and sheep/goats. Some astragali found at both sites, but by no means all of them, show certain kinds of intentional alteration of the bone surface (figure 7.1). This includes:

- One or more deep striations, with some number of lighter scratches surrounding, on the posterior surface
- Ground lateral surface
- Ground medial and lateral surfaces
- Hole bored into the proximal end of the bone
- Divot or pit in anterior face
- Smoothing and polishing (to various degrees)[11]

There is no clear "grammar" governing these modifications. Striations on the posterior surface are the most common, with a single, deep striation more common than multiple striations. Grinding and striations are not mutually exclusive treatments.[12] Proximal holes are only found in astragali with both the medial and lateral sides ground, but not all astragali with medial and lateral grinding have holes. The divot or pit in the anterior face is the least common treatment, found only on three bones. Various levels

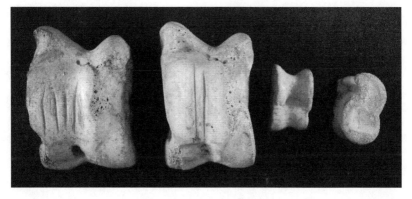

FIGURE 7.1 Photo of altered astragali from Gegharot. Courtesy of Adam T. Smith.

of smoothing and polish are found on about 25% of the worked astragali and is found on bones with all the other treatments. In a number of cases, whatever caused the polishing occurred after the striations were carved in the posterior surface. There is no association between any of these treatments and astragali coming from the right or left sides of the animal or from different species.

These alterations are functionally and aesthetically ambiguous. The striations are informal marks, varying slightly in orientation and length. The variable number of lighter scratches may hint at some kind of handling or manipulation. Similarly, the polishing (and the variability in the level of polish seen) suggests that the polishing was of limited duration or intensity and was produced by handling as part of a process or activity (rather than an intentionally sought aesthetic transformation). These marks do not match the pattern of wear from modern experiments that used astragali as loom weights and shuttles for weaving or as burnishers (Meier 2013; Grabundzija, Schoch, and Ulanowska 2016).[13] The grinding of the medial and lateral sides, along with the proximal holes, seems more aesthetically oriented—though both modifications would also have altered how they felt to the touch and possibly how they moved when manipulated. While these marks and alterations are consistent with regard to the different faces of the bone, this does not seem to have been to demarcate the different sides of a die. At the same time, most of the alterations would not have precluded using them as dice.

Rather than alterations that aimed at aesthetic transformation, the marks on the astragali from the Tsaghkahovit Plain seem to be more immediately connected to working with and on the bones themselves. They are traces of people handling the astragali in particular ways: scratching, grinding, touching, rubbing, boring. Sustained physical contact with, and manipulation of, the bones may have aimed at producing sustained focus on the bones themselves—and at producing the kinds of value they created or indexed. That value may have drawn on the intrinsic potencies and abilities of different kinds of herd animals, on the ability of herd animals to grow human bodies and to generate and sustain social production, including reproduction, on analogies drawn between people and herds, or on all of these. It also possible that these alterations were parts of choreographies that were multisensorial and/or not primarily visual. I've already suggested the importance of the tactile sensation of handling the bones and altering their surfaces. But the presence of bone whistles, made from the toe bones of cattle (and in one case, a horse) may indicate that sound was also an important part of at least some of these practices.

Destinations

In addition to the initial divergence in how the mandibles and tarsals from different herd animals were handled, the data also highlight that these bones moved along different paths of circulation. Perhaps unsurprisingly, there is no clear one-to-one mapping of species, body parts, treatments, or spatial contexts. Sheep/goat mandibles are overabundant both within the site walls of Gegharot and in the TRC, which suggests that the choreographies of value that circulated them were widespread, spanning the potentially different activities that took place at the two different site areas. The pattern for cattle calcanei is more subtle and may reveal two separate choreographies.

The overabundance of cattle calcanei at the TRC seems like a direct counterpart to the overabundant astragali at Gegharot. The difference in which cattle bones are overabundant at each site area may be evidence of how differences between the two spaces were established, maintained, and understood. But if we zoom in to look at the middens at Gegharot, the data reveal that in addition to the many cattle astragali, there are also fairly large numbers of calcanei, central fourth tarsals, phalanges, and maxillae and mandibles. This suggests that people at Gegharot may have started with cattle heads and hind limbs, which were then broken down further— with the meaty upper limbs (bearing most of the meat) circulating elsewhere (possibly off-site) and the lower limbs and skulls deposited in the middens or elsewhere. This may have been separate from, or a smaller component of, the choreographies that circulated other astragali into the walls of Gegharot.

The movement of astragali into Gegharot marks the simultaneous alignment of the itineraries of cattle and sheep/goats postmortem while also pointing to activities that took place with greater frequency (if not exclusively) within the walls of the site. This is clearly true for Gegharot, where we have large assemblages of faunal remains from the citadels and terraces, but it may also be true at Tsaghkahovit. Astragali, while present in the Tsaghkahovit Residential Complex, are not overabundant. However, the very limited excavations of Late Bronze Age contexts on the northern and western terraces at Tsaghkahovit—the direct counterpart to the areas excavated at Gegharot—also encountered noticeable numbers of astragali (Adam T. Smith, Badalyan, and Avetisyan 2004).

Within the larger pattern of circulation, there are a few contexts where excavators found larger numbers of astragali in situ in nonmidden contexts, revealing traces of the activities that astragali were involved in prior to their final deposition on-site. One of these was found in the threshold of the room on the eastern citadel at Gegharot (figure 7.2) that has been described by the excavators as a "shrine" (see chapter 4). On the floor of this room, just in front of the entrance—beneath the destruction layer that sealed it at the end of the second Late Bronze Age occupation—there was a large concentration of animal bones (~220 fragments). While this group did include a large number of astragali, it also included other fragmentary

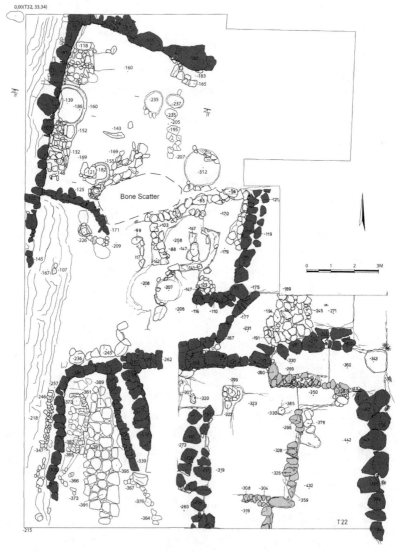

FIGURE 7.2 East citadel "shrine" room. Courtesy of Project ArAGATS.

remains from all other sections of the skeleton (head, axial, forelimb, and hindlimb).[14] Altogether, there were 43 cattle astragali (20 right, 23 left) and 39 sheep or goat astragali (18 right, 21 left) in the scatter of bones, some of which were gnawed and others showing the common kinds of alteration discussed previously. An additional 6 astragali, some worked, were found in the three complete vessels sitting nearby.[15] Approximately one quarter of the astragali had been scratched, polished, or otherwise altered; this was a higher proportion of worked cattle astragali than in the assemblage as a whole.[16]

The location of these astragali and the fact that they were part of a larger scatter of animal bones is puzzling. Why were the bones deposited on the floor, right in front of the entrance to the room? We can say, with some degree of certainty, that these bones were deposited in the room before the conflagration that destroyed the site. If it was a cache or collection, perhaps spilled during the chaos leading up to the destruction, then why would there be other (quite unremarkable) faunal remains included? Nothing else about the situation in the room suggests that the assemblage of faunal remains in the doorway was part of a deliberate closing of the room, at some point prior to the destruction event.

Another in situ collection of astragali were found on the citadel at Tsaghkahovit. Beneath the destruction layer (which is roughly contemporaneous with the second destruction layer at Gegharot), excavators found an occupation floor. On this floor (Trench C2), they found a larger pit filled with ash and a shallow pit covered by two grinding stones (Avetisyan, Badalyan, and Smith 2000, 48). Inside the smaller pit, there were two sheep astragali (unworked) and one tibia, all from the right side. Around the pits, excavators recovered a collection of 15 worked astragali (mixed in with a few cattle first phalanges). Twelve of the worked astragali were from cattle and the remaining astragali were from sheep. In addition to the usual patterns of being worked, all the astragali found in this context were intentionally burned. On some, one of the paired faces is a darker color than the other, reflecting a different length of exposure to heat for aesthetic or other purposes, but none of these worked astragali were gnawed. But nothing like this deliberate burning treatment is seen in any of the worked astragali from Gegharot.

These unusual deposits, which were made on the living surfaces preserved underneath the destruction events, suggest that the itineraries of astragali (or at least of some astragali) involved temporary collection and manipulation followed by subsequent deposition alongside other forms of rubbish elsewhere in the site. They also suggest that the astragali seen in the faunal assemblages may have had multiple trajectories that brought them within the site walls rather than a single practice or use. I read the differences between these unusual collections of astragali as traces of practices that were flexible or improvisational in nature rather than a form of value generation or transaction that was strictly codified.

Deposition

Despite the differences in the itineraries of mandibles, calcanei, and astragali, the treatment of cattle and sheep/goat bones, and the traces of different practices of collection and handling, in the end, most of these bones were deposited among what looks like everyday rubbish at Gegharot and the TRC. While there is some evidence that groups of astragali were collected and perhaps stored together temporarily, the presence of worked and unworked astragali between walls, in middens, and in abandoned spaces on-site suggests that many, if not most, of their choreographies of value ended with the bones being deposited alongside other discarded items. Against this background of ubiquity, there are a couple of places at Gegharot where these isolated elements were either deposited in noticeably larger numbers or as part of structured forms of action. In one, an unusually large number of sheep/goat mandibles was found in a midden deposit from the first occupation at Gegharot. The midden contained many animal bones overall and had a noticeably higher proportion of mandibles from cattle, sheep, and goats. Moreover, these mandibles included an unusually large proportion from very young sheep.[17] The presence of these mandibles from young lambs seems to echo the inclusion of very young sheep and goats in the kurgans below Gegharot.

Astragali are ubiquitous across Gegharot, having been found in nearly all the contexts where excavators found faunal remains. Yet there are also some pits dating to the first period of occupation where astragali were included as part of a structured sequence of actions (figure 7.3). Yet when we look at *all* the pits from the first period of occupation, we see the familiar pattern (table 7.1). Some of the pits are filled with an assortment of everyday materials: animal bones, broken pottery, broken tools, and so forth. Others appear to have had a more intentional sequence of deposition, though the kinds of artifacts found in both kinds of pits show considerable overlap. Astragali, worked and unworked, are found in both kinds of pits—and not all pits have astragali in them. They are also not exclusively found in large concentrations. Instead, the pits may contain none, a few, or a large number of astragali.[18] Astragali are not deposited alone in pits

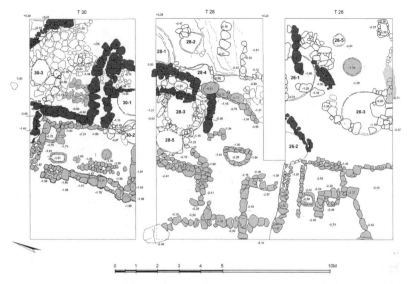

FIGURE 7.3 Pits from the first Late Bronze Age occupation at Gegharot. Dark shading indicates LBA construction. Light shading indicates EBA construction. Courtesy of Project ArAGATS.

or with a consistent repertoire of other items.[19] The bone whistles follow a similar pattern: some of them were recovered in pits on the citadel at both Gegharot and Tsaghkahovit, but a number were also found in the midden deposits on the lower terrace at Gegharot. As a whole, this pattern falls somewhere in the ambiguous middle ground between everyday discard and structured, separate deposition.

MORTUARY CHOREOGRAPHIES

Turning to the fields of tombs adjacent to Gegharot and Tsaghkahovit, we can trace another set of choreographies of value that involved herd animals. Sometime in the fifteenth through sixteenth centuries BCE, a person (aged 35–45 years, skeletally male) died and was interred in a kurgan below the site of Gegharot (Badalyan et al. 2008). The tomb consisted of a large stone circle 11.5 meters in diameter covered by an earthen mound 1.4 meters high. Within the circle, underneath the mound, were two chambers dug below the surface of the earth. In the chamber at the center of the circle, the deceased individual was laid to rest on top of the partial skeletal remains of a very young child (~1.5 years old) and, alongside five ceramic vessels, some bronze weapons, some obsidian arrowheads, and a number of beads. Along the northeastern edge of the central chamber, mourners

TABLE 7.1 Pits at Gegharot from the first period of Late Bronze Age occupation

Name	Description	Contents	No. of astragali	Structured deposition?
26-1	Pit sealed by a clay floor and burned beams, filled with broken ceramics, obsidian fragments, broken stone tools, and a stone bead	Ceramic sherds, obsidian fragments, a bead, stone tools, faunal remains (NISP = 189)	Cattle: 3 (left, 2 worked) Sheep: 1 (right)	No
26-2	Pit filled with charcoal and organic matter interspersed with broken ceramics and astragali	Ceramic sherds, charcoal, faunal remains (NISP = 84)	Cattle: 1 (right) Sheep: 1 (right) Sheep/goat: 1 (right, worked)	No
26-3	Bottom of the pit was filled with large numbers of faunal remains, ceramic sherds, obsidian, stone tools, a spindle whorl, bone whistle, bone tools, and a small cup. The upper part of the pit's fill had large pieces of obsidian and a few ceramic sherds from a single vessel.	Ceramic sherds, obsidian, stone tools, a whistle, bone tools, spindle whorl, faunal remains (NISP = 257)	Cattle: 3 (2 right, 1 left) Sheep: 4 (2 right, 2 left) Sheep/goat: 1 (right, worked)	No
26-5	Small pit containing a nearly complete ceramic vessel set on a semicircle of stones	Ceramic vessel, faunal remains (NISP = 9)	None	Yes
28-1	Pit extending under a later wall, covered by charred beams	Ceramic sherds, a paste bead, faunal remains (NISP = 45)	Goat: 1 (left)	No
28-2	Bottom of the pit was lined with a layer of small stones and filled with broken ceramics, obsidian fragments, and faunal remains	Ceramic sherds, obsidian fragments, faunal remains (NISP = 12)	None	No?
28-3	Large pit filled with three layers of packed stones, separated by yellow clay, topped by a stone "box" that may have served as a post support	Broken and whole tools (pestles, graters, mortars), faunal remains (NISP = 253)	Cattle: 8 (3 right, 5 left) Sheep: 4 (2 right, 2 left)	Yes

28-4	Shallow pit	Model wheel, fragments of tuff, faunal remains (n = 27)	None	No
28-5	Large pit filled with numerous faunal remains as well as a small ceramics vessel and some stone tools	Small pot, pumice polisher, tuff disc, other stone tools, faunal remains (NISP = 364)	Cattle 13 (5 right, 7 left) Sheep: 3 (2 right, 1 left) Sheep/goat: 1 (right)	No
30-1	Lower half of the pit contained large fragments of burned beams, and a complete ceramic bowl and pot sitting on top of a thin layer of yellow clay at the bottom. Upper half of the pit was filled with broken ceramics and animal bones.	Ceramic vessels, sherds, faunal remains (NISP = 103)	Sheep/goat: 1 (left)	Yes?
30-2	Pit containing small fragments of pottery, obsidian flakes, and animal bones	Ceramic sherds, obsidian flakes, faunal remains (NISP = 13)	None	No
30-3	Pit containing animal bones, ceramic sherds, and a fragment of a bone awl	Ceramic sherds, broken bone awl, faunal remains (NISP = 97)	Cattle: 3 (right) Sheep: 1 (right)	No

deposited the skull and forelimb of a horse, and another horse skull was placed along the northwestern wall. In the other chamber, dug in the western area of the stone circle, they laid the bodies of two sheep and two goats, all between 6 and 12 months old, at the bottom of the pit. Then they piled twenty-two ceramic vessels of varying shapes and sizes and partial portions of the carcasses of cattle, sheep, and goats on top of the lambs and covered the chamber with large stones.

The basic elements of these choreographies of value were repeated in the other two kurgans adjacent to this one. Kurgan 2 has both a central and a western chamber (Chazin 2016b). While the original contents of the central chamber were removed and replaced by a later Iron I period burial, the western chamber shows striking similarities to Kurgan 1. The articulated skeletons of two young sheep (aged 8–12 months) were placed at the bottom of the pit, with their bodies positioned to mirror one another and their detached heads placed on top of their rib cages. Piled on top of and around the bodies of the lambs were nineteen ceramic vessels of varying shapes and sizes, a bronze sword, a cache of arrowheads made of translucent obsidian, and an array of carcass portions. Some of the contents of the vessels included animal bones, likely from prepared meals (similar to those found in TsBC12).

Kurgan 3 was constructed slightly differently, with the central chamber surrounded by a smaller stone circle, placed off-center within a larger stone circle (Badalyan and Smith 2017). Along the western edge of the larger circle was an earthen pit containing six ceramic vessels. In the central chamber, the deceased (aged 18–20 and possibly male) was interred with seven complete vessels, obsidian arrowheads, bronze ornaments, the bronze fittings of yoke (including a statuette of a boar), and the partial remains of a large mammal. Along the western wall, mourners placed the heads and hooves (and possibly the hides) of two adult horses with bronze bits in their mouths.

A couple of the excavated burials in Tsaghkahovit Burial Cluster 12 appear to echo parts of the choreographies seen in the kurgans—specifically the deposition of whole animals and the structured deposition of heads and lower limbs. In Burial 02, an individual (aged 35–49 years, skeletally male) was interred on top of the body of a young male goat (aged 6–12 months). The tomb also contained the skulls of two very young sheep, one male and one female (aged 2–6 months), along with some poorly preserved postcranial remains. In Burial 06, another person (too poorly preserved to determine age or skeletal sex) was interred with five ceramic vessels (some of which had animal bones in them). The body was covered with a clayey soil and portions of animals' bodies were laid on top, including the right lower limb of a horse as well as a left cattle hindlimb and the right half of a cattle skull, both of which showed a similar age of death (aged 15–30 months) and may have come from the same individual. This patterned deposition is reminiscent of, and may very well be a variant of, the head and hoof deposit.

Overall, cromlech burials in the Tsaghkahovit Plain vary widely in the types of faunal remains included, just as they as vary in burial architecture and other grave goods. In contrast, the incorporation of herd animals into kurgans seems to have been somewhat more standardized, and it incorporated herd animals in multiple ways. Yet the practices incorporating animal bodies into the kurgans are broadly parallel to those seen in the humbler cromlech burials near Tsaghkahovit (M. Marshall 2014). Those tombs also contained whole animals, meat units, and cooked food. While none of the cromlech burials excavated in the Tsaghkahovit Plain thus far have revealed a head and hoof deposit, at the nearby site of Aparan II, excavators found an Late Bronze Age grave where the head and hoof deposits of two horses were the only grave goods (Badalyan and Avetisyan 2007).[20]

Animals were incorporated into tombs in multiple ways, suggesting that the value of herd animals in this domain was far from singular. While the choreographies differed, they all began with slaughter. This may have taken place at the side of the grave, and it may have been a moment of heightened attention and drama in the proceedings (Hamilakis 2008). Some of the slaughtered animals were placed in the grave whole while others were butchered. Portions of the carcass were placed in the graves, and the rest may have been distributed (raw or cooked) to the living. Some of the meat was also cooked into food and placed in the graves. The inclusion of meat units and cooked food in vessels appears to be directly related to the consumption of animals as food. In contrast, the inclusion of whole animals seems to point to other aspects of human-animal relationships and other forms of value.

This may explain the pattern whereby, in the tombs excavated thus far in the Tsaghkahovit Plain, all the animals deposited whole were very young sheep and goats. In contrast, the structured deposits of partial remains—the head and hoof deposits and the paired limbs in Burial 06—are from adult cattle and horses. Possibly the incorporation of very young animals drew on their connection to the reproductive and social potential of the herds. Likewise, the structured deposition of partial animals, especially for the head and hoof burials, may have been connected to the individual biographies of adult animals and the ways in which their histories or genealogies drew people together (and marked their differences) through the value of living animals.

The evidence from the Late Bronze Age tombs are traces of explicit choreographies of value that sought to transform social spacetime in the wake of the death of a person. The meat units and cooked food point to commensal politics that generated relations of affiliation-distinction through the sharing of food between the living and the dead. Meat was not the only substance that may have been shared and consumed as part of mortuary practices. Both Kurgan 1 and Kurgan 2 contained, in the ceramics deposited with the young lambs, a large pot (sitting on a stand) with four small platforms on the shoulder, each holding a small cup—a vessel form highly suggestive of social consumption, possibly of alcohol (figure 7.4). The division of the carcass into meat units and its distribution also performatively grounded relations of authorization-subjection, as it enacted affiliation-distinction. It is less certain what kinds of claims about the world and the moral-political premises of value were made by including whole lambs and kids or the heads and hooves of herd animals. The inclusion of whole lambs may link mortuary practices to other choreographies

FIGURE 7.4 Late Bronze Age "party pot" from
Kurgan 1. Courtesy of Adam T. Smith.

of value that relied on female animals' capacities to expand and transform social spacetime through reproduction.

The similarities in the incorporation of herd animals in tombs in the Tsaghkahovit Plain, despite differences in the elaboration and quantities of grave goods, might be read as evidence of an explicit choreography making a claim to an authority that was more along the lines of a "first among equals" than the absolute separation of a sovereign from their subjects. Of course, because explicit choreographies of value are contestable claims, not transparent representations of the world, this raises the question of whether mortuary rituals were intended to gloss over or minimize real differences in power or if they were an active part of maintaining a more even distribution of wealth and authority among the Late Bronze Age inhabitants of the Tsaghkahovit Plain.

CHOREOGRAPHING AUTHORITY

Postmortem, different parts of cattle's, sheep's, and goats' bodies entered into a wide variety of choreographies of value. Sometimes the slaughter was an ordinary act, one where the body of the animal was broken down into its various parts. Some of these parts were distributed to different people or groups of people to be consumed elsewhere, with the heads, spines, and lower limbs left behind to return to the soil. At other times, the bodies of slaughtered animals were destined to be part of mortuary rituals, to be consumed by mourners or interred with the dead. In both itineraries, some heads and lower-limb bones were selected, possibly on the basis of age, sex, or other characteristics, and sent along other paths. The tempo of these choreographies varied. The ankle bones of sheep and goats appear to have been put into circulation more quickly after slaughter, whereas some of the cattle bones were left long enough to be gnawed by dogs or other creatures before moving along.

Heads and hooves circulated in patterns that alternately established similarities and differences between cattle and sheep and between different places in the plain. The movement of astragali into Gegharot brought together cattle and sheep/goats. The circulation of cattle astragali and calcanei separated Gegharot from the TRC but the circulation of sheep/goat mandibles linked them. Once within the sites, some of these bones were handled and altered, temporarily collected together for a time, and eventually dispersed to their final deposition in many different places alongside mundane, broken, and discarded objects.

Having traced the complex and overlapping traces of choreographies I see in the archaeological data from the Tsaghkahovit Plain, I want to return to the question of how choreographies of value work to create and maintain forms of political authority. In earlier accounts, a subset of the overabundant astragali at Gegharot were contextualized by their spatial association with certain rooms identified as shrines (see chapter 4), leading to the claim that they were used for divination (Adam T. Smith and Leon 2014).[21] The power of this claim, which helps explain why it was readily adopted as a habit of interpretation, is that it offers a clear and compelling image of felicitous authority: those in power were authorized to rule because they could successfully manage the larger forces of the world and were singled out from others by their nonnormative relationships to both time and power, and they were held apart by the secrecy and exclusivity of esoteric practices confined to small rooms at the top of citadel.

The problem with this interpretation is that it severs these astragali from all the other astragali (and other overabundant bones) within the sites in the Tsaghkahovit Plain. Moreover, my reanalysis of the faunal remains more generally, and my exploration of the abundance of astragali in particular, undermine the case for astragalomancy. Perhaps more importantly, what emerged from my analysis is the fact that the traces of action that we see in the walled sites in the Tsaghkahovit Plain complicate any easy division between domestic and public or everyday and ritual spaces. Both results call into question the compelling vision of political authority underlying the interpretation of these spaces as shrines used for divination. What might be offered in its place?

The complex choreographies of value that incorporated dead animals in multiple ways into the mortuary practices in the Late Bronze Age Tsaghkahovit Plain appear to have, at least in part, drawn on the different kinds of value-in-action made possible by living and dead animals. In that context, the metonymic inclusion of heads and hooves seems to have been connected to the spatiotemporal transformations made possible by living animals (incorporating the differences between male and female animals and large and small stock). But the choreographies involving heads and hooves in nonmortuary contexts in the Tsaghkahovit Plain don't easily map to the distinction between these different kinds of value.

What the messiness of these patterns suggests to me is that these choreographies of value are revealing traces of practices of *fractal recursion*. As I discussed in chapter 3, fractal recursion is the process by which social distinctions, such as public/private, wild/domesticated, masculine/feminine, or religious/secular, are projected on to a variety of actions, actors, places, and things. This process of shifting calibration in social sorting works to naturalize distinctions by subsuming the messiness of social life—the diversity of action and actors—into seemingly stable categorizations of difference and similarity. The categorization appears stable because of the way it moves across scales while erasing the process of recursion from notice. Importantly, fractal recursion is never perfectly mimetic; the distinctions it draws are necessarily messy or even incoherent. Sue Gal (2002) emphasizes that the messiness of these distinctions in practice is not a failure of the process of categorization but rather an essential feature of how it works.

Attending to the possibility that the choreographies of value I've been examining involved practices of fractal recursion around key distinctions shaping social and political life provides an explanation for why the data from the Tsaghkahovit Plain tend to frustrate the process of archaeological interpretation. There is very likely a disjuncture between whatever distinctions were being mapped through and onto the differences between heads and hooves, large and small stock, and the spaces inside and outside walls in the Late Bronze Age Tsaghkahovit Plain, on the one hand, and archaeologists' process of trying to calibrate the data between our categories of public/private, economic/symbolic or quotidian/unexpected, on the other.

In general, much of the work of fractal recursion is at the level of implicit choreographies of value, which is why they often work powerfully to naturalize certain features of social life. For instance, the distinction between masculine and feminine in contemporary US society is fractally recursive in a wide range of quotidian ways. While cleanliness, smelling good, and concern with appearances may be generally associated with femininity in the contemporary United States, the masculine/feminine distinction can be scaled down to the level of hypergendered packaging of products like body wash, deodorant, or even makeup—using differences in scent, color, and design to remap the distinction (and see P. Manning 2012 on "girly" drinks). But there are also explicit choreographies of value that also contribute to the distinction. For instance, traditional heterosexual wedding ceremonies in the United States are explicit choreographies of value that establish claims about the distinction between masculine and feminine at a variety of levels: in the clothes worn by the bride and groom, the text and performance of the ceremony itself, the commentary on marriage made by the participants during the event, and the wide variety of material items made for use at weddings (which are often highly gendered).[22]

The itineraries of animals' bodies postmortem in the Late Bronze Age

Tsaghkahovit Plain almost certainly combined implicit and explicit cho- reographies of value, but we lack the detailed understanding of social life that would allow me to definitively trace how the two were interrelated. Was it through the strong contrast between the explicit choreographies of value that established felicitous authority and those of everyday life—as it was for the overwhelming spectacle of royal sacrifice and feasting in Shang China that separated elites from nonelites by "dialectically constructing and consuming animality to fuel [their] way toward divinity" (R. Camp- bell 2014, 257)? Or was it through the encompassment of the everyday choreographies of value within the explicit choreographies that made claims about the nature of authority, as it was in the "sacrificial ontology" of the Moche, whereby the dead nourished the living and power was "re- lational and interactive, but unequally distributed between the haves and have-nots, the old and the young, the living and the dead" (Weismantel 2021, 131; see also Swenson and Warner 2012)? Or was it perhaps through the ways in which implicit and explicit choreographies of value were wo- ven into each other, through the relations between humans and herd ani- mals, as described by Govindrajan (2018) for contemporary Uttarakhand, where everyday love and labor with herd animals is intricately linked to the relations of authorization-subjection between humans and gods?

Without texts or ethnographies to help us understand what distinc- tions were being upheld through the processes of fractal recursion that emerge from following the archaeological traces, it is difficult to specify the moral-political premises of value that fueled the explicit choreographies in the Late Bronze Age Tsaghkahovit Plain. What is clear, however, is that these explicit choreographies don't seem to have represented a clear break with more mundane choreographies involving animals and that part of their power emerged from the complex relations between the living and the dead—relations that emerged from the ongoing material circulations between the walled sites and the fields of tombs. If, as archaeologists have generally presumed, the mortuary traditions of the Late Bronze Age were a key component of relations of authorization-subjection, then the value of herd animals in its many forms (and the relation between those forms) was a key part of creating and managing those relations.

I have argued that the value of living animals resides in their reproduc- tive futurity, their capacity to draw people together and sustain relation- ships forward through time. In contrast, the body of the dead animal (and its ability to be incorporated in human's bodies through eating) generates the possibility of powerful forms of social affiliation and distinction. What kinds of transformations of social spacetime might have emerged from the circulation of isolated elements? One possibility is that the collection and circulation of isolated elements were actions that self-consciously disrupted or altered the normal circuits of distribution or exchange or normal temporality. Yannis Hamilakis (2014, 87) has argued that part of the importance of feasts—as explicit choreographies of value in my terms—is that they are events "that disrupt normal temporality and produce time as a distinctive moment." The collection of mandibles and ankle bones may have marked the beginning of this alternate pattern, though unlike the mortuary choreographies, this one did not necessarily follow in close temporal succession from the moment of slaughter. Seen in this light, the somewhat unremarkable patterns of deposition alongside more ordinary forms of refuse may be evidence that these choreographies ended with the reintegrating of the heads and hooves with other, more everyday choreographies of slaughter, consumption, and discard.

This reintegration was a marked choice, part of the explicit claims being made about the world, and one that differed from other kinds of choreographies in other times and places where bones serve as material memories of feasts or hunts that are curated and displayed. Perhaps the deposition of these bones all over the various areas of the sites, among the residues of everyday life, was understood as their beneficial incorporation into the site itself, either as the living fabric of the site or as the tangible and sedimented history of the community. Interesting in this regard is the fact that the remains of the first occupation were incorporated into the walls and construction of the site during its second occupation. While the destruction of the site was likely a traumatic event, people at Gegharot did not respond by relocating entirely, clearing the site entirely of debris, or perfectly recreating the site as it once at had been. Instead, they lived in and on top of the remains of their history.

It is possible that the altertemporalities of these choreographies were a response to the need to maintain social relations through the winter, a time when mobility for both humans and animals was limited by snow and bad weather. Caspar Meyer (personal communication, April 12, 2022) has suggested that preserved dairy products like ghee and cheese relocate culinary experiences through time and reactivate memories of the past. Late Bronze Age people and herds in the Tsaghkahovit Plain were improvising practices of reproductive labor that would have changed the temporal experiences of seasons and may have been part of a larger set of choreographies that managed value and social relations through the year. The data could reflect a seasonal cycle whereby bones were collected, circulated, and worked with across the autumn and winter and then gathered and deposited as the seasons changed, perhaps as a part of a more general spring cleaning. If Late Bronze Age herders slaughtered animals that were unlikely to survive the winter in the fall, as contemporary herders in Mongolia do (Fijn 2011), then the collection and deposition of these bones might have been connected to larger claims about the cycle of life and death, and its relation to power and authority.

Another possibility, which is not exclusive of the other, is that the circulation of isolated elements was part of an attempt to expand or enhance the transformation of social spacetime created by the distribution and consumption of meat or the circulation of living animals. Bones contrast with flesh in their material durability—once clean, they can last beyond a human lifetime. Thus, they offer the potential for spacetime transformations that might endure beyond the memory of a meal or the life span of a sheep or cow (cf. Weiner 1992, 38). Yet people at Gegharot and Tsaghkahovit do not appear to have been interested in curating the mandibles and ankles bones they gathered for the long term. Instead, the choreographies that circulated the isolated elements were based on the conscious selection and movement of those bones through interrelating paths of circulation and interaction, after which these circuits were closed by depositing the bones alongside other, more everyday objects.

The patterns of deposition might indicate that these choreographies of value aimed to connect the sites to other parts of the social and political landscape. For contemporary herders in Mongolia, the bones of the animal are where its spirit or soul resides, and they are key to regeneration of life. As such, herders keep dogs away from the bones of herd animals, which are then left in pastures to disintegrate (Fijn 2011, 229). The patterns of circulation in the Tsaghkahovit Plain may suggest a different choreography of value, whereby parts of the carcass (ribs and vertebrae, long bones) are properly returned to pastures and the heads and tarsals are incorporated into social life and the built environments of both the living and the dead. As explicit choreographies of value, this may have staked a claim about the relationship between sites (and the actions that took place inside them) and the parts of social life that took place in the pastures.

The necessary relation between slaughter, consumption, and the availability of bones for further circulation makes it easy to consider that the choreographies involving isolated elements might have been extensions or intensifications of the value of dead animals. But there are aspects of the choreographies that suggest instead that they might have been aimed at synthesizing or mediating the value of living and dead animals. The interplay of similarity and difference between the spatial patterning and choice of bones between cattle and sheep and goats is highly suggestive. These choreographies did not merely replicate the division between cattle and small stock in regard to reproductive futurity and commensal potentiality, but drew on that distinction to make other kinds of claims about the world. This may also help to account for the layering of different kinds of animal bones within the tombs as part of mortuary rituals. Whole animals (especially young ones), head and hoof deposits of adult animals, and the meat units and cooked food drew on different forms of value, knitting them together to manage the relations between mourners and the deceased.

The partitioning of animal bodies—for everyday meals, for inclusion in mortuary rituals, and for the as-yet-opaque processes that brought isolated jaws and ankle bones within the site walls—had a key role in shaping both the hegemonic (naturalized or taken-for-granted) features of everyday life and the explicit statements of political ideology materialized in kurgans, emplaced sites, and the political landscape as a whole (cf. Dawdy 2020). The value transformations and the social differences they engendered (implicitly or explicitly) were woven together into relationships of affiliation-distinction and authorization-subjection, building on the sensorial, metonymic, metaphoric, and iconic possibilities of animals' bodies. But these differences were not merely a static representation of the ordering of society. They were part of active choreographies of value that generated and channeled social potencies. The actions that brought mandibles, calcanei, and astragali into sites, drawing on the potent possibilities of these bones, created topologies of spacetime that channeled the flow of value and shaped the moral-political premises of Late Bronze Age societies in the Tsaghkahovit Plain.

NEW STORIES,
NEW QUESTIONS

In the preceding chapters, I have argued against the metamyth underlying popular and scholarly narratives about human-animal relations in the
past—the idea that contemporary forms of inequality, objectification, and
instrumental relations with animals have their origins in domestication in
the deeper past. There is a further consequence to this line of thought, one
that has remained somewhat implicit in my argument thus far. Trouillot's
mapping of the "Savage slot" highlights the importance of *utopia* in shaping the nexus between Order and the "Savage." This argument is something archaeology must grapple with as archaeologists think about why the
field might or should matter. If the past continues to fill the "Savage slot,"
both within the discipline and in the popular imagination, then we must
attend carefully to how our stories about the past continue to be inflected
by Order and utopias.

When thinking about human-animal relations in particular, I remain
unsettled by the temptation to reduce the deeper past to the positive
counterpart—or even the solution—to the problems of the present, in the
wake of pushing back against seeing it as the origins of modernity. I am
apprehensive of the way that such a move confirms the temporal shape of
traditional stories, remaining content to shift the moment of origins (and
rupture) backward or forward in time. I have tried to resist this temptation by disrupting and complicating the modern/premodern divide in the
examples I used to help me shape my interpretations, placing Neolithic
cattle alongside Dolly the cloned sheep. Asking new questions and building new interpretations of the archaeological data from the Tsaghkahovit
Plain have illuminated unexpected homologies and resonances between

practices and histories that are often separated by the modern/premodern divide.

The past decade of working with the material remains of the past has left me convinced that postdomestication, premodern pasts are much *weirder* than we've allowed them to be. If archaeologists can loosen the bonds of our interpretive habits, we will find many wild and wondrous pasts. This book also makes the case for the intellectual pleasures of confronting the simultaneous promise and difficulty of doing archaeology. For all its frustrations, I have genuinely enjoyed the challenge of trying to conjure worlds from scraps of bones while using my commitment to archaeological materiality and rigorous interpretive work as both a guardrail and a ladder.

Above all, the archaeological data from the Late Bronze Age Tsaghkahovit Plain show that human–herd animals relations in the past were a space of potential—ones where the capacities of both humans and herd animals were altered through novel material practices, multispecies labor relations, and interspecies choreographies of value. Attending to the specific potential of human–herd animal relations in a postdomestication, premodern context makes possible to tell new stories about living with herds in the past by reshaping local histories *and also* broader stories about the past. Starting locally, the preceding chapters have spun various threads of interpretation, pulling and twisting together archaeological data from the sites of Tsaghkahovit and Gegharot and a motley range of models, stories, and questions from the present and the recent and deeper pasts. Here I will try to loosely knit these strands together to suggest some new questions and perspectives on how archaeologists might think about political life in the Late Bronze Age South Caucasus.

The data from Tsaghkahovit and Gegharot reveal traces of a wide variety of forms of labor, all connected to caring for herd animals: vertical mobility to higher-altitude pastures, foddering, and the careful manipulation of reproduction (both restricting and expanding it). All these forms of work emerged from the intrinsic entanglement of human and animal biological and social reproduction—including the unequal stakes for human and animal participants in that reproduction (within and across lines of species difference). Both foddering and the more obvious bodily intimacies of milking and caring for pregnant and newborn animals were potential sites for deepened or intensified human–herd animal relations. The choice to greatly expand the reproductive seasonality of sheep and goats and the absence of evidence for the culling of very young animals suggests that maximization and efficiency were not the main organizing principles of this labor.

Looking across the biographies of sheep by using zooarchaeological and isotopic data, I found evidence suggesting that there were two different sets of labor practices in place during the Late Bronze Age. One practice greatly expanded the seasonality of sheep reproduction, which also expanded the seasonality of certain kinds of labor associated with caring for pregnant ewes and lambs (especially feeding them during the winter). A key part of this choreography of value was likely the extension of the seasonal availability of fresh dairy products. Other sheep had their reproduction carefully controlled to match the timing of the seasonal availability of pasture and limit the human labor associated with their reproduction. Both approaches to colaboring took place in the context of widespread foddering for sheep, goats, and cattle, which solved the problem of herds' need for food in the harsh winter by harnessing human labor through harvesting (and potentially sowing) grasses, rather than through long-distance mobility to warmer locales.

The differentiation of labor activities and schedules, as well as the practice of working together with different herds (composed of animals of different species, ages, sexes, and biographies), shaped relations of affiliation-distinction. While we don't know who did what work, it seems probable that tasks were apportioned on the basis of characteristics like age, gender, and other social statuses while at the same time constituting the people who did the various tasks as particular kinds of people. The work of making human and animal social and biological reproduction possible iteratively established how humans (and herds as well) understood the nature of those relations. This proliferation and differentiation of labor—tied to different potentials for the production of meat, milk, and living sheep—may be traces of two different strategies for composing felicitous authority. This felicity would have emerged both from the labor relations underpinning them and the potential of meat, milk, and living animals to transform social spacetime.

Turning to the other forms of labor that are well represented in the available archaeological data is revealing. Thanks to neutron activation and portable X-ray fluorescence analyses, we know some details about the production and circulation of ceramics in the Late Bronze in the Tsaghkahovit Plain (Lindsay et al. 2008; Adam T. Smith, Badalyan, and Avetisyan 2009; Greene 2013; Lindsay and Greene 2013). These analyses reveal a complex system—one with noticeable differences between groups of potters—and hints that this variation may reflect differently organized labor processes. Vessels with similar forms and using the same source clays were manufactured using different processes of paste preparation. Likewise, analyses also show that the same "technostyle" of paste preparation was used on clays from multiple sources (which may indicate the use of the same technostyle across multiple production loci; see Greene 2013, 222).

Neither the faunal nor the ceramics data from Gegharot and Tsaghka-hovit support the interpretation that the forms of labor connected to herds and pottery were in service of producing goods within a tributary system oriented toward the centralized collection of goods (Greene 2013, 179). Taken together, the ceramics and faunal data suggest a potential repertoire of relations of affiliation-distinction built through divergent and multiple labor practices. It seems likely that the diversity of labor practices also helped establish and maintain relations of authorization-subjection, even if the nature of the connection remains opaque. Thinking about the connections between the organization of labor and the circulation and consumption of its products brings us back to the question of value.

I have argued that we must attend to herd animals' pre- and postmortem values, and the potential differences between those forms of value. Reading across ethnographic and historical examples, I suggest that the value of living herd animals is grounded in the specific futurity of reproduction's ability to transform social spacetime. This futurity works to create connections and obligations between people while also drawing on the material-semiotic potential of genealogies and the wider biological-social reproduction of humans and animals. In many of these examples, the longer lifespans and larger size of cattle make them more closely aligned with (or better suited to) the production and circulation of this kind of value. The data from the Tsaghkahovit Plain appear to conform to this more general pattern in certain ways. Cattle were, on average, slaughtered at older ages than sheep and goats, indicating greater emphasis on the value of the living animal. Moreover, cattle appear to have lived different lives than sheep and goats, as revealed by the isotopic evidence of their different diets, water consumption, and potentially, patterns of mobility. The limited data available on mortality patterns on the basis of sex, which show the traces of a subgroup of young male cattle that were slaughtered and consumed on-site at Gegharot, may indicate the relatively greater value of living female cattle (based on their reproductive futurity).

Yet the complicated practices shaping sheep reproduction and slaughter in the Late Bronze Age Tsaghkahovit Plain don't match what we might expect had sheep and goats been the small change in a system of value where living cattle were the paradigmatic form of wealth. In those models, which were drawn from ethnographic research, small stock were valued mainly for their meat and converted into larger stock whenever possible.

Sheep and goats were slaughtered at younger ages than cattle, but the existence of two approaches to sheep herding complicates the picture (as does the expanded birth seasonality for goats). One set of labor practices does seem to have been organized to limit the labor associated with reproduction, slaughtering most sheep after they had reached their adult size. The other approach expanded the seasonality of reproduction, slaughtering some sheep before they obtained their maximum size but after any production of milk had long ceased and keeping others alive for a long time.

This evidence leads me to conclude that these two labor practices, and thus the two different biographies for sheep, are evidence of the fractal recursion of the division between the different values (potential spacetime transformations) of living and dead animals. The standard ethnographic examples lead us to search for this division at the level of herd animal species (large versus small stock), but it can also explain the differentiation of labor involved in herding sheep. Two things follow from this interpretive move. First, it reorients how we might think about the value of milk. Working from the assumption that the expansion of birth seasonality also was an expansion in the seasonal availability of milk and other dairy products (as well as the labor connected to them), we can ask, What kind of spacetime transformation did this make possible? What kind of relations could it forge?

Milk, more immediately than meat, is a product of the expansion of the social spacetime inherent in reproduction. Sheep's (and goats') shorter lifespans may imply a faster tempo of expansion and connection than cattle—which may have been a boon for some aspects of authorization (because one could establish new connections and obligation more quickly) and a liability in other ways (including the smaller scale of reproductive futurity and redistributive generosity). But because milk can be divided and transformed into a wide variety of substances of varying material qualities, it shares with meat a similar potential to shape and reflect social differences through circulation and consumption. Also, like meat, the circulation and consumption of dairy products are shaped by a trade-off between strategies that expand the circle of people invited to consume versus transformations that extend its edibility (Halstead 2007; McCormick 2002; Towers et al. 2017).

This suggests that the diversity of labor practices connected to sheep herding might be better understood as choreographies of value that attempted to replicate or claim the kinds of felicitous authority that comes from the expansion of social spacetime through the value of living animals, connecting it more directly to the value of smaller stock. If we assume sheep were easier to obtain than cattle, then perhaps this was a path to felicitous authority that was more widely available. But the separation of the two choreographies in the labor practices they require and the differing biographies of sheep that they entail also raises questions about what kinds of felicitous authority generated and sustained those practices and with what wider consequences for other relations of authorization-subjection.

As I discussed in chapter 6, the value of dead animals works to transform social spacetime by establishing and maintaining relations through circulation and consumption. Often, these value transformations rely on material-semiotic mappings of part-whole relationships (which ground relations of affiliation-distinction), though they can also traffic in the material-semiotic potential of incorporation of meat and milk (as a bodily substances) into the bodies of those who eat them. The available archaeological evidence from the Tsaghkahovit Plain provides little illumination on how the consumption of herd animals formed relations of affiliation-distinction or authorization-subjection, in part because the butchery and consumption of many of the animals whose biographies I can trace occurred "off-stage." Nevertheless, the data do suggest that herd animals' postmortem value was comprised of both the implicit choreographies of production and consumption, daily meals and quotidian tasks, as well as more explicit choreographies of value that used their bodies to make material-semiotic claims about the nature of the world (and that likely contributed to the felicity of authority).

What also emerges is evidence that that the postmortem, postbutchery circulation of isolated skeletal elements (mandibles and tarsals) generated and transformed value through time and space. The logics of these practices remain opaque. Possibly, these isolated elements were related to the living animals they came from through a form of material metonymy— bringing some form of herd animals' values into the walled sites. Whatever value was instantiated with these practices, it did not require the careful storage and curation of the objects. Instead, these practices seem to have involved physical handling and light alterations for a limited period of time.

The value of the mandibles and tarsals seems to have been produced and transacted across multiple, overlapping choreographies of value, marking the fractal recursion of the moral-political premises and qualities that shaped their value. This multiplicity helps account for the palimpsest of material traces that make the skeletal element distribution messy, complicating any straightforward link between context and meaning or purpose. These practices seem not to replicate the differences between species of herd animals visible in their premortem biographies. Perhaps the isolated elements channeled a different aspect of herd animals' value, somewhat independently of the values of living and dead animals, or it somehow synthesized the differences between large and small stock to achieve further transformations in value (and instantiate felicitous authority). What is more certain is that the explicit choreographies that circulated bones generated created forms of felicitous authority through their interrelation with, rather than their distinction from, more implicit choreographies.

I have noted that the material metonymy that underpins the circulation of isolated bones within walled sites shares suggestive similarities with, but also differences from, the material metonymy of the head and hoof burials that are widespread in the Caucasus and Eurasia more broadly. A more comprehensive examination of the inclusion of animal remains in Late Bronze Age burials is a promising line of inquiry for future research. Given the evidence considered here, it would be productive to explore in greater depth whether the three forms of including animal remains in mortuary practices—whole and partial animals, meat units, and bones found in ceramic vessels—are practices that harness or incorporate different kinds of value. The cooked food (potentially shared between the living and the dead), the partial portions of a carcass, and the inclusion of whole (or metonymic parts of) bodies would likely have had different spatial and temporal possibilities, as connected to the different choreographies of eating, cooking and butchering and the reproduction of both human and herd animal social life. For the moment, it is enough to suggest that the three ways of incorporating animals in burials appear to bring together the pre- and postmortem value of herd animals, suturing the commensal and sumptuary politicking of mortuary rituals to other kinds of value-in-action.

When we consider the evidence from the faunal remains together with the data on the production and circulation of ceramics, it highlights how archaeologists' image of the political landscape of the Late Bronze Age—as anchored by walled sites and the fields of cromlechs and kurgans—must be supplemented or transformed by acknowledging the wide variety of quotidian taskscapes (pastoralist mobility, foddering, butchery, ceramics production) and the potential for explicit choreographies of value that expanded well beyond site boundaries. This may prove challenging for archaeology, as these choreographies of value may very well have left fewer durable traces than the construction of stone walls and large burial mounds.

Nevertheless, comparing the circulation of ceramics and the movement of animals' bodies postmortem does give us a sense of some of those choreographies and what they might tell us about political life in the Late

Bronze Age. For both, the patterning that we see in the collected data does not reveal much about the differential use of space within the walls of sites. For both animal bones and pots, the available data show patterns of distribution that don't differ notably by site sector, or in the case of herd animals, by depositional context. Further research is needed, possibly at sites with less complex depositional histories than Gegharot and Tsaghkahovit, to better understand how spaces within the walled sites were organized and used. What the ceramic-sourcing data does indicate is that the circulation of pottery containers generated a different mapping of social space within the plain than the activities connected with herding. The inflow of containers from multiple production and clay sources at Gegharot knitted the activities within the site's walls to the production tasks connected to a much wider area, whereas Tsaghkahovit drew heavily on nearby sources for ceramics. In contrast, the faunal data suggest a roughly similar extension of social spacetime at both sites through the circulation of whole and partial animal bodies postmortem—even as the presence of different isolated elements suggests the potential for other differences in choreographies of value.

What this multiplicity in ceramic production and circulation (and perhaps in use) and the production, circulation, and consumption of herd animals suggest is the potential for the composition of various kinds of felicitous authority.[1] Relations of authorization-subjection could have generated and channeled value consisting of differential social potencies from different sources and along different trajectories, thus composing the desired social spacetimes in different ways. At the same time, however, this potential multiplicity of sources and itineraries of value transformations— and the lack of apparent coordination between them—may have represented a real or potential threat to any attempts to centralize or maintain arrangements of authority and power. The expansion of access to mortuary practices and the reduced level of ostentation also give credence to this emerging picture of a dynamic palimpsest of practices intended to create and maintain felicitous authority.

Taking this interpretation a bit further, I'd like to forward a hypothesis. The data from the contexts that can be securely dated to the second phase of occupation at Gegharot have a higher proportion of cattle bones than those dating securely to the first phase. Perhaps, after the events that led to the destruction of the site, the people who returned and rebuilt Gegharot found it necessary or expedient to double down on the choreographies of value built around cattle. Perhaps these are traces of a change in politics where the value of sheep or meat was reduced and that of living cattle was more strongly emphasized. What ripple effects might that change have had? Did it narrow the range of people who could successfully use cattle to generate felicitous authority? Is it connected to the abandonment of the site after the second destruction event? Were these local events part of a wider context of political authority and interaction? What kinds of archaeological data and what new methods would we need to begin to answer these questions?

If the logics of value in the Late Bronze Age Tsaghkahovit Plain generally saw cattle (versus sheep/goats) as the more stable and durable media for commanding the labor, affiliation, and subjection of others (and therefore more felicitous in generating both affiliation-distinction and authorization-subjection), then there are at least two possible interpretations of this shift. First, we might consider whether it is evidence that the people and groups who were creatively composing authority—using the forms of value generated through the choreographies of value connected to expanded seasonal reproduction of sheep and thus the production of milk—eventually shifted the performative practice of authority away from sheep to choreographies grounded in the value of cattle. In essence, this would posit that together, sheep and people were able to generate an alternate path to authority without overturning the larger order of moral-political premises of value.

The other possibility is that the creative assembling of sheep, people, and milk (and maybe also bones) generated new kinds of value, which in turn created uncertainty about, or even a direct challenge to, the value of cattle and the relations of authorization-subjection and affiliation-distinction that composed it (and that it composed).[2] This interpretation assumes that at some point prior to the initial phase of occupation at Gegharot, the constellations of choreographies producing the value of cattle as the main route to composing authority and political collectivities were hegemonic. *Hegemonic*, in the sense that Shannon Dawdy (2020, 158) proposes, these choreographies were perceived to be "non-agentive, explicit, and natural," as opposed to the aspects of politics that require explicit justification. Following her reading of the politics of *beiläufigkeit* (the incidental, taken-for-granted), I wonder if the choreographies of value that shaped and shifted human and sheep labor in the Late Bronze Age also worked to call into question certain assumed aspects of the composition of authority; in essence, moving them from hegemony to ideology in Dawdy's terms. If this was the case, then perhaps the higher numbers of cattle after the first destruction of the site reveals a partial reassertion (or reassembling) of an orthodoxy in the face of the challenges of heterodoxic practices.

Thinking along these lines illuminates a resonance between the evidence from the faunal assemblages and Maureen Marshall's (2014, 289–90) analysis of mortuary practices in the Tsaghkahovit Plain. She notes that the differences in mortuary practices between those interred on the northern and southern slopes of TsBC12 can be read simultaneously as evidence of a potential shift in mortuary practices over time *and also* as evidence of different relations of affiliation-distinction. She writes, "It seems significant that there was a rebuilding project at Gegharot at the same time that a new area of TsBC12 was used for interring the dead. It was not only a new area, but was marked as unique with its terracing walls and distinguished visually in in the densely packed overlapping of tombs" (229). It remains to be seen what else we might learn about what changed, or didn't change, between the first and second occupations at Gegharot and how this related to the dramatic episodes of site destruction and their absence at Tsaghkahovit.

While the scope for future work on the shape of political life in the Late Bronze Age South Caucasus remains wide open, the data from the past decade of work at sites in Tsaghkahovit Plain have allowed me to provide a basic demonstration of how archaeologists can explore the political potentialities of living with herds. Attending to practices of feeding and eating, labor and reproduction, and pre- and postmortem value departs from, or at least transforms, the archaeological inclination to treat domesticated herd animals (among others) as mere resources for human political action. Zoopolitics locates the political importance of herd animals in the interrelationships between the social and biological reproduction of humans and herd animals. But it simultaneously insists that we must attend to the specifics of those relationships and the ways they matter in the performance of felicitous authority. The relations of use between humans and herd animals are historically constituted and specific; it is their specificity that enables their enmeshment in the wider field of practices (which are also historically specific and diverse) that form relations of affiliation-distinction and authorization-subjection.

By this point, I hope to have convinced you that there is no straightforward, linear path between human–herd relations in the Late Bronze Age and contemporary relationships with cattle, sheep, and goats. So why is it that so many archaeologists and nonarchaeologists alike seem committed to telling stories that posit an origin point in the deeper past? Archaeologists, at least, may simply be drawn to stories that increase the sense that our discipline is relevant beyond our personal interests and obsessions. But that doesn't really explain the wider traction and incredible staying power of the ontostories of domestication for people with wildly different political and intellectual commitments. Domestication ontostories remain important, and attractive, because of the ways that two different but related contemporary concerns traffic in them: (1) contemporary debates about the moral status of meat consumption and (2) questions about the entanglement of the politics of animal exploitation and the politics of human inequality and violence. Both concerns end up tangled with stories about domestication because domestication ontostories start from the fixed point provided by the objectification of livestock in the present, but they don't intersect with them in exactly the same way.

Contemporary debates over meat consumption are fought over the terrain of whether eating meat is key to being human ("natural" and therefore normal, or even necessary) or whether it is, in fact, both optional and ethically problematic (vis-à-vis animal suffering or environmental impacts; see, e.g., Berson 2019; Zaraska 2016). The terrain of this debate stretches into deeper time than animal domestication stories, back to the earliest eras of our species. In doing so, they recast animal domestication as the second act in the human history of meat-eating. Rejecting any relations of use between humans and animals—seeing any killing as a form of unwarranted objectification—shifts the role that domestication plays in explaining contemporary human-animal relations.

If killing is the problem, then the origin of the problem is not domestication. Instead, the problem is carnivory itself, along with the stories that attempt to naturalize, and thereby valorize, the human consumption of meat. These stories provide competing readings of the evidence for, and interpretations of, the role of meat-eating in the development of *Homo sapiens* as a species, accepting or rejecting the idea that meat-eating is what made (and makes) us human. The mistreatment of livestock animals in industrial production shapes the affective register of these arguments, but the specific history of domestication is not the central issue. Nevertheless, domestication stories are woven into accounts and arguments that make the case against meat and other forms of instrumental relations.

There are other critiques of the cost of contemporary instrumental and objectifying relations with animals that start from different premises. These stories allow the possibility of relations of use that are ethically positive, even if they involve killing animals. Collectively, they raise questions about what kinds of relations between humans and animals are capable of generating both good lives and good deaths for animals. These narratives imagine the possibility of premodern, nonmodern, or non-Western relations with animals (e.g., Armstrong Oma 2010; Hage 2017; Norton 2015; Porcher 2017b; Tani 1996). The stories differ in whether they imagine the possibility of being in good relation to *domesticated* animals. This, to a large extent, seems to depend on to what extent deep-time histories of domestication are seen as the source of problematic contemporary forms of objectification and instrumental use.

This leads me to the other factor that keeps us coming back to domestication ontostories and shapes their narrative beats. There is an appealing symmetry in the mirrored logics of animal domestication as the originary moment that links the origins of human and animal domination through the objectification and domination of animals and the rise of unequal and exploitative political orders in the deep past. This symmetry is echoed in, and reinforced by, the historical narratives that identify capitalism, colonialism, and imperialism as the source of entrenched human inequalities (based on gender, class, race, etc.) *and also* the suffering of animals and ecologies under capitalist accumulation. This seductive parallelism is precisely what turns certain places and times into flyover country in ontostories about the past.

What would a history of objectification look like if it made different assumptions about the connections between the present, past, and future? What other stories might we tell about the long-term histories of human–herd animal relations and their stakes? I'm not entirely sure—but it's an important question to consider. Archaeologists and historians could have an important role to play in thinking about how to remap the relationships between the future and the past. Animal work, as a subject of critical inquiry in the present, offers one possible entry point for this kind of revision. In their recent books, both Alex Blanchette (2020) and Jocelyne Porcher (2017b) build their thoughts about animal work into a wider critique of capitalism in contemporary life, exploring how it negatively impacts both humans and animals. Despite the considerable differences between their arguments, both critiques of the present (and imaginaries of possible futures) point to a need to reshape the relationship between the present, futures, and past.

Blanchette (2020, 244) argues that "we are not *when* some think we are" inasmuch as we are not actually living in a "postindustrial" present in the United States. He contends that the temporal narratives about postindustrialization obscure the intense effort required to maintain the increasingly precarious arrangements of industrialized life and that this misrecognition prevents effective political action. Porcher (2017b, 43), in contrast, starts from a clear separation between *zootechnics* (i.e., industrial agriculture) and animal husbandry (work relationships between humans and animals). She argues that we have mistakenly seen the history of our working relationships with animals through the theory provided by zootechnics. Yet she is clear that the solution to the horrors of contemporary industrial agriculture cannot be a return to "traditional farming." She wants to imagine a utopia that invents another "life at work, which has learned the lessons of the past and seizes the potential in the present" (103–4). Taking the two arguments together, what I want to highlight is that rejecting the (post)industrial might need to involve rethinking what we know about preindustrial human–herd animal relations. Even if we cannot return to a golden age that never existed, we don't have to accept the futures that are naturalized by the stories we have told about the past.

What remains to be seen is what will emerge if we can better map the entanglements *and* the disjunctures between: (1) human–herd animal relations in the past and the present and (2) the ways we are tempted to use our histories with herd animals to narrate the links between the present and the deeper past as means of addressing contemporary issues and future concerns. The particular history of some human-animal relations—those that Anna Tsing rightly notes as having world-historical consequences— are the *origins* of the stories we tell about early domestication, and not vice versa. We need to firmly reverse the arrow of causality or connection between our scholarly understandings of human-animal relations in the more recent past and our stories about living with animals in the deeper past, and especially those about living with herd animals. I have sought to do this within the pages of this book while avoiding enacting a counterproductive rupture between the more recent and deeper pasts.

Rather than seeing the deeper past as a point of origin or as essentially irrelevant, we need to find new ways of telling stories about how we, both humans and domesticated animals, are shaped in multiple ways by the long-term histories of our relations. I have tried to develop a set of tools for thinking about human–herd animal relationships of use that does not presume that objectification is the foundational basis but also does not preclude the possibility of finding relations in the past that shared similarities with the particular nexus of ontology, property, and power that defines contemporary industrial animal farming and legal frameworks. I have insisted that we slow down and not presume we already know what the consequences of killing herd animals in other times and places were. Key to new narratives will be rethinking what went on in the long gaps between the old narrative beats, exploring in greater richness and texture how domestication may have been important to what followed—but not determinative in the way the old ontostories insisted.

ACKNOWLEDGMENTS

This book has deep roots, and as a result, I have many people to thank for helping me along the way. I would not have been able to do this work without the generous welcome and ongoing support I received from my Armenian colleagues. Many, many thanks go to Ruben Badalyan and Armine Harutyunyan for welcoming me to Project ArAGATS, and also to Artur Petrosyan, Lilit Ter-Minasyan, Roman Hovsepyan, and Levon Aghikyan for their hospitality, kindness, teaching, and camaraderie. My gratitude as well goes to Durik for all the delicious meals that she prepared for the ArAGATS team in Aparan and for introducing me to the delights of *gata* and *spas*. Thanks also go to the American side of the ArAGATS team, and especially to Adam T. Smith, who invited me to come to Armenia, thus setting all this in motion. And I also thank Kate Franklin, Maureen Marshall, and Elizabeth Fagan, who have been excellent mentors and even better friends for the last decade.

The foundations of this work were laid during my time at the University of Chicago. Kate Grossman and Belinda Monahan generously showed me the ropes of zooarchaeological analysis and spent many hours with me in the basement of the Institute for the Study of Ancient Cultures, teaching me about bones. My research benefited from the convivial intellectual atmosphere I encountered at U of C, especially as a member of the Inter-disciplinary Archaeology Workshop, and later on, in the early years of the Animal Studies Workshop. The conversations in these spaces set me on the path to writing this book. While at Chicago, I benefited from the mentorship of faculty in the Department of Anthropology: Adam T. Smith, Alan Kolata, Mickey Dietler, and François Richard. Shannon Dawdy and

Alice Yao gave generous guidance at crucial moments in the formation of my project, for which I am grateful.

I was especially lucky to spend at semester at Cornell and take a class with the incomparable Nerissa Russell, who expanded my horizons of possibility for a rigorous and daring zooarchaeology. The very earliest inklings of the ideas in this book began from a number of deep and convivial conversations with Emma Hite during that semester and with the other half of our seminar dream team, Jana Eger and Kathryn Weber. Emily Schach, Kristen Nado, and Sofia Pacheco-Flores helped me as I learned the basics of isotope analysis, and their friendship made my time in Tempe, Arizona, much more pleasant. Kelly J. Knudson kindly allowed me to spend a semester working in the Archaeological Chemistry Laboratory at ASU. I am also deeply grateful to Gwyn Gordon, who shared her deep expertise and provided practical support for the strontium isotopic analyses I undertook.

As I worked on the manuscript, I benefited from the intellectual generosity and practical support of many people and institutions. My first steps toward the book you are now reading were taken in a talk I gave at the Stanford Archaeology Center during my postdoc there. I am especially thankful for Andrew Bauer's intellectual companionship and for Barb Voss's brief but effective mentorship while I was there. I owe a debt as well to Radhika Govindrajan, whose research I first encountered when I heard her give a talk at Stanford. Not only has her work deeply influenced my own intellectual development, she also generously gave me practical advice about the process of writing a book and getting published. The early stages of writing and conceptualizing the manuscript were made possible by the intellectual space and camaraderie provided by a year in the School of Historical Studies at the Institute for Advanced Study (funded through the Andrew W. Mellon Fellowship for Assistant Professors). I am especially grateful for Kira Thurman's and Sarah Quinn's friendship, support, and wisdom.

This book was indelibly shaped by a number of colleagues who generously engaged with it and commented on many drafts over the years. I have been extremely lucky to have been writing and thinking with Anna Weischelbraun for nearly a decade now, and she, along with Colin Halverson, Britta Ingebretson, and Zeb Dingley, have read and reread nearly every word of this manuscript. They helped me achieve my most ambitious goals for this book. Mara Greene was the best writing buddy I could have asked for, and I am so grateful for the space we created to write together during that first terrible year of the COVID pandemic. My colleagues at Columbia and Barnard (and elsewhere in New York City) generously read and discussed chapters with me at various points: Camilla Sturm, Zoë Crossland, Brian Boyd, Naor Ben-Yehoyada, Sev Fowles, Terry D'Altroy, Ellen Morris, and Rod Campbell. Many thanks go as well to Andrea Ford, Xiao-Bo Yuan, Meghan Morris, Christien Tompkins, and Joseph Weiss for their comments on chapter drafts.

Brian Boyd, Yannis Hamilakis, and Mary Weismantel were kind enough to read the entire manuscript in fall 2022. Their generous and insightful comments helped me bring my vision for the work to fruition. I am also grateful for the comments from the anonymous reviewers, who helped to improve the book and also gave me the confidence that this somewhat unusual book would find an audience. Thanks go as well to Mary Al-Sayed, Jane Desmond, and Barbara J. King for believing in my book and giving it a home in the Animal Lives series. And I thank Dylan Montanari and Fabiola Enríquez Flores for seeing the book across the finish line and into readers' hands. I am grateful for the work of copyediting team Nicole Balant and Caterina MacLean, as well as Kristen Raddatz and the many other people at the press who helped produce and market this book.

Finally, this book would never have been written without the love and support of my family and friends. Thanks go to my parents and my sisters, Becca and Lillian, for supporting me on this long journey. Tuan, I thank you for everything. I could not have done this without you—thank you for making dinner, listening to me talk endlessly about sheep and goats and the Bronze Age, being the best hype man I could ever ask for, helping to make the figures for this book, and all the million other ways that you supported me. And a final thank you goes to Bronson, who has, in his own feline way, taught me many things and helped make the writing of this book possible.

NOTES

Introduction

1. In contrasting how sheep and primates are studied, Rowell characterizes the situation as a "hierarchical scandal" in ethology (quoted in Despret 2006, 361).

2. By postdomestication, I mean times and places that come after the initial period of domestication; where the local history of relations with domesticated herd animals may have considerable time-depth but is also premodern in that they are older than the last five hundred years or so. In general, this roughly coincides with post-Neolithic periods in the Old World, but the argument of this book questions the logics underlying that periodization (see chapter 1). As I discuss in the next chapter, domestication can be thought of as both a process and a category, potentially making the term *postdomestication* somewhat awkward.

3. These practices are fundamentally and simultaneously material and semiotic.

4. Haraway's (2003, 2008) term *companion species* is often mistaken for *companion animal*, thereby reducing the scope to those species we are used to living with as pets and focusing on individual relationships with individual animals (e.g., Fijn 2011, 119).

5. Doing so avoids reducing animals to an undifferentiated and homogeneous category (see Russell 2021, 53).

6. Joyce (2012) explores the complex connections, as well as the disconnects, between archaeology's approach to materiality in comparison with the material turn more broadly.

7. Parallel to this debate in archaeology are the philosophical interventions around the "question of the animal" within critical animal studies. These scholars are deeply concerned with the ethical stakes of the politics of thinking about and living with animals but start from a different set of questions and concerns (e.g.,

Wolfe 2010). A key point of overlap between these conversations is Agamben's (1998) work on *bios* and *zoe*, which is both political theory and a philosophical perspective on the animal.

8. My work in this book to include animals in the political, as situated within a particular set of intellectual communities and traditions (mainly anthropological archaeology and political anthropology), is an attempt to build an orientation to animals that is commonplace within Indigenous philosophies and scholarship. The so-called problem of including animals in political theory is established by the terrain of Western thought and its traditional ontological commitments. In contrast, recognition of the political import of ethical relations with animals is noncontroversial and foundational in many forms of Indigenous thought because they foreground social-political relationships between humans and animals (e.g., Todd 2016, 18; V. Watts 2013).

9. My approach to the performative is shaped by the work of Karen Barad (2006), who insists on the material-semiotic nature of performativity, and the work of Judith Butler (1997, 2015) on the performativity of gender, and their ongoing work on politics that followed from it.

10. The term *ancient Near East* is increasingly controversial, as it emerges from, and retains, the orientalist orientations of earlier Western scholarship on the deeper past of the Levant, ancient Egypt, Nubia, Mesopotamia, Persia, and Anatolia. When merely referring to the geographical area, I use the term *Southwest Asia* or refer to a more specific geographic region. And I retain the term *Near East* when invoking the specific genealogy of archaeological scholarship.

11. African cattle pastoralism has, for a long time, been an enduring anthropological trope of the difference of African societies (e.g., Herskovits 1926; Evans-Pritchard 1940b; Kuper 1982; Hall 1986). The value of living cattle in these societies is a foil to the (normatively) instrumental and utilitarian logics of agriculture, as assumed either explicitly or implicitly. This difference in value intertwines in complex ways with other anthropological ideas about political organization and social evolution in Africa. These logics are not limited to political anthropology— they also crop up in animal studies (Fijn 2011; Tani 1996). However, there is also a competing tendency in critical animal studies to assimilate pastoralists (often citing ethnographic work on the Nuer) into the teleological narratives of objectification of domesticated animals (e.g., Mason 2017; Shepard 1996; Tsing 2018).

12. Here cash is a metonymic stand-in for capitalist regimes of value that emphasize efficiency, maximization, and depersonalized economic relations in the market.

Chapter 1

1. Animal and plant domestication, both as actual messy histories and as cosmogonic narratives, share important similarities but also meaningful differences. In this chapter, my focus is on the story about animals.

2. See, for instance, K. Anderson (1997); Brighenti and Pavoni (2018); Cassidy and Mullin (2007); Harris and Hamilakis (2014); Noske (1989); Russell (2002); Swanson, Lien, and Ween (2018).

3. A valuable exception to this trend within archaeology is Kristin Armstrong Oma's work on the Scandinavian Bronze Age (e.g., 2013a, 2013b, 2017, 2018).

4. Other examples include Mason (2017); Rose (2004); Tani (1996); Tuan (1984); Wilkie (2010).

5. See Franklin (2007) for a detailed account.

6. For a detailed and thought-provoking discussion of this burial, see Russell and Düring (2006).

7. Scholarship examining this history includes V. Anderson (2004); Cronon (1991); Crosby (2015); Franklin (2007); Sayre (2017); Ficek (2019).

8. Although beyond the scope of this book, it would be interesting to think about how starting from human-animal relationships with these species might yield a very different perspective on pastoralism. While archaeologists and anthropologists have produced very interesting research on these nonnormative types of pastoralism, it has done little to dislodge the master narratives.

9. Recent genetic evidence suggests, however, another, as yet unidentified, center of domestication that was the main ancestral source for populations of ancient and modern horses (Gaunitz et al. 2018; Librado et al. 2017; Guimaraes et al. 2020).

10. However, there is historical and ethnographic evidence for mobile pig herding in the South Caucasus and nearby regions (Kohl 2009, 97).

11. These ontostories neglect the important role manure played as a secondary product.

12. I get the formula "it's something we did to them" from John Hartigan's discussion of the anthropocentric master narrative of domestication: "The core certainty and conceit behind a long tradition of narrating the history of domestication is that, simply, *it's something we did to them*" (2014, 72).

13. The literature on domestication, both plant and animal, is vast and ever-expanding, as archaeologists continue to sift through new and old evidence for the domestication histories of particular species and regions as well as debating how we should understand domestication as an analytical category and particular historical event or trajectory. Clutton-Brock's (1999, 2012) reviews are a touchstone for nonarchaeologists writing about domestication. Other relatively recent analytical syntheses include Leach (2003); Losey (2022); O'Connor (2013); Russell (2002, 2007); Stépanoff and Vigne (2018); Zeder (2012).

14. It was unintentional inasmuch as people weren't setting out to domesticate animals, master nature, enter the Neolithic, or become civilized. Nevertheless, the diverse practices of early domestication were actions that stemmed from a range of locally meaningfully intentions, not the intentions presumed by the domestication ontostory.

15. Scholars who use evolutionary frameworks like selection and niche con-

struction to understand domestication treat it as an "ongoing relationship" and a process that has a beginning but not an end (see the discussion in Losey 2022, 145).

16. James Scott's *Against the Grain* (2017) is an interesting mix of domestication maximalism and minimalism. In the first half of the book, he presents the arguments and data for an expanded understanding of domestication (as unintentional and delinked from civilizational progress). Yet in his account of agriculture's role in the early state's domestication of its subjects, he replicates much of the flavor of the original (negative) ontostory, retaining the connections between ancient polities and modern predicaments.

17. Lien's (2015) discussion of farmed salmon uses the concept of *domus* in an altogether different fashion, questioning the ontostory by examining the similarities and differences between farmed salmon and other livestock.

18. Hodder (1990, 275) himself is somewhat ambiguous about whether the *domus* extends from the Neolithic to the present: "I have not wanted to claim that modern words such as domestication, form, and agriculture have roots in the Neolithic, although I do think such a claim would be reasonable. Rather my use of the Indo-European terms results from a desire to show that the concepts though which we think the origins of agriculture are constructed in the past, perhaps even in the very deep past."

Chapter 2

1. There are important similarities between my turn toward "relationships of use" and Porcher's (2017b) definition of "animal husbandry" as a category (and set of practices and histories) that is simultaneously separate from both domestication and industrial agriculture.

2. Important works on these relations include K. Anderson (1997), Blanchette (2020), Crosby (2015), Franklin (2007), Smith-Howard (2014), Sayre (2017).

3. This is not the only way to think about castration and the relations between livestock and humans. Evans-Pritchard (1956, 254) notes that the very close identification of a Nuer man with the animal given to him by his father as part of his initiation is a relationship between the man and an ox, not a bull; and he indicates that in general, oxen are more highly and elaborately valued than bulls. Furthermore, the Nuer make repeated and explicit equivalences between the bodily alteration of ox's bodies (including but not limited to castration) and the alteration of young men's bodies during and after initiation.

4. Tani's jump from the Vedic term *paśú* to the Roman terms *dominus* and *dominatus* ignores the real and substantial differences between Roman and Vedic ideas about property (Sharma 1973).

5. This is an assertion that sits uncomfortably for many people, for whom such arguments are anthropocentric rationalizations that hunters make to deal with the moral quandary of the violent taking of the lives of sentient beings (Arm-

strong Oma 2010; Mason 2017; Serpell 1996; also see the discussion in Russell 2012, 160–62). Nadasdy (2007) counters, based on his own encounter with a rabbit who escaped his snares only later to return to his house to be killed, that our rejection of the possibility of such relationships only shows our anthropocentric assumptions about subjectivity and personhood.

6. This may help to explain the simultaneous proliferation of characterizations of the relationships between hunters and their quarry as seduction or a battle of wits, in which the hunter's success is far from assured (see citations in Nadasdy 2007; Russell 2012).

7. Its social nature differentiates familiarizing predation from ecological and evolutionary models of predation.

8. There is a strong resonance between the emphasis on the potential for humans to be prey in the literature on Amazonian perspectivalism (Fausto 2007; Kohn 2013) and a fascinating essay by feminist philosopher Val Plumwood (1999), in which she recounts her near-death encounter with a crocodile (in which she almost became its prey). Plumwood explores how the potential for crocodiles to eat humans "threatens the dualistic vision of human mastery of the planet in which we are predators but can never ourselves be prey" (88).

9. Crucially, it is not the moment of death that transforms *someone* into *something*, for either human or nonhuman persons. Rather, the body of the animal killed by hunters must be transformed into food (by cooking).

10. At first glance, these might seem like strange places to look for new ways to think about pastoralism and our relationships with herd animals. Hunting (as an anthropological category) is generally understood as referring to lifeways and human-animal relationships that are markedly different from both pastoralism and contemporary, Western society.

11. Roderick Campbell's (2014) analysis of humans, animals, and divinities in Shang China also suggests ways that feeding and eating can help us think about power and authority beyond the human-animal divide.

12. The insistent typological impulse that plagues studies of pastoralism is driven in part by the basic acknowledgment that there are many different ways in which human and herd animal labor and reproduction can interrelate and the intuition that these differences might matter.

13. Bioarchaeologist Pam Geller (2012) coined the term *death history* to describe a community's "ongoing engagement with descendents' bodies" after death (Geller and Suri 2014, 501).

Chapter 3

1. There has also been a strong tendency in archaeology, abetted by its "epistemic pessimism" (Wylie 2000), to reduce the political as epiphenomenal to ecology or economy (Adam T. Smith 2011a).

2. David Graeber (e.g., 2001, 2013) and I share a similar orientation to the

relationship between value and politics—and we have a similar debt to Nancy Munn's (1992) work on value—but my approach to value differs from Graeber's, not least of all because I am asking different questions and using value theory to inform archaeological, not ethnographic, methods and interpretations.

3. Performativity has largely been developed by feminist thinkers writing about gender, politics, and science. My use of the term draws on the writings of Karen Barad (2003, 2006), as well as Judith Butler's (1997, 2006, 2015) work on the performativity of gender and politics. Barad and Butler's work has been taken up by other archaeologists, but not within the archaeology of politics directly (e.g., Govier 2019; Y. Marshall and Alberti 2014; Perry and Joyce 2005; Thomas 2002). Birke, Bryld, and Lykke (2004) highlight the importance of Barad's analytic at the interface of animal studies and feminist STS.

4. My efforts here are related to, but distinct from, other attempts to incorporate things and other nonhumans into archaeologists' theorizations of political life (e.g., Bauer and Kosiba 2016; Adam T. Smith 2015; Swenson and Warner 2012). Because of their distinct positions within Cartesian dualisms and narratives of deep history, things and animals give us different perspectives on the political.

5. I use the term *political orders* for two interrelated reasons. First, it shifts the emphasis from starting from a group of people ("the polity") and explaining how that group maintains its coherence (or fails to) to how coordinated activity works to produce political communities and political projects (cf. Graeber 2013, 220), both of which can vary widely in scale and composition. It also helps to move our vision of the political away from the state, especially the emphasis on territoriality and centralization that it presumes (Honeychurch 2015; Adam T. Smith 2003).

6. Affiliation-distinction and authorization-subjection as relations have emerged as key concerns in the archaeology of politics in the long wake of critiques of neoevolutionary models of political institutions within archaeology (Honeychurch 2015; Johansen and Bauer 2011; Adam T. Smith 2003, 2011b; see also Weismantel 2021).

7. Govindrajan (2018, 79) writes, "while the leaders of cow-protection organizations might declare that only *desi* [Indian] cows are worthy of love, care, and veneration, any cow, even a Jersey, becomes a mother cow when it comes to the difficult issue of slaughter. For them, the Dalits and Muslims who kill a cow, any cow, are enemies of the Hindu nation and, by extension, killable."

8. Fractal recursion as a process relies on a particular kind of indexical sign. As an account of semiotics, it is compatible with my larger performative framework for politics, since as Gal (2002, 86) notes, the process of shifting reiteration is never fully mimetic, but instead both establishes and alters subjectivities through the very practices that constitute them.

9. Austin (1975) labels these kinds of speech acts "performative." Butler takes up Austin's ideas about performatives in their elaboration of performativity, especially in the book *Excitable Speech* (1997).

10. Addressing the question of authority in this way also eliminates the issue of distinguishing between secular and religious authority raised by Fleisher and Wynne-Jones (2010, 186) in their discussion of power and authority in African prehistory. It recasts the question as, What aspects of religious practices or beliefs—or the actions and rites involved in the maintenance of a secular authority—compose the felicity of authority in a specific historical context?

11. Rosenberg (2020, 366) argues that, overall, the eugenic logics of the "Better Sires—Better Stock" campaign were so successfully instilled that they managed to persevere in the face of mounting evidence that pure breeding did not actually produce better stock or increased value. Some of that felicity was linked to the two-way traffic between human and animal reproduction in eugenics, where practices and ideas from each domain could serve as evidence and justification in the other.

12. A more detailed analysis could trace the fractal distinctions between human and animals as they shifted scales and were then erased and assimilated into the nature/culture binary.

13. One potential point of failure is revealed by eugenicists' concerns that drawing too close a connection between human and livestock reproduction would result in "sex-radicalism" due to systematic polygamy and incest in livestock breeding (Rosenberg 2020, 376).

14. In a happy moment of analytical recursion, this framework also neatly bridges between production and reproduction as potential sites for political life.

Chapter 4

1. This discussion in partially inspired by Zoë Crossland's (2013) discussions of Peirce's ([1903] 1998) triad of interpretants (affective, energetic, and habitual). One way of thinking about archaeological traces is as uncertain indexicals, where the uncertainty of what a trace might index provokes a line of further inquiry. The canonical example of the index is smoke, which causally points to fire. A large part of archaeological work is exploring what a material trace might be indexical of. However, archaeologists may also begin to take for granted that there is or must be an indexical connection between a material trace and its assumed cause as part of a habit of interpretation.

2. The periodization of the Middle and Late Bronze Ages in the Caucasus (and other regions) is an example of this upshifting between indexical and symbolic sign-object relations. The original logics of the Three Age System (Stone Age, Bronze Age, Iron Age) were highly indexical. The development of different technologies was read as the progressive evolution of technology, which provided a chronological anchor for early archaeologists trying to make sense of the archaeological record. In the contemporary moment, the persistence of these categories is generally understood to be more symbolic than indexical, inasmuch

as the divisions of chronological time are retained and used but their link to the progressive development of technology is downplayed. This is especially true in the South Caucasus, where the boundary between the Late Bronze Age and the Early Iron Age is extremely muddy, both in terms of metal artifacts and also in terms of the wider range of material culture (Adam T. Smith, Badalyan, and Avetisyan 2009; Sagona 2018). Iron appears in the Late Bronze Age (Chernykh 1992) and the regional archaeological material culture horizon of Lchashen-Metsamor spans the chronological division between the Bronze and Iron Ages.

3. *Material culture horizon*, rather than *archaeological culture*, refers to shared styles of artifact production across a geographic area, avoiding *a priori* assumptions that it represents a group united by other things like language, genetic descent, or culture. The Lchashen-Metsamor material culture horizon is defined by black-burnished pottery and an increase in the scale and intensity of metal production (including both open work and lost wax casting; Gevorkyan 1982). *Lchashen-Tsitelgori* is Sagona's alternate term for the same material cultural horizon, also called the Central Caucasian or East Georgian culture in some of the Georgian literature. Sagona (2018) also includes the Ghodshali-Kedabeg culture from the Azerbaijani literature in this group. Castelluccia (2018) has argued that there is a distinct Lchashen culture centered in the Sevan Basin (and the site of Lchashen), which extends across the Late Bronze and Early Iron Ages (see also Pogrebova 2011).

4. The idea that nomads couldn't be feudal was firmly anchored in Engels's (1972, 90–92) comments on nomads, and it aligned better with the positions taken by Western scholars (Gellner 1984). Yet as Sneath (2007) demonstrates, arguments that pastoralist societies in Central Asia never developed classes required a lot of intellectual and historiographic gymnastics.

5. The publications by the Project ArAGATS team are extensive and span from the Early Bronze Age to the Achaemenid era. Publications on the Late Bronze Age occupations in the plain include Avetisyan, Badalyan, and Smith (2000); Badalyan, Smith, and Avetisyan (2003); Adam T. Smith, Badalyan, and Avetisyan (2004); I. C. Lindsay (2006); Badalyan et al. (2008); Lindsay et al. (2008); Adam T. Smith, Badalyan, and Avetisyan (2009); Lindsay, Smith, and Badalyan (2010); Monahan (2012); Greene and Lindsay (2012); Greene (2013); M. Marshall (2014); Adam T. Smith and Leon (2014); Badalyan et al. (2014); Badalyan and Smith (2017); S. Manning et al. (2018); Chazin, Gordon, and Knudson (2019); Chazin (2021, 2023, n.d.).

6. The sites located on peaks are substantially smaller than the foothill sites and are difficult to access. They may be connected to the location of routes over and through the Pambakh into the neighboring valleys or to obsidian sources in the Tsaghkunyats Mountains. Analyses of a small number of obsidian artifacts from Late Bronze Age layers at Gegharot and Tsaghkahovit showed that they came from sources in the Tsaghkunyats and on the southern part of the Aragats

massif, indicating trade connections to both the east and west (Badalyan, Smith, and Avetisyan 2003).

7. In earlier publications, this area of the site was called the South Lower Town (SLT), a name that is preserved in the unit and artifact designations for this area of the site.

8. Initial identification and analysis of the faunal assemblages in the Tsagh-kahovit Plain was done by Belinda Monahan (Badalyan, Smith, and Avetisyan 2003; Badalyan et al. 2008, 2014; Monahan 2012), with assistance from me in identifying and recording the faunal assemblage from the TRC and Kurgan 2. I (Chazin 2016b) reanalyzed the entire corpus of Late Bronze Age faunal data from the Project ArAGATS excavations to explore intrasite depositional contexts and evidence for changing patterns in faunal use between the first and second occupations of Gegharot.

9. Similar objects are commonly encountered at Paleolithic sites (Caldwell 2009).

10. The identification is based on the vessel form and has not been confirmed by residue analysis.

11. Excavators found charred grains and the ribs, scapula, and humerus of a sheep or goat in the vessel. One of the grains of emmer showed clear traces of boiling (M. Marshall 2014, 212). Other vessels in the cemetery also had bones (ribs and upper-limb bones) and grains (wheat, barley, and other cereals).

12. At Aragatsiberd and Gegharot, most of the sherds identified as being made from clays from the southern Aragats and Pambakh Valley sources were from small and medium jars, which is consistent with the idea that the circulation of ceramics was the circulation of full containers (see Greene 2013, 96–98).

13. Additional Late Bronze Age and Early Iron Age burials near Gegharot were excavated by Esayan and Martirosian in the mid-twentieth century (Bada-lyan and Avetisyan 2007, 99–111; Martirosian 1964).

14. This problem is exacerbated by early and incomplete analyses of the fau-nal remains that interpreted them as evidence of tribute or provisioning of sites by mobile pastoralists. As I discuss in chapter 6, the faunal data actually present a different picture.

15. Two of the three rooms identified as shrines are clearly dated to the second occupation of the site, and it is possible that the third does as well (S. Manning et al. 2018).

16. Adam T. Smith et al. (2004, 29) connect the room at Gegharot with the shrines dating to the Iron I period identified at Metsamor (Avetisyan and Bobo-khyan 2019; Khanzadyan, Mkrtchyan, and Parsamyan 1973, 110–15). Yet the altars and basins at Metsamor are different from those at Gegharot, being much more elaborate in form and larger in size. Any interpretation of the spaces as a shrine should attend to the differences as well as the similarities between the spaces at Metsamor and at Gegharot.

17. This is an example of how classification works to "clean" the data produced by archaeologists, highlighting the power of that move, as well as perils that Gero (2015, 14) is more concerned with.

18. Adam T. Smith and Leon (2014) acknowledge that the evidence for aleuromancy rests on the thinnest evidential basis.

Chapter 5

1. Not all water sources retain this seasonal isotopic signal. Sources of water that collect over many years, like large rivers, lakes, aquifers, and wells, will average the isotopic composition of seasonal inputs. Similarly, each sample of enamel that is analyzed is a time-averaged sample representing a few weeks (rather than a single moment in time). Practically, this means that the annual variation is damped, but that doesn't preclude the use of the technique in the analysis of birth seasonality.

2. There is a delay between the dietary inputs and when the enamel is formed. Experimental studies have shown that this delay is approximately six months (Balasse 2003b; Zazzo, Balasse, and Patterson 2005). But it is consistent, and archaeologists can use studies of modern sheep with known birth seasons to establish the exact calendrical season of birth. Given the nature of archaeological data and the practicalities of animal husbandry, being able to identify the general season (spring, summer, fall, or winter) of birth is very useful and generally, greater precision isn't required.

3. There are two different ways to model the length of the annual cycle, a parametric approach that uses the fact that annual variation in oxygen isotope ratios is sinusoidal (Balasse et al. 2012; Tornero et al. 2013) and a nonparametric approach (Chazin et al. 2019). Regardless of the method used, the data from the Tsaghkahovit Plain indicate that sheep were born across the annual cycle (Chazin 2021).

4. Balasse et al. (2020, 9) developed a statistical rule of thumb to describe the distribution of births across the season to account for the fact that restricted birth seasonality (whether restricted by climate or human intervention) doesn't mean there will be no out-of-season births. The data from the plain show a much wider main season of births (see Chazin 2021, 455, for a detailed analysis).

5. Unsurprisingly, there is more evidence for aseasonal reproduction in cattle in the deeper past. Multiple seasons of birth have been documented at fourth millennium BCE sites in Scandinavia (Gron, Montgomery, and Rowley-Conwy 2015) and at Bronze and Iron Age sites in the British Isles (Towers et al. 2011, 2017). A recent study documented slightly extended seasonality for cattle in Linearbandkeramik sites across Europe (Balasse et al. 2021). Intentional lamb deseasoning has also been documented in the sixth millennium BCE in the western Mediterranean (Tornero et al. 2020).

6. For sheep and goats, this practice is historically and ethnographically at-

tested (Cranstone 1969), and now also archaeologically attested (Balasse et al. 2003; Hadjikoumis et al. 2019).

7. Extending the birth season for sheep would necessarily extend the potential availability of both milk and young animals, regardless of which was the "primary" goal.

8. Doing so would be quite risky, as it can endanger the health of ewes and the reproductive viability of the herd. Much more likely, and ethnographically common, is the patterns of two lambings over a period of three years (see discussion in Balasse et al. 2003).

9. For contemporary Mongolian herders, milk is contrasted to meat as the appropriate food for summer and winter seasons respectively, a pattern that is also attested in William of Rubruck's thirteenth-century account of his travels through the Mongol empire (Fijn 2011, 187). Many of the dairy products that these herders prepare from fresh, fluid milk are consumed exclusively during the summer months. Others, such as dried curds, fermented butter, and distilled alcohol, are intended for consumption in the winter, when fresh milk is no longer produced.

10. The previous solution to milk's perishability (as well as the seasonal nature of its production) was to preserve dairy products as yogurt, cheese, butter, and so on. In the nineteenth century, because the primary focus was the use of cow's milk to replace human breast milk, this solution would no longer suffice. I discuss this transformation in more detail in the following section.

11. Naomi Sykes (2014) analyzes the role of "revolutions" in organizing and shaping zooarchaeological accounts of the long-term history of human-animal relationships. DuPuis's (2002, 136) account of industrial milk production highlights the way in which that history is also narrated through the figure of a series of revolutions that resulted in industrial progress and development.

12. Both Greenfield and Arnold (2015) and Roffet-Salque et al. (2018) give recent summaries of the state of the debate. Older summaries and assessments of the debate can be found in Sherratt (1997), Vigne and Helmer (2007), Greenfield (2010), and Marciniak (2011).

13. When possible, zooarchaeologists try to look at the combined age and sex profiles of slaughtered animals—but for cattle, sheep, and goats, it is generally much easier to collect data on age than on sex.

14. Yet these models, like all discussions of surplus, are doubly haunted. They are haunted by the never fully excised problem of nonuniversal, local, contextual, and historical ideas of surplus (cf. Bogaard 2017; Hastorf and Foxhall 2017; Morehart and De Lucia 2015a). But, perhaps as equally, they are haunted by their genealogical connections to the socioevolutionary models of both Marx and Adam Smith. I am less optimistic than other archaeologists that the appeal and comfort of surplus, as a robust and familiar methodological and analytical framework, outweighs these problems. That being said, I do think it is worthwhile to see what might be salvaged methodologically from some familiar tools, like survivorship curves, while radically reconstituting the logics of interpretation.

15. Morehart and De Lucia's (2015b, 22–24) defense of the importance of the idea of *absolute surplus* for archaeologists is a good example of the archaeological necessity and appeal of the "visibility" of surplus (see also Bogaard 2017; Hastorf and Foxhall 2017).

16. Sherratt's account of the SPR was originally aimed at explaining precisely the question that Diamond raises about the differences between the historical "trajectories" in the Old and New World (1981, 261).

17. One that ignores or downplays lactase persistence in non-European populations and the historical evidence for dairy consumption by people lacking the genes for lactase persistence.

18. It is precisely this stance that frames lactase nonpersistence as a problem for health and even a potential risk for disease (see Wiley 2011).

19. The disruption of women's labor and mutual support networks and increasing suspicion of women breastfeeding occurred at the same time as the rise of the Romantic cult of motherhood. Amid these transformations, women were told that their value came from their role as the caretakers of the domestic space (as set apart from the competitive, masculine, urban public space) and their duty was to guarantee the moral and physical health of their children.

20. Nineteenth-century reformers in the United States framed the moral and social problems of infant nutrition and mortality differently from French physicians in the eighteenth century. The extreme popularity of wet-nursing in eighteenth-century Europe was perceived as a key cause of infant mortality (Schiebinger 1993, 66). As a result, authorities grew concerned about the loss of labor power due to infant deaths and began to encourage women to breastfeed their own children as a moral duty. Notably, Linnaeus was one of a number of physicians who advocated abolishing wet-nursing, arguing that it violated the laws of nature (67). In the nineteenth century in Sweden, the conflicts over breastfeeding, women's roles, and male expertise played out differently as well (Asdal 2014).

21. This rhetoric of perfection and nutritional completeness enabled the process by which "a food that needed to be produced every day for a specific group of consumers became an everyday food for everyone" (DuPuis 2002, 64). Ironically, it was the limited understanding of the biochemical make-up of milk in the nineteenth century that led scientists and reformers to conclude that women's breastmilk and cow's milk were equivalent nutritionally (46).

22. The process of industrialization proceeded differently in cheese production in the United States because cheese-making did not require the year-round production of milk (see DuPuis 2002 for an in-depth discussion).

23. Mlekuž (2015, 279) has argued that when cattle are reared to produce milk, they are no longer food but rather are workers. My argument goes further in suggesting that all herd animals can be thought of as working.

24. Thinking through differences between capital or resources and labor is muddied by the turn toward talking about human labor in terms of resources

NOTES TO CHAPTER 5

or capital (as driven by developments within economics). These shifts in terminology have important political consequences (see Battistoni 2017; Weeks 2011).

25. Battistoni (2017, 11–13) is responding to ethical critiques that reject the instrumental valuation of animal lives (and nature more broadly) within capitalism. She argues, along with Haraway (2008), that the idea of intrinsic value is not sufficient to provide satisfactory alternatives to the problems of capitalist value. Here, I am extending and transforming that argument to assert that archaeological interpretations need to encompass and account for value systems where there is not as stark an ethical divide between intrinsic and instrumental value. Moreover, for me, herd animals are an especially good focus in that project because of the immediacy of both instrumental and intrinsic value.

26. Work and labor are often defined in opposition to each other, making a cut that then sets the terms of the subsequent debate. For example, Hannah Arendt (1958) makes a tripartite division between labor, work, and action. In contrast, Marxian thought is organized through the distinction between (living) labor and (waged) work. Labor in general is an intrinsic, creative (human) capacity—"species being"—that is, a category that is simultaneously more expansive than (waged) work and more valued (Weeks 2011, 14). Unlike in other texts, I am writing about labor and work in a context where wage labor in a capitalist system is not directly relevant. It remains relevant only inasmuch as it plays such an important role in how we think about work from the vantage point of the present. For this reason, I use *labor* and *work* somewhat interchangeably when speaking about noncapitalist pasts. I use both terms to evoke a sense purposive practices and processes, but not in contrast to (or exclusion of) reproduction or animals. For humans and animals alike, by invoking work and labor, I am insisting on the political stakes of productive activities.

27. For herd animals, it also short-circuits the idea that pastoralists' herds are a "self-reproducing" form of wealth.

28. It is possible that during the winter months, milk could be refrigerated or frozen by storing outside.

29. Within these logics, milk is different from other pastoralist products. While secondary products are grouped together as strategies to produce more calories for less input of labor and land, milk is often seen as less valuable than other forms of pastoralist wealth; milk is more perishable than meat on the hoof and more difficult to store and transport (Zeder 1988, 10; Wapnish and Hesse 1988, 94).

30. While isotopic studies of human diet can identify the relative amount that dairy proteins may have contributed to an individual's diet, they cannot distinguish between fresh milk and other forms of dairy. We also do not know how individuals and groups in the Late Bronze Age Tsaghkahovit Plain differed in their levels of dairy consumption seasonally or in terms of age, gender, or other forms of social status or belonging.

Chapter 6

1. This phrase originated to describe Chicago meatpackers' pursuit of new profits by industrializing the processing of hog carcasses (Swift and Van Vlissingen 1927).

2. Faunal remains were assigned to contexts of deposition post hoc, on the basis of excavation notes, database entries, and personal communication with excavators. Loci were assigned to these categories: midden, pit, intramural trash, cultural fill, destruction debris, wash, vessel, special feature, and indeterminate (see Chazin 2016b). The first two categories—middens and pits—are delimited spaces where relatively large numbers of faunal remains (along with other things) are deposited, possibly in a relatively short amount of time. In contrast, cultural fill and wash contexts are places where faunal remains accumulate in small quantities, sometimes over long periods of time. Destruction debris is separated out, because of the specific temporality of its formation and the unique taphonomic factors linked to the destruction events.

3. In contrast, skeletal element analysis is more focused on meat sharing and transport decisions when dealing with hunter-foragers and small-scale agriculturalists.

4. Previous analyses of the faunal assemblages from Gegharot and Tsaghkahovit had suggested that provisioning might explain the high numbers of infant and juvenile sheep and goats found in the assemblage. Those analyses looked at site and site-sector assemblages, rather than depositional contexts within sites, and used different methods for examining skeletal element distribution.

5. Animal hides may be prepared in such a way that the phalanges are left attached to the hide, especially if the animal is small. However, that is unlikely to be the case for hides from larger animals (Zeder et al. 2013, 117), and it would not include the tarsals.

6. This is based on the analysis of anatomical regions by weight of remains identified to mammalian size classes. This approach solves the problem of the underrepresentation of cranium fragments in MNE counts, because skull fragments are often difficult to identify as to genus or the specific bone of the cranium (due to some skull bones being relatively delicate). However, it is less difficult to separate out skull fragments from other small pieces of bone.

7. No mandibles or calcanei from either site showed any signs of working. Some astragali were worked, but not to make tools (see chapter 7). It's possible the astragali were used as loom weights, but the ubiquity of the astragali (and the distribution of worked astragali) argue against that hypothesis (Grabundzija, Schoch, and Ulanowska 2016).

8. *Determinative* here means "decisive," rather than the more specialized linguistic meaning referring to something that contributes to meaning.

9. Munn (1992, 6) emphasizes that "actors construct this meaningful order in the process of being constructed in its terms." Graeber (2001, 59, 77, 249, 251)

also ends up laying out something akin to performativity, although arriving via a different set of questions and analytical tools and using different terms.

10. Graeber's (2001, 88) "struggle to establish what value is" seems akin to what Kockelman (2007) describes as residential agency.

11. Tsing's (2013) analysis of matsutake mushrooms explores the complicated moral-political premises of noncapitalist forms of value in their trajectories as transnational commodities.

12. Munn calls these qualities *qualisigns*, taking the term from C. S. Peirce's semiotic framework. Peirce describes a qualisign as a type of sign—something that links an object and an interpretant in his framework—that signifies an abstract property like "lightness" or "red." As he notes, a qualisign "cannot actually act as a sign until it is embodied, but the embodiment has nothing to with its character as a sign" (Peirce [1903] 1998, 291). Munn's key insight is that this gap between the sign and its material embodiment, along with the potential for this qualisign to be embodied materially by different media, is what makes the generation of value (as homogenous potency) semiotically possible.

13. Peirce ([1903] 1998) categorizes the relationship between the sign and its object into three categories. Icons resemble the object they represent (e.g., a portrait resembles the person), indexes have an actual connection to the object (e.g., smoke indexes a fire), and symbols have an arbitrary or conventional connection to their object (e.g., the relationship between a flag and the country it represents).

14. Munn (1992, 17) notes that certain acts have outcomes that can be "considered icons of the acts that produce them—in other words they can be said to involve iconic signs of the spatiotemporal value transformation (positive or negative) generated by the act." It is this interplay between indexical relations of causality (the outcome of an action) and the iconic potentiality of its material parameters to instantiate qualisigns that enable movement between different orders of meaning (270–72).

15. Giddens (1984, 34) sees his approach as making it possible to address the use of allocative resources in noncapitalist contexts (he uses the term "primitive") without subsuming them under the logics of market economics. Similarly, he is arguing against those who would claim that "the primitive" did not have politics.

16. Hall's transformation of the question of how and when the African Cattle Complex arose into how to understand the sociopolitical dynamics of cattle as authoritative resources leads him to argue that cattle were adopted by African farmers and foragers because of the stability they provided compared to agricultural crops. Here, Hall and Tswana pastoralists are in perfect agreement (see Comaroff and Comaroff 1990). What is odd about this assertion is that the southern African truism that cattle are the more stable form of agricultural wealth is directly opposed to the assumption (or truism) of the literature on Eurasian pastoralism. There, the assumption is that herds are a risky form of wealth, prone to epidemics and losses to winters and droughts (e.g., Dahl 1979; Gellner 1984, xi; Salzman 2004, 105). It is this line of reasoning that leads to the claim that

pastoralists couldn't generate the surpluses necessary to develop complex forms of political organization.

17. I have some reservations about the dichotomy Guyer and Belinga (1995) introduced between accumulation and composition, which they frame as the opposition between quantitative and qualitative, between addition and synergy. It excludes the question of whether there is quantitative accumulation that is outside capitalism or different from neoclassical economic logics. This is a pressing issue for Near Eastern archaeology, where the evidence is usually subsumed into models of accumulation lumped together as "wealth-in-things." The wider literature on value in anthropology has shown that rather than sorting societies into the categories of gift and commodity, we must attend to the range of logics that exist across societies and can coexist within in them.

18. The same distinction in reproductive potential between animals of different ages, sexes, and species is used in the survivorship models for different production orientations (see chapter 5) and in the models of provisioning discussed earlier in this chapter.

19. It also helps to mitigate the issues highlighted by Guyer and Belinga's (1995, 108–13) critique of the "shorthand" use of the concept, which, in its reliance on Marxist accumulation stripped of its theoretical content, tends to reinforce assumptions about the material and kinship basis of organization in "simple societies" as well as requiring an essential analytical separation between people and things that is problematic.

20. At the heart of this difference, for Ingold (1988), is a difference in the form of instrumental relationships between humans and animals. In his analysis, the two types of pastoralism represent different solutions to the problem of risk. Milch pastoralism shares the risk, because herders who lose their flocks have ways of making claims on animals belonging to others to whom they are connected through relationships grounded in practices of circulation. In contrast, carnivorous pastoralists must strive to accumulate as large a flock as possible to protect themselves from disaster. For Ingold, these different property relations are ultimately social, even if they are grounded in the material realities of production. He stresses that pastoralist accumulation may appear similar to capitalist accumulation yet the two are essentially different, not least of all because capitalist accumulation requires exchange and pastoralist accumulation does not.

21. What is less clear, because of Ingold's (1988) focus on refuting ecological and adaptationist accounts of pastoralist logics, is how much potential the wealth accumulated in herds in carnivorous pastoralism has to create other forms of social *spacetime*. In other words, what might be the value of herds as *wealth* beyond an insurance policy against famine?

22. Ray and Thomas (2003, 41) make a similar argument about the importance of cattle as wealth in the British Neolithic. They mainly focus on the differences between the ways in which cattle were wealth in the Neolithic and more contemporary ways of thinking about wealth: "If for Karl Marx commodities

in modern societies are congealed lumps of labor, then it is possible to envisage that, for people in the Neolithic, cattle were congealed lumps of social relations." Unlike Hall, they do not emphasize a contrast between practices that circulate living animals and those that circulate meat and other products.

23. Norton's (2015, 52) analysis of Indigenous pet-keeping in the Caribbean and South America suggests this is not the only way that the circulation of living animals might create value. In particular, living animals that had been tamed were often exchanged between people to establish a social relationship.

24. Govindrajan's (2018) ethnographic work reminds us that slaughter and sacrifice also shape human-animal relations in important ways (see chapter 7).

25. In-and-in breeding is the practice of repeatedly crossing closely related animals.

26. Zeb Dingley (personal communication, March 3, 2022) provided this insight into the Nuer materials.

27. The distinction between people and things shapes how we imagine the material nature of things and their relationship to social life. The framing as gift versus commodity emphasizes the distinction between goods that stand apart from people (to be accumulated and exchanged for other goods) and goods that are deeply imbricated in the formation of *social* or *intersubjective* selves. In doing so, the material nature of the things themselves tends to drop out of the frame—especially in many cases where the things in question can be found as both gifts and commodities. In contrast, the archaeological literature emphasizes the idea that things have an important role in materializing and solidifying social relationships.

28. Henrichsen's (2013) careful historical analysis of Herero "(re-)pastoralization" in the nineteenth century suggests that small stock can potentially have an important role in (re-)establishing pastoralist wealth. Hoag (2018) indicates that differences between large and small stock are relative and are contextually shaped.

29. There is now a very robust literature on feasting in archaeology, with a variety of theoretical positions and replete with examples of feasts in a wide range of times and places. Some of the key synthetic works are those by Bray (2003); Dietler and Hayden (2001); Hayden and Villeneuve (2011).

30. *Metonymy* refers to figures of speech where the substitution of one term for another is based on association or contiguity, whereas *metaphor* refers to substitutions based on analogy. Strictly speaking, *synecdoche* is the figure of speech where a part is substituted for a whole. Synecdoche is a subclass of metonymy, and I have chosen to use the broader term here.

31. This variation, as well as the potential for differential valuation, is not limited to meat and fat. Blanchette (2020, 228) describes how one Japanese firm prefers pigs' front leg bones for making the flavorings for packaged ramen, since they are thought to produce a higher quality product than other bones.

32. Sykes (2010, 187) suggests that another important aspect of this transfor-

mation was a shift in the temporality of elite meat consumption: "As the market economy developed, the functional necessity of communal feasting as a mechanism for meat redistribution would have been reduced as aristocratic households could obtain meat as required, rather than having to eat up the glut received at particular times of the year, such as at Martinmas."

33. Birtalan (2003) suggests that this practice has a long history, extending back at least to the Mongol period.

34. For Mongolian herders, the tibia signifies genealogical connections and lineages, in line with the wider practice of referring to descent groups with the term *bone* (i.e., white bone, black bone; see Fijn 2011; Sneath 2007).

35. The exception to this is the calcaneus, which does fuse over the lifetime of an animal, starting sometime after the second year (Silver 1969; Zeder 2006).

36. Due to the lack of systematic study of faunal remains in the region, it is difficult to say for certain that either practice never involved nondomesticated taxa (particularly in the case of the head and hoof burial).

Chapter 7

1. I use the term *itineraries*, instead of *biographies*, because the term is more open-ended and less linear, and it leaves more space to consider the dynamics of motion and rest (Joyce 2015a, 2012).

2. Moreover, even if I could explain the astragali through reference to these hoards, there would still be the problem of explaining the excess calcanei and mandibles.

3. In this framework, astragali hoards are recontextualized as a kind of choreography of value that has specific potentialities, shifting the process of interpretation described by Susnow et al. (2021, 75).

4. After reading an early version of this chapter, Anna Weichselbraun pointed me in the direction of STS scholars who also use choreography as a metaphor (Pickering 1995, 102; Cussins 1996, 604). Later, I found it in work by STS scholars studying animals (Law 2010; Lien 2015). Birke, Bryld, and Lykke (2004) use choreography as loose metaphor in their discussion of human-animal relations in lab work. These authors use "choreography" to evoke the relationships between humans and nonhumans within a performative understanding of scientific practice and social life. The metaphor helps to convey a sense of coordination or stabilization within the more-than-human flow of action and agency. Cussins's (1996) use of "ontological choreographies" emphasizes how artificial reproductive technologies draw together things that are usually separate ontological orders. In contrast, I'm interested in thinking about how choreographies of value allow us to see how performative practices structure value and its relation to the moral-political premises of social life. As such, the concept is closer to Lien's (1015, 189) discussion of choreographies as practices that "enact specific orderings in and of time and space."

5. Govindrajan (2018, 49) suggests that these acts may also be understood as resolution of the debt between herder and herd animal for the care given and received.

6. Within the ceremony itself, this is evidenced by the sprinkling of water and uncooked rice on the goats' backs and interpreting the shaking of their bodies as a sign of the goats' consent to participate (Govindrajan 2018, 33).

7. Part of this explicit counterchoreography of value, which takes place in the newspapers and the courts, is the claim that animal sacrifice is essentially nonmodern and must be rejected. This claim insists on separating the religious logics of value in sacrifice from the economic or material value of the slaughtered animal. This division resembles the way in which archaeological practice has tended to treat the postmortem value of herd animals, as either straightforwardly utilitarian or resolutely nonutilitarian. Nevertheless, animal rights activism in India also involves important and meaningful "unmarked" choreographies of value (Dave 2014).

8. Because the astragalus is a nonfusing element, smaller-bodied individuals may be either younger or female animals.

9. Statistical analysis suggests that this is a real difference, not noise in the data. The difference between the number of gnawed calcanei and the overall rate of gnawing at the Tsaghkahovit Residential Complex produces a Fisher exact test statistic < 0.00001. This is also true of the less abundant, but still anomalous, cattle astragali (Fisher exact test statistic = 0.00001).

10. The differences between the number of gnawed astragali and gnawed calcanei and the overall level of gnawing at Gegharot appear to be meaningful based on statistical analysis (astragali: X^2 = 19.7319, p < 0.00001; calcanei: Fisher exact test statistic value is < 0.00001).

11. Polish is an ambiguous category that describes both the visual glossiness of the bone surface and the intentional (or perhaps unintentional) alteration of bone surface (Bradfield 2020).

12. Archaeologists have found medially and laterally ground astragali in other times and places (Meier 2013; Minniti and Peyronel 2005; Sasson 2007; Susnow et al. 2021).

13. Meier (2013) suggests, on the basis of experimental studies, that the worn medial and lateral surfaces of the astragali from Middle Bronze Age sites in Hungary are the result of using the bones to smooth leather-hard ceramics. The astragali from the Tsaghkahovit Plain show comparatively little grinding, however. From the experimental studies, Meier (2013, 171) notes that the astragali worked better as polishers the more they were ground down, which suggests that the astragali from Gegharot and Tsaghkahovit were not used for that purpose.

14. This assemblage also included a large number of cattle phalanges, though this represents a much smaller MNE because an individual cow has eight first phalanges and only two astragali. Oddly, the assemblage didn't have any cattle metapodials or second and third phalanges.

15. Locus 50, a large jar, had two cattle astragali (1 right, 1 left), no worked astragali, and a single lumbar vertebra. Locus 51, another large jar, had three striated cattle astragali (1 right, 2 left). Locus 52, a nearly complete vessel, had one left cattle astragali that had striations and had been ground.

16. Out of the 88 astragali, 24 of them were worked, and the majority of worked astragali were from cattle (n = 16). This is a much higher proportion of worked cattle astragali than in the assemblage as a whole, and it is statistically significant. The Fisher exact test statistic value is 0.0001.

17. The survivorship profile for all sheep/goats in this midden is equivalent to the general pattern for sheep/goats from the Late Bronze Age assemblages at the two sites, with 60% of animals being slaughtered before two years of age (see Chazin 2016b). In contrast, the survivorship curve for sheep mandibles in the midden shows a much larger offtake of young animals, where 90% of animals were slaughtered before two years of age (and nearly 60% before 12 months of age).

18. The total number of astragali in a pit is roughly correlated (R^2 = 0.88) with the total Number of Identified Specimens (NISP) for the pit, though the association is stronger for cattle (R^2 = 0.74) than for sheep/goats (R^2 = 0.58).

19. This is also true of other pits that cannot be dated securely to either phase of occupation during the Late Bronze Age.

20. In the Late Bronze Age South Caucasus, archaeologists have found head and hoof deposits of cattle, sheep, and goats, not just horses.

21. Initial larger-scale analyses suggested there were caches of astragali associated with the other shrines (Adam T. Smith and Leon 2014), but subsequent analyses on a locus-by-locus basis indicate that only the east citadel shrine has a collection of astragali and that there is no meaningful patterning in the number of left and right astragali.

22. The explicit choreography of value of the traditional, patriarchal wedding is self-consciously rejected and reworked by queer, gender nonconforming, and feminist communities, establishing their own explicit choreographies by shifting dress, the text and performances of the ceremonies, and so on in a wide variety of creative ways.

New Stories, New Questions

1. Metallurgy and metalworking are another domain that probably also generated and channeled value. Ceramics, herd animals, and metalworking were, importantly, sources of value that crossed between the lives of the living and the spaces of the dead. An important question for future research is the way in which mortuary practices and cemeteries figured into these choreographies of value.

2. It is worth noting that this is also a hypothesis about the value of herd animals in the preceding Middle Bronze Age period. Very little direct evidence is available for the value of herd animals in that period, let alone the differences

in the value of large and small stock or the role secondary products and meat played in political life. If it turns out that sheep played a key role in the political life in the Middle Bronze Age, then the shifts that occur at Gegharot after the first destruction can perhaps be read as the rise of a new way of composing authority, one in which cattle played a larger role. Nevertheless, if we continue to assume higher levels of mobility in the Middle Bronze Age, it does seem likely that the expanded birth seasonality for sheep in the Late Bronze Age represents a new practice.

REFERENCES

Abramishvili, Mikheil, and Michelle Orthmann. 2008. "Excavations at Sajoge, 2003: Preliminary Report." In *Archaeology in Southern Caucasus: Perspectives from Georgia*, edited by Antonio Sagona and Mikheil Abramishvili, 275–89. Leuven: Peeters Press.

Abramishvili, Rostom, and Mikheil Abramishvili. 2008. "Late Bronze Age Barrows at Tsitelgori." In *Archaeology in the Southern Caucasus: Perspectives from Georgia*, edited by Antonio Sagona and Mikheil Abramishvili, 351–63. Leuven: Peeters Press.

Agamben, Giorgio. 1998. *Homo Sacer: Sovereign Power and Bare Life*. Stanford, CA: Stanford University Press.

Agbe-Davies, Anna. 2015. *Tobacco, Pipes, and Race in Colonial Virginia: Little Tubes of Mighty Power*. Walnut Creek, CA: Left Coast Press.

Alberti, Benjamin, Severin Fowles, Martin Holbraad, Yvonne Marshall, and Christopher Witmore. 2011. "'Worlds Otherwise': Archaeology, Anthropology, and Ontological Difference." *Current Anthropology* 52 (6): 896–912.

Allentuck, Adam. 2015. "Temporalities of Human–Livestock Relationships in the Late Prehistory of the Southern Levant." *Journal of Social Archaeology* 15 (1): 94–115.

Anderson, Kay. 1997. "A Walk on the Wild Side: A Critical Geography of Domestication." *Progress in Human Geography* 21 (4): 463–85.

Anderson, Virginia DeJohn. 2004. *Creatures of Empire: How Domestic Animals Transformed Early America*. New York: Oxford University Press.

Anthony, David W. 2007. *The Horse, the Wheel, and Language: How Bronze-Age Riders from the Eurasian Steppes Shaped the Modern World*. Princeton, NJ: Princeton University Press.

Arbuckle, Benjamin. 2012. "Pastoralism, Provisioning, and Power at Bronze Age Acemhöyük, Turkey." *American Anthropologist* 114 (3): 462–76.

Arbuckle, Benjamin, and Emily L. Hammer. 2019. "The Rise of Pastoralism in the Ancient Near East." *Journal of Archaeological Research* 27 (3): 391–449.

Arbuckle, Benjamin, and Sue Ann McCarty, eds. 2014. *Animals and Inequality in the Ancient World*. Boulder: University Press of Colorado.

Arbuckle, Benjamin, Aliye Oztan, and Sevil Gulcur. 2009. "The Evolution of Sheep and Goat Husbandry in Central Anatolia." *Anthropozoologica* 44 (1): 129–57.

Arendt, Hannah. 1958. *The Human Condition*. Chicago: University of Chicago Press.

Argent, Gala. 2013. "Inked: Human-Horse Apprenticeship, Tattoos, and Time in the Pazyryk World." *Society & Animals* 21 (2): 178–93.

Armstrong Oma, Kristin. 2010. "Between Trust and Domination: Social Contracts between Humans and Animals." *World Archaeology* 42 (2): 175–87.

———. 2013a. "Human-Animal Meeting Points: Use of Space in the Household Arena in Past Societies." *Society & Animals* 21 (2): 162–77.

———. 2013b. "Past and Present Farming: Changes in Terms of Engagement." In *Humans and the Environment: New Archaeological Perspectives for the 21st Century*, edited by Matthew I. J. Davies and Freda Nkirote M'Mbogori, 181–92. Oxford: Oxford University Press.

———. 2017. *The Sheep People: The Ontology of Making Lives, Building Homes and Forging Herds in Early Bronze Age Norway*. Sheffield: Equinox Publishing.

———. 2018. "Making Space from the Position of Duty of Care—Early Bronze Age Human-Sheep Entanglements." In *Multispecies Archaeology*, edited by Suzanne E. Pilaar Birch, 214–29. Abingdon, UK: Routledge.

Armstrong Oma, Kristin, and Lynda Birke. 2013. "Guest Editors' Introduction Archaeology and Human-Animal Studies." *Society & Animals* 21 (2): 113–19.

Asad, Talal. 1978. "Equality in Nomadic Social Systems? (Notes towards the Dissolution of an Anthropological Category)*." *Critique of Anthropology* 3 (11): 57–65.

Asdal, Kristin. 2014. "Versions of Milk and Versions of Care: The Emergence of Mother's Milk as an Interested Object and Medicine as a Form of Dispassionate Care." *Science in Context* 27 (2): 307–31.

Atkins, Peter William. 2010. *Liquid Materialities: A History of Milk, Science and the Law*. Critical Food Studies. Farnham, UK: Ashgate.

Austin, J. L. 1975. *How to Do Things with Words*. 2nd ed. Cambridge, MA: Harvard University Press.

Avetisyan, Pavel S., Ruben S. Badalyan, and Adam T. Smith. 2000. "Preliminary Report on the 1998 Archaeological Investigations of Project ArAGATS in the Tsakahovit Plain, Armenia." *Studi micenei ed egeo-anatolici* 42 (1): 19–59.

Avetisyan, Pavel S., and Arsen Bobokhyan. 2019. "Cult-Places of Ancient Armenia: A Diachronic View and an Attempt of Classification." In *Over the Mountains and Far Away: Studies in Near Eastern History and Archaeology Pre-*

sented to Mirjo Salvini on the Occasion of His 80th Birthday, edited by Pavel S. Avetisyan, Roberto Dan, and Yervand H. Grekyan, 19–33. Summertown, UK: Archaeopress.

Badalyan, Ruben S., and Pavel S. Avetisyan. 2007. *Bronze and Early Iron Age Archaeological Sites in Armenia*. Oxford: Archaeopress.

Badalyan, Ruben S., and Adam T. Smith. 2017. "The Kurgans of Gegharot: A Preliminary Report on the Results of the 2013–2014 Excavations of Project ArAGATS." In *Bridging Times and Spaces: Papers in Ancient Near Eastern, Mediterranean and Armenian Studies*, edited by Pavel S. Avetisyan and Yervand H. Grekyan, 11–28. Oxford: Archaeopress.

Badalyan, Ruben S., Adam T. Smith, and Pavel S. Avetisyan. 2003. "The Emergence of Sociopolitical Complexity in Southern Caucasia: An Interim Report on the Research of Project ArAGATS." In *Archaeology in the Borderlands: Investigations in Caucasia and Beyond*, edited by Adam T. Smith and Karen S. Rubinson, 144–66. Los Angeles: University of California, Cotsen Institute of Archaeology.

Badalyan, Ruben S., Adam T. Smith, Ian C. Lindsay, Lori Khatchadourian, and Pavel S. Avetisyan. 2008. "Village, Fortress, and Town in Bronze and Iron Age Southern Caucasia: A Preliminary Report on the 2003–2006 Investigations of Project ArAGATS on the Tsaghkahovit Plain, Republic of Armenia." *Archäologische Mitteilungen aus Iran und Turan* 40:45–105.

Badalyan, Ruben S., Adam T. Smith, Ian Lindsay, Armine Harutyunyan, Alan Greene, Maureen Elizabeth Marshall, Belinda Monahan, and Roman Hovsepyan. 2014. "A Preliminary Report on the 2008, 2010, and 2011 Investigations of Project ArAGATS on the Tsaghkahovit Plain, Republic of Armenia." *Archäologische Mitteilungen aus Iran und Turan* 46:149–222.

Balasse, Marie. 2003a. "Keeping the Young Alive to Stimulate the Production of Milk? Differences between Cattle and Small Stock." *Anthropozoologica* 7:3–10.

———. 2003b. "Potential Biases in Sampling Design and Interpretation of Intra-Tooth Isotope Analysis." *International Journal of Osteoarchaeology* 13 (1–2): 3–10.

Balasse, Marie, Loïc Boury, Joël Ughetto-Monfrin, and Anne Tresset. 2012. "Stable Isotope Insights ($\delta18O$, $\delta13C$) into Cattle and Sheep Husbandry at Bercy (Paris, France, 4th Millennium BC): Birth Seasonality and Winter Leaf Foddering." *Environmental Archaeology* 17 (1): 29–44.

Balasse, Marie, Rosalind Gillis, Ivana Živaljević, Rémi Berthon, Lenka Kovačiková, Denis Fiorillo, Rose-Marie Arbogast, et al. 2021. "Seasonal Calving in European Prehistoric Cattle and Its Impacts on Milk Availability and Cheese-Making." *Scientific Reports* 11 (1): 8185.

Balasse, Marie, Léo Renault-Fabregon, Henri Gandois, Denis Fiorillo, John Gorczyk, Krum Bacvarov, and Maria Ivanova. 2020. "Neolithic Sheep Birth Distribution: Results from Nova Nadezhda (Sixth Millennium BC, Bulgaria) and a Reassessment of European Data with a New Modern Reference Set Including Upper and Lower Molars." *Journal of Archaeological Science* 118 (June): 105139.

Balasse, Marie, Andrew B. Smith, Stanley H. Ambrose, and Steven R. Leigh. 2003. "Determining Sheep Birth Seasonality by Analysis of Tooth Enamel Oxygen Isotope Ratios: The Late Stone Age Site of Kasteelberg (South Africa)." *Journal of Archaeological Science* 30:205–16.

Balasse, Marie, and Anne Tresset. 2007. "Environmental Constraints on Reproductive Activity of Domestic Sheep and Cattle: What Latitude for the Herder?" *Anthropozoologica* 42 (2): 71–88.

Barad, Karen. 2003. "Posthumanist Performativity: Toward an Understanding of How Matter Comes to Matter." *Signs* 28 (3): 801–31.

———. 2006. *Meeting the Universe Halfway: Quantum Physics and the Entanglement of Matter and Meaning*. Durham: Duke University Press.

Barua, Maan. 2019. "Animating Capital: Work, Commodities, Circulation." *Progress in Human Geography* 43 (4): 650–69.

Battistoni, Alyssa. 2017. "Bringing in the Work of Nature: From Natural Capital to Hybrid Labor." *Political Theory* 45 (1): 5–31.

Baudrillard, Jean. 1975. *The Mirror of Production*. Translated by Mark Poster. St. Louis: Telos Press.

Bauer, Andrew M., and Steve Kosiba. 2016. "How Things Act: An Archaeology of Materials in Political Life." *Journal of Social Archaeology* 16 (2): 115–41.

Bennett, Joshua. 2020. *Being Property Once Myself: Blackness and the End of Man*. Cambridge, MA: Harvard University Press.

Berson, Josh. 2019. *The Meat Question: Animals, Humans, and the Deep History of Food*. Cambridge, MA: MIT Press.

Besky, Sarah, and Alex Blanchette. 2019. *How Nature Works: Rethinking Labor on a Troubled Planet*. Albuquerque: University of New Mexico Press.

Bhandar, Brenna. 2018. *Colonial Lives of Property: Law, Land, and Racial Regimes of Ownership*. Durham: Duke University Press.

Birke, Lynda, Mette Bryld, and Nina Lykke. 2004. "Animal Performances: An Exploration of Intersections Between Feminist Science Studies and Studies of Human/Animal Relationships." *Feminist Theory* 5 (2): 167–83.

Birtalan, Agnes. 2003. "Ritualistic Use of Livestock Bones in the Mongolian Belief System and Customs." In *Proceedings of the 45th Permanent International Altaistic Conference (PIAC), Budapest, Hungary, June 23–28, 2002*, edited by A. Sarkozi and A. Rakos, 33–62. Budapest: Hungarian Academy of Sciences, Research Group for Altaic Studies.

Blackstone, William. 1803. *Blackstone's Commentaries*. Philadelphia: W. Y. Birch and A. Small.

Blanchette, Alex. 2015. "Herding Species: Biosecurity, Posthuman Labor, and the American Industrial Pig." *Cultural Anthropology* 30 (4): 640–69.

————. 2018. "Blood Mares and the Work of Naturalization." *Fieldsights*, July. https://culanth.org/fieldsights/introduction-the-naturalization-of-work.

————. 2020. *Porkopolis: American Animality, Standardized Life, and the Factory Farm*. Durham: Duke University Press.

Bocci, Paolo. 2017. "Tangles of Care: Killing Goats to Save Tortoises on the Galápagos Islands." *Cultural Anthropology* 32 (3): 424–49.

Bogaard, Amy. 2017. "The Archaeology of Food Surplus." *World Archaeology* 49 (1): 1–7.

Bökönyi, Sándor. 1974. *History of Domestic Mammals in Central and Eastern Europe*. Budapest: Akadémiai Kiadó.

————. 1994. "The Role of the Horse in the Exploitation of the Steppes." In *The Archaeology of the Steppes: Methods and Strategies*, edited by Bruno Genito, 17–30. Naples: Istituto Universitario Orientale Dipartimento di Studi Asiatici.

Boyd, Brian. 2017. "Archaeology and Human–Animal Relations: Thinking Through Anthropocentrism." *Annual Review of Anthropology* 46 (1): 299–316.

————. 2018. "An Archaeological Telling of Multispecies Co-Inhabitation." In *Multispecies Archaeology*, edited by Suzanne E. Pilaar Birch, 251–70. New York: Routledge.

Bradfield, Justin. 2020. "The Perception of Gloss: A Comparison of Three Methods for Studying Intentionally Polished Bone Tools." *Journal of Archaeological Science: Reports* 32 (August): 102425.

Bray, Tamara L. 2003. *The Archaeology and Politics of Food and Feasting in Early States and Empires*. New York: Kluwer Academic/Plenum Publishers.

Brighenti, Andrea Mubi, and Andrea Pavoni. 2018. "Urban Animals—Domestic, Stray, and Wild: Notes from a Bear Repopulation Project in the Alps." *Society & Animals* 26 (6): 576–97.

Brittain, Marcus, and Nick Overton. 2013. "The Significance of Others: A Prehistory of Rhythm and Interspecies Participation." *Society & Animals* 21 (2): 134–49.

Brück, Joanna. 1999. "Ritual and Rationality: Some Problems of Interpretation in European Archaeology." *European Journal of Archaeology* 2 (3): 313–44.

Bulkin, V. A., Leo S. Klejn, and G. S. Lebedev. 1982. "Attainments and Problems of Soviet Archaeology." *World Archaeology* 13 (3): 272.

Burney, Charles Allen, and David M. L. Lang. 1971. *The Peoples of the Hills: Ancient Ararat and Caucasus*. London: Weidenfeld and Nicolson.

Butler, Judith. 1997. *Excitable Speech: A Politics of the Performative*. New York: Routledge.

————. 2006. *Gender Trouble: Feminism and the Subversion of Identity*. New York: Routledge.

————. 2015. *Notes toward a Performative Theory of Assembly*. Cambridge, MA: Harvard University Press.

Caldwell, Duncan. 2009. "Palaeolithic Whistles or Figurines? A Preliminary

Survey of Pre-Historic Phalangeal Figurines." *Rock Art Research* 26 (1): 65–82.

Campbell, Ben. 2005. "On 'Loving Your Water Buffalo More Than Your Own Mother': Relations of Animal and Human Care in Nepal." In *Animals in Person: Cultural Perspectives on Human-Animal Intimacy*, edited by John Knight, 79–100. Oxford: Berg.

Campbell, Roderick. 2012. "On Sacrifice: An Archaeology of Shang Sacrifice." In *Sacred Killing: The Archaeology of Sacrifice in the Ancient Near East*, edited by Anne Porter and Glen Schwartz, 305–23. Winona Lake, IN: Eisenbrauns.

———. 2014. "Animal, Human, God: Pathways of Shang Animality and Divinity." In *Animals and Inequality in the Ancient World*, edited by Benjamin S. Arbuckle and Sue Ann McCarty, 251–74. Boulder: University Press of Colorado.

Cassidy, Rebecca, and Molly H. Mullin, eds. 2007. *Where the Wild Things Are Now: Domestication Reconsidered*. Oxford: Berg.

Castelluccia, Manuel. 2018. "The Lčašen Culture and Its Archaeological Landscape." *Iran and the Caucasus* 22 (3): 215–31.

Chazin, Hannah. 2016a. "The Life Assemblage: Rethinking the Politics of Pastoral Practices." In *Incomplete Archaeologies: Assembling Knowledge in the Past and Present. Proceedings from a Session at the 2013 EAA Meetings in Pilsen, CZ.*, edited by Emily Miller-Bonney, Kathryn Jane Franklin, and James Johnson, 28–47. Oxford: Oxbow.

———. 2016b. "The Politics of Pasture: The Organization of Pastoral Practices and Political Authority in the Late Bronze Age in the South Caucasus." PhD thesis, University of Chicago.

———. 2021. "Multi-Season Reproduction and Pastoralist Production Strategies: New Approaches to Birth Seasonality from the South Caucasus Region." *Journal of Field Archaeology* 46 (7): 448–60.

———. 2023. "Animal Work before Capitalism: Sheep's Reproductive Labor in the Ancient South Caucasus." *American Anthropologist* 125 (4): 809–23.

———. "Herding in mountain pastures: Diverse isotopic biographies across species in the Late Bronze Age South Caucasus." Unpublished manuscript, submitted to *Archaeological and Anthropological Sciences*, last modified March 22, 2024. Microsoft Word file.

———. "Animal power: Rethinking cattle and caprines' role in Late Bronze Age political organization." Unpublished manuscript, submitted to *Journal of Anthropological Archaeology*, last modified June 5, 2024. Microsoft Word file.

Chazin, Hannah, Soudeep Deb, Joshua Falk, and Arun Srinivasan. 2019. "New Statistical Approaches to Intra-Individual Isotopic Analysis and Modeling Birth Seasonality in Studies of Herd Animals." *Archaeometry* 61 (2): 478–93.

Chazin, Hannah, Gwyneth W. Gordon, and Kelly J. Knudson. 2019. "Isotopic

Perspectives on Pastoralist Mobility in the Late Bronze Age South Caucasus." *Journal of Anthropological Archaeology* 54 (June): 48–67.

Chemineau, P., B. Malpaux, J. A. Delgadillo, Y. Guérin, J. P. Ravault, J. Thimonier, and J. Pelletier. 1992. "Control of Sheep and Goat Reproduction: Use of Light and Melatonin." *Animal Reproduction Science* 30 (1): 157–84.

Chernykh, Evgenij N. 1992. *Ancient Metallurgy in the USSR: The Early Metal Age.* Cambridge: Cambridge University Press.

Childe, V. Gordon. 1951. *Man Makes Himself.* Rev. ed. New York: New American Library.

Clutton-Brock, Juliet. 1999. *A Natural History of Domesticated Mammals.* 2nd ed. Cambridge: Cambridge University Press.

———. 2012. *Animals as Domesticates: A World View through History.* East Lansing: Michigan State University Press.

Cobb, Charles R. 2005. "Archaeology and the 'Savage Slot': Displacement and Emplacement in the Premodern World." *American Anthropologist* 107 (4): 563–74.

Comaroff, John L., and Jean Comaroff. 1990. "Goodly Beasts, Beastly Goods: Cattle and Commodities in a South African Context." *American Ethnologist* 17 (2): 195–216.

Cook, C. Justin. 2014. "The Role of Lactase Persistence in Precolonial Development." *Journal of Economic Growth* 19 (4): 369–406.

Crabtree, Pam J. 1990. "Zooarchaeology and Complex Societies: Some Uses of Faunal Analysis for the Study of Trade, Social Status, and Ethnicity." *Archaeological Method and Theory* 2 (January): 155–205.

Cramp, Lucy J. E., Jennifer Jones, Alison Sheridan, Jessica Smyth, Helen Whelton, Jacqui Mulville, Niall Sharples, and Richard P. Evershed. 2014. "Immediate Replacement of Fishing with Dairying by the Earliest Farmers of the Northeast Atlantic Archipelagos." *Proceedings: Biological Sciences* 281 (1780): 1–8.

Cranstone, B. A. L. 1969. "Animal Husbandry: The Evidence from Ethnography." In *The Domestication and Exploitation of Plants and Animals*, edited by Peter J. Ucko and G. W. Dimbleby, 247–63. London: Duckworth & Co.

Crellin, Rachel J., Craig N. Cipolla, Lindsay M. Montgomery, Oliver J. T. Harris, and Sophie V. Moore. 2020. *Archaeological Theory in Dialogue: Situating Relationality, Ontology, Posthumanism, and Indigenous Paradigms.* New York: Routledge.

Cronon, William. 1991. *Nature's Metropolis: Chicago and the Great West.* New York: W. W. Norton.

Crosby, Alfred W. 2015. *Ecological Imperialism: The Biological Expansion of Europe, 900–1900.* 2nd ed. Cambridge: Cambridge University Press.

Crossland, Zoë. 2013. "Signs of Mission: Material Semeiosis and Nineteenth-Century Tswana Architecture." *Signs and Society* 1 (1): 79–113.

———. 2014. *Ancestral Encounters in Highland Madagascar: Material Signs and Traces of the Dead*. New York: Cambridge University Press.

Crumley, Carole L., and William H. Marquardt, eds. 1987. *Regional Dynamics: Burgundian Landscapes in Historical Perspective*. San Diego: Academic Press.

Cussins, Charis. 1996. "Ontological Choreography: Agency through Objectification in Infertility Clinics." *Social Studies of Science* 26 (3): 575–610.

Dahl, Gudrun. 1979. "Ecology and Equality: The Boran Case." In *Pastoral Production and Society = Production Pastorale et Société: Proceedings of the International Meeting on Nomadic Pastoralism, Paris 1–3 Dec. 1976*, edited by L'Equipe écologie et anthropologie des sociétés pastorales, 261–81. Cambridge: Cambridge University Press.

Dahl, Gudrun, and Anders Hjort. 1976. *Having Herds: Pastoral Herd Growth and Household Economy*. Stockholm: University of Stockholm, Dept. of Social Anthropology.

Dalrymple, John. 1757. *An Essay towards a General History of Feudal Property in Great Britain*. London: A. Millar.

Dave, Naisargi N. 2014. "Witness: Humans, Animals, and the Politics of Becoming." *Cultural Anthropology* 29 (3): 433–56.

———. 2019. "Kamadhenu's Last Stand: On Animal Refusal to Work." In *How Nature Works: Rethinking Labor on a Troubled Planet*, edited by Sarah Besky and Alex Blanchette, 211–24. Albuquerque: University of New Mexico Press.

Davis, Whitney. 1992. "The Deconstruction of Intentionality in Archaeology." *Antiquity* 66 (251): 334–47.

Dawdy, Shannon Lee. 2020. "Talking Trash and the Politics of Disregard." *Cambridge Archaeological Journal* 30 (1): 156–60.

Debono Spiteri, Cynthianne, Rosalind E. Gillis, Mélanie Roffet-Salque, Laura Castells Navarro, Jean Guilaine, Claire Manen, Italo M. Muntoni, et al. 2016. "Regional Asynchronicity in Dairy Production and Processing in Early Farming Communities of the Northern Mediterranean." *Proceedings of the National Academy of Sciences of the United States of America* 113 (48): 13594–99.

deFrance, Susan D. 2009. "Zooarchaeology in Complex Societies: Political Economy, Status, and Ideology." *Journal of Archaeological Research* 17 (2): 105–68.

DeMarrais, Elizabeth, Luis Jaime Castillo, and Timothy Earle. 1996. "Ideology, Materialization, and Power Strategies." *Current Anthropology* 37 (1): 15–31.

Descola, Philippe. 2013. *Beyond Nature and Culture*. Chicago: University of Chicago Press.

Despret, Vinciane. 2004. "The Body We Care for: Figures of Anthropo-zoogenesis." *Body & Society* 10 (2–3): 111–34.

———. 2006. "Sheep Do Have Opinions?" In *Making Things Public: Atmospheres of Democracy*, edited by Bruno Latour and Peter Weibel, 360–70. Cambridge: MIT Press.

———. 2015. "Do Animals Work? Creating Pragmatic Narratives." In *Animots:*

Postanimality in French Thought, edited by Matthew Senior, David L. Clark, and Carla Freccero, 124–42. New Haven: Yale University Press.

———. 2016. *What Would Animals Say if We Asked the Right Questions?* Minneapolis: University of Minnesota Press.

Devejyan, S. G. 1981. *Lori-Berd 1: Rezul'taty Raskopok 1969–1973 G.g.* Yerevan, Armenia: Izdatel'stvo AN Armyanskoj SSR.

———. 2006. *Lori Berd 2.* Yerevan, Armenia: Nairi.

Diamond, Jared M. 1997. *Guns, Germs, and Steel: The Fates of Human Societies.* New York: W. W. Norton.

Dietler, Michael, and Brian Hayden, eds. 2001. *Feasts: Archaeological and Ethnographic Perspectives on Food, Politics, and Power.* Washington, DC: Smithsonian Institution Press.

Dolukhanov, P. M. 1995. "Archaeology in Russia and Its Impact on Archaeological Theory." In *Theory in Archaeology: A World Perspective*, edited by Peter J. Ucko, 327–42. London: Routledge.

Donaldson, Sue, and Will Kymlicka. 2017. "Animals in Political Theory." In *The Oxford Handbook of Animal Studies*, edited by Linda Kalof, 43–64. Oxford: Oxford University Press.

Dunne, J., K. Rebay-Salisbury, R. B. Salisbury, A. Frisch, C. Walton-Doyle, and R. P. Evershed. 2019. "Milk of Ruminants in Ceramic Baby Bottles from Prehistoric Child Graves." *Nature* 574 (7777): 1–3.

DuPuis, E. Melanie. 2002. *Nature's Perfect Food: How Milk Became America's Drink.* New York: New York University Press,

Dyson-Hudson, Rada, and Neville Dyson-Hudson. 1980. "Nomadic Pastoralism." *Annual Review of Anthropology* 9 (1): 15–61.

Engels, Friedrich. 1972. *The Origin of the Family, Private Property, and the State, in the Light of the Researches of Lewis H. Morgan.* New York: International Publishers.

Erb-Satullo, Nathaniel L. 2021. "Technological Rejection in Regions of Early Gold Innovation Revealed by Geospatial Analysis." *Scientific Reports* 11:20255.

Erb-Satullo, Nathaniel L., and Dimitri Jachvliani. 2022. "Fortified Communities in the South Caucasus: Insights from Mtsvane Gora and Dmanisis Gora." *Journal of Field Archaeology* 47 (5): 305–23.

Evans-Pritchard, E. E. 1940a. *The Nuer, a Description of the Modes of Livelihood and Political Institutions of a Nilotic People.* Oxford: Clarendon Press.

———. 1940b. "The Nuer of the Southern Sudan." In *African Political Systems*, edited by Meyer Fortes and E. E. Evans-Pritchard, 272–96. London: Oxford University Press.

———. 1956. *Nuer Religion.* Oxford: Clarendon Press.

Evershed, Richard P., Sebastian Payne, Andrew G. Sherratt, Mark S. Copley, Jennifer Coolidge, Duska Urem-Kotsu, Kostas Kotsakis, et al. 2008. "Earliest Date for Milk Use in the Near East and Southeastern Europe Linked to Cattle Herding." *Nature* 455 (7212): 528–32.

Ezanno, Pauline, Alexandre Ickowicz, and Renaud Lancelot. 2005. "Relationships between N'Dama Cow Body Condition Score and Production Performance under an Extensive Range Management System in Southern Senegal: Calf Weight Gain, Milk Production, Probability of Pregnancy, and Juvenile Mortality." *Livestock Production Science* 92 (3): 291–306.

Fausto, Carlos. 2007. "Feasting on People: Eating Animals and Humans in Amazonia." *Current Anthropology* 48 (4): 497–530.

Fausto, Carlos, and Luiz Costa. 2013. "Feeding (and Eating): Reflections on Strathern's 'Eating (and Feeding).'" *Cambridge Journal of Anthropology* 31 (1): 156–62.

Federici, Silvia. 2021. *Caliban and the Witch: Women, the Body and Primitive Accumulation*. London: Penguin Books.

Ferguson, Adam. 1767. *An Essay on the History of Civil Society*. Edinburgh: A. Millar & T. Caddel.

Ficek, Rosa E. 2019. "Cattle, Capital, Colonization: Tracking Creatures of the Anthropocene in and Out of Human Projects." *Current Anthropology* 60 (S20): S260–S271.

Fijn, Natasha. 2011. *Living with Herds: Human-Animal Coexistence in Mongolia*. New York: Cambridge University Press.

Fleisher, Jeffrey, and Stephanie Wynne-Jones. 2010. "Authorisation and the Process of Power: The View from African Archaeology." *Journal of World Prehistory* 23 (4): 177–93.

Foucault, Michel. 1990. *The History of Sexuality. Vol. 1, An Introduction*. Reissue. New York: Vintage.

———. 1994. *The Order of Things: An Archaeology of the Human Sciences*. Reissue. New York: Vintage.

Fowles, Severin. 2012. *An Archaeology of Doings: Secularism and the Study of Pueblo Religion*. Santa Fe, NM: School for Advanced Research Press.

Frachetti, Michael. 2012. "Multiregional Emergence of Mobile Pastoralism and Nonuniform Institutional Complexity across Eurasia." *Current Anthropology* 53 (1): 2–38.

Franklin, Sarah. 1997. "Dolly: A New Form of Transgenic Breedwealth." *Environmental Values* 6 (4): 427–37.

———. 2007. *Dolly Mixtures: The Remaking of Genealogy*. Durham: Duke University Press.

Fraser, Nancy. 2014. "Behind Marx's Hidden Abode." *New Left Review* 86 (March–April). https://newleftreview.org/issues/ii86/articles/nancy-fraser-behind-marx-s-hidden-abode.

Gal, Susan. 2002. "A Semiotics of the Public/Private Distinction." *Differences: A Journal of Feminist Cultural Studies* 13 (1): 77–95.

Gaunitz, Charleen, Antoine Fages, Kristian Hanghøj, Anders Albrechtsen, Naveed Khan, Mikkel Schubert, Andaine Seguin-Orlando, et al. 2018. "Ancient

Genomes Revisit the Ancestry of Domestic and Przewalski's Horses." *Science* 360 (6384): 111–14.

Geller, Pamela L. 2012. "Parting (with) the Dead: Body Partibility as Evidence of Commoner Ancestor Veneration." *Ancient Mesoamerica* 23 (1): 115–29.

Geller, Pamela L., and Miranda Stockett Suri. 2014. "Relationality, Corporeality and Bioarchaeology: Bodies Qua Bodies, Bodies in Context." *Cambridge Archaeological Journal* 24 (3): 499–512.

Gellner, Ernest. 1984. "Foreword." In *Nomads and the Outside World*, by Anatoly M. Khazanov, ix–xxvi. Cambridge: Cambridge University Press,

Gero, Joan. 2015. *Yutopian: Archaeology, Ambiguity, and the Production of Knowledge in Northwest Argentina*. Austin: University of Texas Press.

Gevorkyan, A. T. 1982. "Progress v razvitii metalloproizvostva pozdnebronzovoy epokhi armenii." In *Kulturniy progress v epokhu bronzi and rannego zheleza*, edited by B. N. Arakelyan, 76–77. Yerevan, Armenia: Akademiya nauk armianskoe SSR.

Giddens, Anthony. 1984. *The Constitution of Society: Outline of the Theory of Structuration*. Berkeley: University of California Press.

Govier, Eloise. 2019. "Do You Follow? Rethinking Causality in Archaeology." *Archaeological Dialogues* 26 (1): 51–55.

Govindrajan, Radhika. 2018. *Animal Intimacies: Interspecies Relatedness in India's Central Himalayas*. Chicago: University of Chicago Press.

Grabundzija, Ana, Chiara Schoch, and Agata Ulanowska. 2016. "Bones for the Loom. Weaving Experiment with Astragali Weights." *Prilozi instituta za arheologiju u zagrebu* 33:287–306.

Graeber, David. 2001. *Toward an Anthropological Theory of Value: The False Coin of Our Own Dreams*. New York: Palgrave.

———. 2013. "It Is Value That Brings Universes into Being." *HAU: Journal of Ethnographic Theory* 3 (2): 219–43.

Graeber, David, and David Wengrow. 2021. *The Dawn of Everything: A New History of Humanity*. London: Allen Lane.

Grant, Annie. 1975. "Appendix B: The Use of Tooth Wear as a Guide to the Age of Domestic Animals." In *Excavations at Portchester Castle I: Roman*, edited by Barry Cunliffe, 437–50. London: Society of Antiquaries.

Greene, Alan F. 2013. "The Social Lives of Pottery on the Plain of Flowers: An Archaeology of Pottery Production, Distribution, and Consumption in the Late Bronze Age South Caucasus." PhD thesis, University of Chicago.

Greene, Alan F., and Ian Lindsay. 2012. "Mobility, Territorial Commitments, and Political Organization among Late Bronze Age Polities in Southern Caucasia." *Archaeological Papers of the American Anthropological Association* 22 (1): 54–71.

Greenfield, Haskel J. 2010. "The Secondary Products Revolution: The Past, the Present and the Future." *World Archaeology* 42 (1): 29–54.

Greenfield, Haskel J., and Elizabeth R. Arnold. 2015. "'Go(a)t Milk?' New Perspectives on the Zooarchaeological Evidence for the Earliest Intensification of Dairying in South Eastern Europe." *World Archaeology* 47 (5): 792–818.

Gregory, C. A. 2015. *Gifts and Commodities.* 2nd ed. Chicago: Hau Books.

Gron, Kurt J., Janet Montgomery, and Peter Rowley-Conwy. 2015. "Cattle Management for Dairying in Scandinavia's Earliest Neolithic." *PLOS ONE* 10 (7): e0131267.

Grossman, Kathryn, and Tate Paulette. 2020. "Wealth-on-the-Hoof and the Low-Power State: Caprines as Capital in Early Mesopotamia." *Journal of Anthropological Archaeology* 60 (December): 101207.

Guimaraes, Silvia, Benjamin S. Arbuckle, Joris Peters, Sarah E. Adcock, Hijlke Buitenhuis, Hannah Chazin, Ninna Manaseryan, et al. 2020. "Ancient DNA Shows Domestic Horses Were Introduced in the Southern Caucasus and Anatolia during the Bronze Age." *Science Advances* 6 (38): eabb0030.

Guyer, Jane I. 1995. "Wealth in People, Wealth in Things—Introduction." *Journal of African History* 36 (1): 83–90.

Guyer, Jane I., and Samuel M. Eno Belinga. 1995. "Wealth in People as Wealth in Knowledge: Accumulation and Composition in Equatorial Africa." *Journal of African History* 36 (1): 91–120.

Hadjikoumis, Angelos, Jean-Denis Vigne, Alan Simmons, Jean Guilaine, Denis Fiorillo, and Marie Balasse. 2019. "Autumn/Winter Births in Traditional and Pre-Pottery Neolithic Caprine Husbandry in Cyprus: Evidence from Ethnography and Stable Isotopes." *Journal of Anthropological Archaeology* 53 (March): 102–11.

Hage, Ghassan. 2017. *Is Racism an Environmental Threat?* Cambridge: Polity Press.

Hakansson, N. Thomas. 1994. "Grain, Cattle, and Power: Social Processes of Intensive Cultivation and Exchange in Precolonial Western Kenya." *Journal of Anthropological Research* 50 (3): 249–76.

Hall, Martin. 1986. "The Role of Cattle in Southern African Agropastoral Societies: More Than Bones Alone Can Tell." *Goodwin Series* 5:83–87.

Halstead, Paul. 1996. "The Development of Agriculture and Pastoralism in Greece: When, How, Who and What?" In *The Origins and Spread of Agriculture and Pastoralism in Eurasia*, edited by D. R. Harris, 296–309. London: University College London Press.

———. 1998. "Mortality Models and Milking: Problems of Uniformitarianism, Optimality and Equifinality Reconsidered." *Anthropozoologica* 27:3–20.

———. 2007. "Carcasses and Commensality: Investigating the Social Context of Meat Consumption in Neolithic and Early Bronze Age Greece." In *Cooking up the Past: Food and Culinary Practices in the Neolithic and Bronze Age Aegean*, edited by C. B. Mee and J. Renard, 25–48. Oxford: Oxbow.

Hamilakis, Yannis. 2008. "Time, Performance, and the Production of a Mnemonic Record: From Feasting to an Archaeology of Eating and Drinking." In

Dais: The Aegean Feast, edited by L. A. Hitchcock, R. Laffineur, and J. Crowley, 3–20. Liège: Université de Liège.

———. 2014. *Archaeology and the Senses: Human Experience, Memory, and Affect.* Cambridge: Cambridge University Press.

———. 2017. "Sensorial Assemblages: Affect, Memory and Temporality in Assemblage Thinking." *Cambridge Archaeological Journal* 27 (1): 169–82.

Hamilakis, Yannis, and Andrew Meirion Jones. 2017. "Archaeology and Assemblage." *Cambridge Archaeological Journal* 27 (1): 77–84.

Hammond, John. 1971. *Hammond's Farm Animals.* 4th ed. London: Edward Arnold.

Haraway, Donna. 2003. *The Companion Species Manifesto: Dogs, People, and Significant Otherness.* Chicago: Prickly Paradigm.

———. 2008. *When Species Meet.* Minneapolis: University of Minnesota Press.

Harris, Kerry, and Yannis Hamilakis. 2014. "Beyond the Wild, the Feral, and the Domestic." In *Routledge Handbook of Human-Animal Studies*, edited by Marvin Garry, 97–113. London: Routledge.

Hartigan, John. 2014. *Aesop's Anthropology: A Multispecies Approach.* Minneapolis: University of Minnesota Press.

Hastorf, Christine A., and Lin Foxhall. 2017. "The Social and Political Aspects of Food Surplus." *World Archaeology* 49 (1): 26–39.

Hayden, Brian, and Suzanne Villeneuve. 2011. "A Century of Feasting Studies." *Annual Review of Anthropology* 40: 433–49.

Helvétius. 1810. *A Treatise on Man; His Intellectual Faculties and His Education.* Translated by William Hooper. London: Vernor, Hood and Sharpe.

Henrichsen, Dag. 2013. "Establishing a Precolonial 'Modern' Cattle-and-Gun Society: (Re-)Pastoralisation, Mercantile Capitalism and Power Amongst Herero in Nineteenth-Century Central Namibia." In *Pastoralism in Africa*, edited by Michael Bollig, Michael Schnegg, and Hans-Peter Wotzka, 201–29. New York: Berghahn Books.

Herskovits, Melville J. 1926. "The Cattle Complex in East Africa." *American Anthropologist* 28:230–72, 361–80, 494–528, 633–64.

Hesse, Brian, and Paula Wapnish. 1998. "Pig Use and Abuse in the Ancient Levant: Ethnoreligious Boundary-Building and Swine." In *Ancestors for the Pigs*, edited by Sarah M. Nelson, 123–35. Philadelphia: University of Pennsylvania, Museum of Archaeology and Anthropology.

Hoag, Colin. 2018. "The Ovicaprine Mystique: Livestock Commodification in Postindustrial Lesotho." *American Anthropologist* 120 (4): 725–37.

Hodder, Ian. 1990. *The Domestication of Europe: Structure and Contingency in Neolithic Societies.* Oxford: B. Blackwell.

———. 1998. "The Domus: Some Problems Reconsidered." In *Understanding the Neolithic of NW Europe*, edited by E. Edmonds and C. Richards, 84–101. Glasgow: Cruithne Press.

Honeychurch, William. 2015. *Inner Asia and the Spatial Politics of Empire: Archaeology, Mobility, and Culture Contact*. New York: Springer.

Honeychurch, William, Joshua Wright, and Chunag Amartuvshin. 2009. "Re-Writing Monumental Landscapes as Inner Asian Political Process." In *Social Complexity in Prehistoric Eurasia: Monuments, Metals, and Mobility*, edited by Bryan K. Hanks and Katheryn M. Linduff, 330–57. Cambridge: Cambridge University Press.

Ingold, Tim. 1988. *Hunters, Pastoralists, and Ranchers: Reindeer Economies and Their Transformations*. Cambridge: Cambridge University Press.

———. 2011a. "From Trust to Domination: An Alternative History of Human-Animal Relations." In *The Perception of the Environment: Essays in Livelihood, Dwelling and Skill*, 61–76. London: Routledge.

———. 2011b. *Perception of the Environment: Essays on Livelihood, Dwelling and Skill*. London: Routledge.

Johansen, Peter G., and Andrew M. Bauer, eds. 2011. *The Archaeology of Politics: The Materiality of Political Practice and Action in the Past*. Newcastle upon Tyne: Cambridge Scholars Publishing.

Joyce, Rosemary A. 2006. "The Monumental and the Trace: Archaeological Conservation and the Materiality of the Past." In *Of the Past, for the Future: Integrating Archaeology and Conservation*, edited by Neville Agnew and Janet Bridgland, 13–18. Los Angeles: Getty Conservation Institute.

———. 2012. "Life with Things: Archaeology and Materiality." In *Archaeology and Anthropology: Past, Present and Future*, edited by D. Shanklin, 119–32. Oxford: Berg.

———. 2015a. "Things in Motion: Itineraries of Ulua Marble Vases." In *Things in Motion: Object Itineraries in Anthropological Practice*, edited by Rosemary A. Joyce and Susan D. Gillespie, 21–38. Santa Fe: School of Advanced Research Press.

———. 2015b. "Transforming Archaeology, Transforming Materiality." *Archaeological Papers of the American Anthropological Association* 26 (1): 181–91.

Kames, Henry Home. 1792. *Historical Law-Tracts*. 4th ed. Edinburgh: Bell & Bradfute and W. Creech.

Keane, Webb. 2005. "Signs Are Not the Garb of Meaning: On the Social Analysis of Material Things." In *Materiality*, edited by Daniel Miller, 182–205. Durham: Duke University Press.

Khachatrian, Telemak Surenovich. 1975. *Drevniaia kul'tura shiraka: III-I tys. do n. e.* Yerevan, Armenia: Izd-vo erevanskogo universiteta.

Khanzadyan, E. V., K. Mkrtchyan, and E. Parsamyan. 1973. *Metsamor*. Yerevan, Armenia: Haykakan SSR GA hrataraktsutyun.

Kockelman, Paul. 2007. "Agency: The Relation between Meaning, Power, and Knowledge." *Current Anthropology* 48 (3): 375–401.

Kohl, Philip L. 1992. "The Transcaucasian 'Periphery' in the Bronze Age." In

Resources, Power, and Interregional Interaction, edited by Edward M. Schortman and Patricia A. Urban, 117–37. New York: Plenum Press.

———. 2007. *The Making of Bronze Age Eurasia*. Cambridge: Cambridge University Press.

———. 2009. "The Maikop Singularity: The Unequal Accumulation of Wealth on the Bronze Age Eurasian Steppe?" In *Social Complexity in Prehistoric Eurasia: Monuments, Metals and Mobility*, edited by Bryan K. Hanks and Katheryn M. Linduff, 91–106. Cambridge: Cambridge University Press.

Kohn, Eduardo. 2013. *How Forests Think: Toward an Anthropology beyond the Human*. Berkeley: University of California Press.

Kosiba, Steve. 2020. "The Nature of the World, the Stuff of Politics: Exploring Animacy and Authority in the Indigenous Americas." In *Sacred Matter: Animacy and Authority in the Americas*, edited by Steve Kosiba, John W. Janusek, and Thomas Cummins, 1–35. Washington DC: Dumbarton Oaks Research Library and Collection.

Kradin, Nikolay N. 2002. "Nomadism, Evolution and World-Systems: Pastoral Societies in Theories of Historical Development." *Journal of World-Systems Research* 8 (3): 368–88.

Kuper, Adam. 1982. *Wives for Cattle: Bridewealth and Marriage in Southern Africa*. International Library of Anthropology. Boston: Routledge.

Kushnareva, Karinė Khristoforovna. 1997. *The Southern Caucasus in Prehistory: Stages of Cultural and Socioeconomic Development from the Eighth to the Second Millennium B.C.* Translated by H. N. Michael. Philadelphia: University of Pennsylvania, University Museum.

Law, John. 2010. "Care and Killing: Tensions in Veterinary Practice." In *Care in Practice: On Tinkering in Clinics, Homes and Farms*, edited by Annemarie Mol, Ingunn Moser, and Jeannette Pols, 57–73. Bielefeld, Germany: Transcript Verlag.

Leach, Helen M. 2003. "Human Domestication Reconsidered." *Current Anthropology* 44 (3): 349–68.

———. 2007. "Selection and the Unforeseen Consequences of Domestication." In *Where the Wild Things Are Now: Domestication Reconsidered*, edited by Rebecca Cassidy and Molly H. Mullin, 71–100. Oxford: Berg.

Librado, Pablo, Cristina Gamba, Charleen Gaunitz, Clio Der Sarkissian, Mélanie Pruvost, Anders Albrechtsen, Antoine Fages, et al. 2017. "Ancient Genomic Changes Associated with Domestication of the Horse." *Science* 356 (6336): 442–45.

Lien, Marianne E. 2015. *Becoming Salmon: Aquaculture and the Domestication of a Fish*. Oakland: University of California Press.

Lien, Marianne E., Heather Anne Swanson, and Gro B. Ween. 2018. "Naming the Beast—Exploring the Otherwise." In *Domestication Gone Wild: Politics and Practices of Multispecies Relations*, edited by Heather Anne Swanson, Marianne E. Lien, and Gro B. Ween, 1–30. Durham: Duke University Press.

Lindsay, Ian. 2006. "Late Bronze Age Power Dynamics in Southern Caucasia: A Community Perspective on Political Landscapes." University of California, Santa Barbara.

Lindsay, Ian, and Alan Greene. 2013. "Sovereignty, Mobility, and Political Cartographies in Late Bronze Age Southern Caucasia." *Journal of Anthropological Archaeology* 32 (4): 691–712.

Lindsay, Ian, Leah Minc, Christophe Descantes, Robert J. Speakman, and Michael D. Glascock. 2008. "Exchange Patterns, Boundary Formation, and Sociopolitical Change in Late Bronze Age Southern Caucasia: Preliminary Results from a Pottery Provenance Study in Northwestern Armenia." *Journal of Archaeological Science* 35:1673–82.

Lindsay, Ian, and Adam T. Smith. 2006. "A History of Archaeology in the Republic of Armenia." *Journal of Field Archaeology* 31 (2): 165–84.

Lindsay, Ian, Adam T. Smith, and Ruben Badalyan. 2010. "Magnetic Survey in the Investigation of Sociopolitical Change at a Late Bronze Age Fortress Settlement in Northwestern Armenia." *Archaeological Prospection* 17:15–27.

Locke, John. 1980. *Second Treatise of Government.* Edited by C. B. Macpherson. Cambridge, MA: Hackett Publishing Company.

Lokuruka, Michael N. I. 2006. "Meat Is the Meal and Status Is by Meat: Recognition of Rank, Wealth, and Respect through Meat in Turkana Culture." *Food and Foodways* 14 (3–4): 201–29.

Losey, Robert J. 2022. "Domestication Is Not an Ancient Moment of Selection for Prosociality: Insights from Dogs and Modern Humans." *Journal of Social Archaeology* 22 (2): 131–48.

Lysaght, Patricia. 1994. *Milk and Milk Products from Medieval to Modern Times.* Edinburgh: Canongate Academic.

Manning, Paul. 2012. *Semiotics of Drink and Drinking.* London: Continuum.

Manning, Sturt W., Adam T. Smith, Lori Khatchadourian, Ruben Badalyan, Ian Lindsay, Alan Greene, and Maureen Marshall. 2018. "A New Chronological Model for the Bronze and Iron Age South Caucasus: Radiocarbon Results from Project ArAGATS, Armenia." *Antiquity* 92 (366): 1530–51.

Marciniak, Arkadiusz. 2011. "The Secondary Products Revolution: Empirical Evidence and Its Current Zooarchaeological Critique." *Journal of World Prehistory* 24 (2–3): 117–30.

Marom, Nimrod, and Guy Bar-Oz. 2009. "Culling Profiles: The Indeterminacy of Archaeozoological Data to Survivorship Curve Modelling of Sheep and Goat Herd Maintenance Strategies." *Journal of Archaeological Science* 36:1184–87.

Marshall, Maureen Elizabeth. 2014. "Subject(ed) Bodies: A Bioarchaeological Investigation of Late Bronze Age—Iron I (1500–800 B.C.) Armenia." PhD thesis, University of Chicago.

Marshall, Yvonne, and Benjamin Alberti. 2014. "A Matter of Difference: Karen Barad, Ontology and Archaeological Bodies." *Cambridge Archaeological Journal* 24 (1): 19–36.

Martirosian, A. A. 1964. *Armeniia v epokhu bronzy i rannego zheleza*. Yerevan, Armenia: Izd-vo. akademii nauk armianskoi SSR.

Marx, Karl. 1977. *Capital: A Critique of Political Economy*, translated by Ben Fowkes. *Vol. 1*. New York: Vintage Books.

Mason, Jim. 2017. "Misothery: Contempt for Animals and Nature, Its Origins, Purposes, and Repercussions." In *The Oxford Handbook of Animal Studies*, edited by Linda Kalof, 134–51. Oxford University Press.

Masson, V. M. 1997. "'Kavkazskiy put' k tsivilizatsii: Voprosy sotsiokul'turnoy interpretatsii." In *Drevnie obshchestva kavkaza v epokhu paleometalla (rannie kompleksnnye obshchestva i voprosy kul'turnoy transformatsii)*, 124–33. Saint Petersburg: IIMK RAN.

McCormick, Finbar. 1992. "Early Faunal Evidence for Dairying." *Oxford Journal of Archaeology* 11 (2): 201–9.

———. 2002. "The Distribution of Meat in a Hierarchy Society: The Irish Evidence." In *Consuming Passions and Patterns of Consumption*, edited by Preston Miracle and Nicki Milner, 25–31. Cambridge: McDonald Institute for Archaeological Research.

Meier, Jacqueline. 2013. "More Than Fun and Games? An Experimental Study of Worked Bone Astragali from Two Middle Bronze Age Hungarian Sites (2013)." In *From These Bare Bones: Raw Materials and the Study of Worked Osseous Objects*, edited by Alice M. Choyke and Sonia O'Connor, 166–73. Oxford: Oxbow.

Miers, Suzanne, and Igor Kopytoff, eds. 1977. *Slavery in Africa: Historical and Anthropological Perspectives*. Madison: University of Wisconsin Press.

Minniti, Claudia, and Luca Peyronel. 2005. "Symbolic or Functional Astragali from Tell Mardikh-Ebla (Syria)." *Archaeofauna* 14:7–26.

Mlekuž, Dimitrij. 2015. "Archaeological Culture, Please Meet Yoghurt Culture: Towards a Relational Archaeology of Milk." *Documenta praehistorica* 42: 275–88.

Mnatsakanian, A. O. 1965. *Lchasheni mshakuyti zargatsman himnakan etapnery*. Yerevan. Armenia: Patma banasirakan handes.

Monahan, Belinda. 2012. "Beastly Goods: Pastoral Production in the Late Bronze Age Tsaghkahovit Plain." In *The Archaeology of Power and Politics in Eurasia: Regimes and Revolutions*, edited by Charles W. Hartley and B. Bike Yazicioglu, 337–47. Cambridge: Cambridge University Press.

Montgomery, Lindsay M. 2020. "Indigenous Alterity as Archaeological Praxis." In Rachel J. Crellin, Craig N. Cipolla, Lindsay M. Montgomery, Oliver J. T. Harris, and Sophie V. Moore, *Archaeological Theory in Dialogue: Situating Relationality, Ontology, Posthumanism, and Indigenous Paradigms*, 51–66. London: Routledge.

Montón-Subías, Sandra, and Margarita Sánchez Romero, eds. 2008. *Engendering Social Dynamics: The Archaeology of Maintenance Activities.* Oxford: Hadrian Books.

Morehart, Christopher T., and Kristin De Lucia, eds. 2015a. *Surplus: The Politics of Production and the Strategies of Everyday Life.* Boulder: University Press of Colorado.

Morehart, Christopher T., and Kristin De Lucia. 2015b. "Surplus: The Politics of Production and the Strategies of Everyday Life: An Introduction." In *Surplus: The Politics of Production and the Strategies of Everyday Life*, edited by Christopher T. Morehart and Kristin De Luca, 3–44. Boulder: University Press of Colorado.

Mullin, Molly H. 1999. "Mirrors and Windows: Sociocultural Studies of Human-Animal Relationships." *Annual Review of Anthropology* 28 (1): 201–24.

Munn, Nancy D. 1992. *The Fame of Gawa: A Symbolic Study of Value Transformation in a Massim (Papua New Guinea) Society.* Durham: Duke University Press.

Nadasdy, Paul. 2007. "The Gift in the Animal: The Ontology of Hunting and Human–Animal Sociality." *American Ethnologist* 34 (1): 25–43.

Nakassis, Constantine V. 2012. "Brand, Citationality, Performativity." *American Anthropologist* 114 (4): 624–38.

Narimanishvili, Goderdzi, and J. Amiranashvili. 2010. "Jinisi Settlement." In *Rescue Archaeology in Georgia: The Baku-Tbilisi-Ceyhan and South Caucasian Pipelines*, edited by G. Gamkrelidze, 224–53. Tbilisi: Georgian National Museum.

Norton, Marcy. 2015. "The Chicken or the Iegue: Human-Animal Relationships and the Columbian Exchange." *American Historical Review* 120 (1): 28–60.

Noske, Barbara. 1989. *Humans and Other Animals: Beyond the Boundaries of Anthropology.* Winchester, MA: Unwin Hyman.

———. 1993. "The Animal Question in Anthropology: A Commentary." *Society & Animals* 1 (2): 185–90.

"No Use Crying." 2015. *Economist*, March 28. http://www.economist.com/finance-and-economics/2015/03/28/no-use-crying.

O'Connor, Terence P. 1997. "Working at Relationships: Another Look at Animal Domestication." *Antiquity* 71 (271): 149–56.

———. 2013. *Animals as Neighbors: The Past and Present of Commensal Species.* East Lansing: Michigan State University Press.

———. 2018. "Animals and the Neolithic: Cui Bono?" In *Multispecies Archaeology*, edited by Suzanne E. Pilaar Birch, 201–13. New York: Routledge.

O'Donovan, Maria. 2002. *The Dynamics of Power.* Center for Archaeological Investigations, Southern Illinois University Carbondale.

Olsen, Sandra L. 2006. "Early Horse Domestication on the Eurasian Steppe." In *Documenting Domestication: New Genetic and Archaeological Paradigms*, edited by Melinda A. Zeder, D. G. Bradley, E. Emshwiller, and B. D. Smith, 245–69. Berkeley: University of California Press.

Orton, David C. 2010a. "Both Subject and Object: Herding, Inalienability and Sentient Property in Prehistory." *World Archaeology* 42 (2): 188–200.

———. 2010b. "Taphonomy and Interpretation: An Analytical Framework for Social Zooarchaeology." *International Journal of Osteoarchaeology* 22 (3): 320–37.

Outram, Alan K., Natalie A. Stear, Robin Bendrey, Sandra Olsen, Alexei Kasparov, Victor Zaibert, Nick Thorpe, and Richard P. Evershed. 2009. "The Earliest Horse Harnessing and Milking." *Science* 323 (5919): 1332–35.

Overton, Nick J., and Yannis Hamilakis. 2013. "A Manifesto for a Social Zooarchaeology. Swans and Other Beings in the Mesolithic." *Archaeological Dialogues* 20 (2): 111–36.

Panopoulos, Panayotis. 2003. "Animal Bells as Symbols: Sound and Hearing in a Greek Island Village." *Journal of the Royal Anthropological Institute* 9 (4): 639–56.

Parreñas, Juno Salazar. 2018. *Decolonizing Extinction: The Work of Care in Orangutan Rehabilitation*. Durham: Duke University Press Books.

Patterson, Orlando. 1982. *Slavery and Social Death: A Comparative Study*. Cambridge, MA: Harvard University Press.

Payne, Sebastian. 1973. "Kill-Off Patterns in Sheep and Goats: The Mandibles from Aşvan Kale." *Anatolian Studies* 23 (January): 281–303.

Peirce, Charles S. (1903) 1998. "Nomenclature and Division of Triadic Relations, as Far as They Are Determined." In *The Essential Peirce, Selected Philosophical Writings: Volume 2 (1893–1913)*, 289–99. Bloomington: Indiana University Press.

Perry, Elizabeth, and Rosemary A. Joyce. 2005. "Past Performance: The Archaeology of Gender as Influenced by the Work of Judith Butler." In *Butler Matters: Judith Butler's Impact on Feminist and Queer Studies*, edited by Warren J. Blumenfeld and Margaret Sönser Breen, 113–26. Florence, UK: Routledge.

Pickering, Andrew. 1995. *The Mangle of Practice: Time, Agency, and Science*. Chicago: University of Chicago Press.

Piotrovskii, Boris. 1941. "Urartu (Vanskoe Tsarstvo)." In *Istoriya drevnego vostoka*, edited by V. V. Struve, 307–23. Leningrad: Ogiz gospolitizdat.

Pluciennik, Mark. 2001. "Archaeology, Anthropology and Subsistence." *Journal of the Royal Anthropological Institute* 7 (4): 741–758.

———. 2002. "The Invention of Hunter-Gatherers in Seventeenth-Century Europe." *Archaeological Dialogues* 9: 98–151.

Plumwood, Val. 1993. *Feminism and the Mastery of Nature*. London: Routledge.

———. 1999. "Being Prey." In *The New Earth Reader. The Best of Terra Nova*, edited by D. Rothenberg and M. Ulvaeus, 76–92. Cambridge: MIT Press.

Pogrebova, M. N. 2011. *Istoriia vostochnogo zakavkaz'ia: Vtoraia polovina II–nachalo I tys. do n.è., po arkheologicheskim dannym*. Moscow: Vostochnaia literatura RAN.

Pollock, Susan, Reinhard Bernbeck, Lena Appel, Anna K. Loy, and Stefan Schreiber. 2020. "Are All Things Created Equal? The Incidental in Archaeology." *Cambridge Archaeological Journal* 30 (1): 141–49.

Porcher, Jocelyne. 2017a. "Animal Work." In *The Oxford Handbook of Animal Studies*, edited by Linda Kalof, 302–18. New York: Oxford University Press.

———. 2017b. *The Ethics of Animal Labor: A Collaborative Utopia*. Cham, Switzerland: Palgrave Macmillan.

Porter, Anne. 2012. *Mobile Pastoralism and the Formation of Near Eastern Civilizations: Weaving Together Society*. New York: Cambridge University Press.

Porter, Benjamin W. 2010. "Near Eastern Archaeology: Imperial Pasts, Postcolonial Presents, and the Possibilities of a Decolonized Future." In *Handbook of Postcolonial Archaeology*, edited by Jane Lydon and Uzma Z. Rizvi, 41–60. New York: Routledge.

Povinelli, Elizabeth A. 1993. *Labor's Lot: The Power, History, and Culture of Aboriginal Action*. Chicago: University of Chicago Press.

Price, Max. 2020. *Evolution of a Taboo: Pigs and People in the Ancient Near East*. New York: Oxford University Press.

Price, Max, and Cheryl A. Makarewicz. 2024. "Wealth in Livestock, Wealth in People, and the Pre-Pottery Neolithic of Jordan." *Cambridge Archaeological Journal*, 34 (1): 65–82.

Price, Max, Jesse Wolfhagen, and Erik Otárola-Castillo. 2016. "Confidence Intervals in the Analysis of Mortality and Survivorship Curves in Zooarchaeology." *American Antiquity* 81 (1): 157–73.

Ray, Keith, and Julian S. Thomas. 2003. "In the Kinship of Cows: The Social Centrality of Cattle in the Earlier Neolithic of Southern Britain." In *Food, Culture and Identity in the Neolithic and Early Bronze Age*, edited by Mike Parker Pearson, 37–51. Oxford: Archaeopress.

Reid, Andrew. 1996. "Cattle Herds and the Redistribution of Cattle Resources." *World Archaeology* 28 (1): 43–57.

Richards, Michael P., Rick J. Schulting, and Robert E. M. Hedges. 2003. "Archaeology: Sharp Shift in Diet at Onset of Neolithic." *Nature* 425 (6956): 366–67.

Ristvet, Lauren, Hilary Gopnik, Veli Bakhshaliyev, Hannah Lau, Safar Ashurov, and Robert Bryant. 2012. "On the Edge of Empire: 2008 and 2009 Excavations at Oğlanqala, Azerbaijan." *American Journal of Archaeology* 116 (2): 321–62.

Ritvo, Harriet. 1987. *The Animal Estate: The English and Other Creatures in the Victorian Age*. Cambridge, MA: Harvard University Press.

———. 1994. "Possessing Mother Nature. Genetic Capital in Eighteenth-Century Britain." In *Early Modern Conceptions of Property*, edited by John Brewer and Susan Staves, 413–26. London: Routledge.

Roffet-Salque, Mélanie, Rosalind Gillis, Richard P. Evershed, and Jean-Denis Vigne. 2018. "Milk as a Pivotal Medium in the Domestication of Cattle, Sheep and Goats." In *Hybrid Communities: Biosocial Approaches to Domesti-*

cation and Other Trans-Species Relationships, edited by Charles Stépanoff and Jean-Denis Vigne, 127–43. 1st ed. Abingdon, UK: Routledge.

Rose, Deborah Bird. 2004. *Reports from a Wild Country: Ethics for Decolonisation.* Sydney: UNSW Press.

Rosenberg, Gabriel N. 2020. "No Scrubs: Livestock Breeding, Race, and State Power in the Early Twentieth-Century United States." *Journal of American History* 107 (2): 362–87.

Rowley-Conwy, Peter. 2007. *From Genesis to Prehistory: The Archaeological Three Age System and Its Contested Reception in Denmark, Britain, and Ireland.* Oxford: Oxford University Press.

Russell, Nerissa. 2002. "The Wild Side of Animal Domestication." *Society & Animals* 10 (3): 285–302.

———. 2007. "The Domestication of Anthropology." In *Where the Wild Things Are Now: Domestication Reconsidered*, edited by Rebecca Cassidy and Molly Mullin, 27–48. Oxford: Berg.

———. 2012. *Social Zooarchaeology: Humans and Animals in Prehistory.* Cambridge: Cambridge University Press.

———. 2021. "Power and Othering." *Current Swedish Archaeology* 29 (1): 52–55.

Russell, Nerissa, and Bleda S. Düring. 2006. "Worthy Is the Lamb: A Double Burial at Neolithic Çatalhöyük (Turkey)." *Paléorient* 32 (1): 73–84.

Russell, Nerissa, and Louise Martin. 2005. "The Çatalhöyük Mammal Remains." In *Inhabiting Çatalhöyük: Reports from the 1995–1999 Seasons*, edited by Ian Hodder, 33–98. Cambridge: McDonald Institute for Archaeological Research.

Sagona, Antonio G. 2018. *The Archaeology of the Caucasus: From the Earliest Settlements to the Iron Age.* New York: Cambridge University Press.

Sagona, Antonio G., and Paul E. Zimansky. 2009. *Ancient Turkey.* London: Routledge.

Saha, Jonathan. 2017. "Colonizing Elephants: Animal Agency, Undead Capital and Imperial Science in British Burma." *BJHS Themes* 2:169–89.

Sahlins, Marshall. 1974. *Stone Age Economics.* New Brunswick, NJ: Aldine Transaction.

Salzman, Philip Carl. 2004. *Pastoralists: Equality, Hierarchy, and the State.* Boulder, CO: Westview Press.

Sasson, Aharon. 2007. "Corpus of 694 Astragali from Stratum II at Tel Beersheba." *Tel Aviv* 34 (2): 171–81.

Sayre, Nathan F. 2017. *The Politics of Scale: A History of Rangeland Science.* Chicago: University of Chicago Press.

Schiebinger, Londa L. 1993. *Nature's Body: Gender in the Making of Modern Science.* Boston: Beacon Press.

Scott, Ashley, Sabine Reinhold, Taylor Hermes, Alexey A. Kalmykov, Andrey Belinskiy, Alexandra Buzhilova, Natalia Berezina, et al. 2022. "Emergence and Intensification of Dairying in the Caucasus and Eurasian Steppes." *Nature Ecology & Evolution* 6 (6): 813–22.

Scott, James C. 2017. *Against the Grain: A Deep History of the Earliest States*. New Haven: Yale University Press.

Serpell, James. 1996. *In the Company of Animals: A Study of Human-Animal Relationships*. New York: Cambridge University Press.

Shanshashvili, Nino, and Goderdzi Narimanishvili. 2012. "Late Bronze / Early Iron Age Sites in Trialeti—External Relations and Cultural Contacts." In *Austasch und Kulturkontakt im Südkaukasus und Seinen Angrenzenden Regionen in der Spätbronze-/Früheisenzeit*, edited by Andreas Mehnert, Gundula Mehnert, and Sabine Reinhold, 175–94. Langenweißbach, Germany: Beier & Beran.

Sharma, R. S. 1973. "Forms of Property in the Early Portions of the Rig Veda." *Proceedings of the Indian History Congress* 34:94–103.

Sharp, Lesley Alexandra. 2019. *Animal Ethos: The Morality of Human-Animal Encounters in Experimental Lab Science*. Oakland: University of California Press.

Shepard, Paul. 1996. *The Others: How Animals Made Us Human*. Washington, DC: Island Press.

———. 1998. *Thinking Animals: Animals and the Development of Human Intelligence*. Athens: University of Georgia Press.

Sherratt, Andrew G. 1981. "Plough and Pastoralism: Aspects of the Secondary Products Revolution." In *Pattern of the Past: Studies in Honor of David Clarke*, edited by Ian Hodder, G. Isaac, and N. Hammond, 261–306. Cambridge: Cambridge University Press.

———. 1983. "The Secondary Exploitation of Animals in the Old World." *World Archaeology* 15 (1): 90–104.

———. 1997. *Economy and Society in Prehistoric Europe: Changing Perspectives*. Edinburgh: Edinburgh University Press.

Shukin, Nicole. 2009. *Animal Capital Rendering Life in Biopolitical Times*. Minneapolis: University of Minnesota Press.

Silver, I. A. 1969. "The Ageing of Domestic Animals." In *Science in Archaeology*, edited by D. Brothwell and E. S. Higgs, 283–302. 2nd ed. London: Thames and Hudson.

Smith, Adam. 1978. *Lectures on Jurisprudence*. Edited by Ronald L. Meek, D. D. Raphael, and Peter Stein. Oxford: Clarendon Press. Lectures first presented 1762–1763.

Smith, Adam T. 2003. *The Political Landscape: Constellations of Authority in Early Complex Polities*. Berkeley: University of California Press.

———. 2011a. "Archaeologies of Sovereignty." *Annual Review of Anthropology* 40 (1): 415–32.

———. 2011b. "Figuring the Political: The Stuff of Sovereignty in a Post-Evolutionary Archaeology." In *The Archaeology of Politics: The Materiality of Political Practice and Action in the Past*, edited by Peter G. Johansen and Andrew M. Bauer, 354–62. Newcastle upon Tyne: Cambridge Scholars.

———. 2015. *The Political Machine: Assembling Sovereignty in the Bronze Age Caucasus*. Princeton: Princeton University Press.

Smith, Adam T., Ruben S. Badalyan, and Pavel S. Avetisyan. 2004. "Early Complex Societies in Southern Caucasia: A Preliminary Report on the 2002 Investigations by Project ArAGATS on the Tsakahovit Plain, Republic of Armenia." *American Journal of Archaeology* 108:1–41.

———. 2009. *The Archaeology and Geography of Ancient Transcaucasian Societies, Volume 1: The Foundations of Research and Regional Survey in the Tsaghkahovit Plain, Armenia*. Chicago: Oriental Institute of the University of Chicago.

Smith, Adam T., and Jeffrey F. Leon. 2014. "Divination and Sovereignty: The Late Bronze Age Shrines at Gegharot, Armenia." *American Journal of Archaeology* 118:549–63.

Smith-Howard, Kendra. 2014. *Pure and Modern Milk: An Environmental History since 1900*. Oxford: Oxford University Press.

Sneath, David. 2007. *The Headless State: Aristocratic Orders, Kinship Society, and Misrepresentations of Nomadic Inner Asia*. New York: Columbia University Press.

Sterling, Kathleen. 2011. "Inventing Human Nature." In *Ideologies in Archaeology*, edited by Reinhard Bernbeck and Randall H. McGuire, 175–93. Tucson: University of Arizona Press.

Stépanoff, Charles, and Jean-Denis Vigne, eds. 2018. *Hybrid Communities: Biosocial Approaches to Domestication and Other Trans-species Relationships*. London: Routledge.

Strathern, Marilyn. 2012. "Eating (and Feeding)." *Cambridge Journal of Anthropology* 30 (2): 1–14.

Susnow, Matthew, Nimrod Marom, Ariel Shatil, Nava Panitz-Cohen, Robert Mullins, and Naama Yahalom-Mack. 2021. "Contextualizing an Iron Age IIA Hoard of Astragali from Tel Abel Beth Maacah, Israel." *Journal of Mediterranean Archaeology* 34 (1): 59–83.

Swanson, Heather Anne, Marianne E. Lien, and Gro Ween, eds. 2018. *Domestication Gone Wild: Politics and Practices of Multispecies Relations*. Durham: Duke University Press.

Swenson, Edward, and John P. Warner. 2012. "Crucibles of Power: Forging Copper and Forging Subjects at the Moche Ceremonial Center of Huaca Colorada, Peru." *Journal of Anthropological Archaeology* 31 (3): 314–33.

Swift, Louis Franklin, and Arthur Van Vlissingen. 1927. *Yankee of the Yards: The Biography of Gustavus Franklin Swift*. Chicago: A. W. Shaw Company.

Sykes, Naomi. 2010. "Deer, Land, Knives and Halls: Social Change in Early Medieval England." *Antiquaries Journal* 90 (September): 175–93.

———. 2014. *Beastly Questions: Animal Answers to Archaeological Issues*. London: Bloomsbury Academic.

Symmons, Robert. 2002. "A Re-Examination of Sheep Bone Density and Its Role in Assessing Taphonomic Histories of Zooarchaeological Assemblages." PhD thesis, University College London.

Tani, Yutaka. 1996. "Domestic Animal as Serf: Ideologies of Nature in the Mediterranean and the Middle East." In *Redefining Nature: Ecology, Culture and Domestication*, edited by R. F. Ellen and K. Fukui, 387–415. Oxford: Berg.

———. 2017. *God, Man and Domesticated Animals: The Birth of Shepherds and Their Descendants in the Ancient Near East*. Kyoto: Trans Pacific Press.

Thomas, Julian S. 2002. "Taking Power Seriously." In *The Dynamics of Power*, edited by Maria O'Donovan, 35–50. Carbondale: Southern Illinois University Carbondale, Center for Archaeological Investigations.

Todd, Zoe. 2016. "An Indigenous Feminist's Take on the Ontological Turn: 'Ontology' Is Just Another Word for Colonialism." *Journal of Historical Sociology* 29 (1): 4–22.

Tornero, Carlos, Adrian Bălășescu, Joël Ughetto-Monfrin, Valentina Voinea, and Marie Balasse. 2013. "Seasonality and Season of Birth in Early Eneolithic Sheep from Cheia (Romania): Methodological Advances and Implications for Animal Economy." *Journal of Archaeological Science* 40 (11): 4039–55.

Tornero, Carlos, Marie Balasse, Stéphanie Bréhard, Isabelle Carrère, Denis Fiorillo, Jean Guilaine, Jean-Denis Vigne, and Claire Manen. 2020. "Early Evidence of Sheep Lambing de-Seasoning in the Western Mediterranean in the Sixth Millennium BCE." *Scientific Reports* 10 (1): 12798.

Torosyan, R. M., O. S. Khnkikyan, and L. Petrosyan. 2002. *Drevnij shirakavan*. Yerevan, Armenia: Izdatel'stvo gitutyun.

Towers, Jacqueline, Mandy Jay, Ingrid Mainland, Olaf Nehlich, and Janet Montgomery. 2011. "A Calf for All Seasons? The Potential of Stable Isotope Analysis to Investigate Prehistoric Husbandry Practices." *Journal of Archaeological Science* 38 (8): 1858–68.

Towers, Jacqueline, Ingrid Mainland, Janet Montgomery, and Julie Bond. 2017. "Calving Seasonality at Pool, Orkney during the First Millennium AD: An Investigation Using Intra-Tooth Isotope Ratio Analysis of Cattle Molar Enamel." *Environmental Archaeology* 22 (1): 40–55.

Trigger, Bruce. 2006. *A History of Archaeological Thought*. 2nd ed. Cambridge: Cambridge University Press.

Tringham, Ruth. 1991. "Households with Faces: The Challenge of Gender in Prehistoric Architectural Remains." In *Engendering Archaeology: Women and Prehistory*, edited by Joan Gero and Margaret W. Conkey, 93–131. Oxford: Basil Blackwell.

Tronti, Mario. 1979. "The Strategy of Refusal." In *Working Class Autonomy and the Crisis: Italian Marxist Texts of the Theory and Practice of a Class Movement, 1964–79*, edited by Mario Tronti, 7–21. London: Red Notes.

Trouillot, Michel-Rolph. 1995. *Silencing the Past: Power and the Production of History*. Boston: Beacon Press.

———. 2003. *Global Transformations: Anthropology and the Modern World*. New York: Palgrave Macmillan.

Tsing, Anna Lowenhaupt. 2013. "Sorting Out Commodities: How Capitalist Value Is Made Through Gifts." *HAU: Journal of Ethnographic Theory* 3 (1): 21–43.

———. 2018. "Nine Provocations for the Study of Domestication." In *Domestication Gone Wild: Politics and Practices of Multispecies Relations*, edited by Heather Anne Swanson, Marianne E. Lien, and Gro Ween, 231–51. Durham: Duke University Press.

Tuan, Yi-fu. 1984. *Dominance and Affection: The Making of Pets*. New Haven: Yale University Press.

Uerpmann, Magarethe, and Hans-Peter Uerpmann. 1994. "Animal Bone Finds from Excavation 520 at Qala'at Al-Bahrain." In *Qala'at Al-Bahrain. Vol. 1. The Northern City Wall and the Islamic Fortress*, edited by Høljund Flemming and H. Hellmuth Anderson, 417–44. Aarhus, Denmark: Jutland Archaeological Society Publications.

Vigne, Jean-Denis, and Daniel Helmer. 2007. "Was Milk a "Secondary Product" in the Old World Neolithisation Process? Its Role in the Domestication of Cattle, Sheep and Goats." *Anthropozoologica* 42 (2): 9–40.

Vivieros de Castro, Eduardo. 1998. "Cosmological Deixis and Amerindian Perspectivism." *Journal of the Royal Anthropological Institute* 4 (3): 469–89.

Wapnish, Paula, and Brian Hesse. 1988. "Urbanization and the Organization of Animal Production at Tell Jemmeh in the Middle Bronze Age Levant." *Journal of Near Eastern Studies* 47 (2): 81–94.

Warinner, C., J. Hendy, C. Speller, E. Cappellini, R. Fischer, C. Trachsel, J. Arneborg, et al. 2014. "Direct Evidence of Milk Consumption from Ancient Human Dental Calculus." *Scientific Reports* 4 (November): 7104.

Wattenmaker, Patricia. 1998. *Household and State in Upper Mesopotamia: Specialized Economy and the Social Uses of Goods in an Early Complex Society*. Washington, DC: Smithsonian Institution Press.

Watts, Christopher M. 2008. "On Mediation and Material Agency in the Peircean Semeiotic." In *Material Agency*, edited by Carl Knappett and Lambros Malafouris, 187–207. Boston: Springer.

Watts, Vanessa. 2013. "Indigenous Place-Thought & Agency amongst Humans and Non-Humans (First Woman and Sky Woman Go on a European World Tour!)." *Decolonization: Indigeneity, Education & Society* 2 (1): 20–34.

Weeks, Kathi. 2011. *The Problem with Work: Feminism, Marxism, Antiwork Politics, and Postwork Imaginaries*. Durham: Duke University Press.

Weiner, Annette B. 1992. *Inalienable Possessions: The Paradox of Keeping-While-Giving*. Berkeley: University of California Press.

Weismantel, Mary J. 2015. "Seeing Like an Archaeologist: Viveiros de Castro at Chavín de Huantar." *Journal of Social Archaeology* 15 (2): 139–59.

———. 2021. *Playing with Things: Engaging the Moche Sex Pots*. Austin: University of Texas Press.

Wiley, Andrea S. 2011. *Re-Imagining Milk*. New York: Routledge.

————. 2014. *Cultures of Milk: The Biology and Meaning of Dairy Products in the United States and India*. Cambridge, MA: Harvard University Press.

Wilkie, Rhoda M. 2010. *Livestock/Deadstock: Working with Farm Animals from Birth to Slaughter*. Philadelphia: Temple University Press.

————. 2017. "Animals as Sentient Commodities." In *The Oxford Handbook of Animal Studies*, edited by Linda Kalof, 279–301. New York: Oxford University Press.

Wilmot, Sarah. 2007. "From 'Public Service' to Artificial Insemination: Animal Breeding Science and Reproductive Research in Early Twentieth-Century Britain." *Studies in History and Philosophy of Science Part C: Studies in History and Philosophy of Biological and Biomedical Sciences* 38 (2): 411–41.

Wolfe, Cary. 2010. *What Is Posthumanism?* Minneapolis: University of Minnesota Press.

Wylie, Alison. 2000. "Questions of Evidence, Legitimacy, and the (Dis)Unity of Science." *American Antiquity* 65 (2): 227–37.

Zaraska, Marta. 2016. *Meathooked: The History and Science of Our 2.5-Million-Year Obsession with Meat*. New York: Basic Books.

Zazzo, Antoine, Marie Balasse, and William P. Patterson. 2005. "High-Resolution δ13C Intratooth Profiles in Bovine Enamel: Implications for Mineralization Pattern and Isotopic Attenuation." *Geochimica et cosmochimica acta* 69 (14): 3631–42.

Zeder, Melinda A. 1988. "Understanding Urban Process Through the Study of Specialized Subsistence Economy in the Near East." *Journal of Anthropological Archaeology* 7:1–55.

————. 1991. *Feeding Cities: Specialized Animal Economy in the Ancient Near East*. Washington, DC: Smithsonian Institution Press.

————. 2006. "Reconciling Rates of Long Bone Fusion and Tooth Eruption and Wear in Sheep (*Ovis*) and Goat (*Capra*)." In *Recent Advances in Ageing and Sexing Animal Bones*, edited by Deborah Ruscillo, 87–118. Oxford: Oxbow Press.

————. 2012. "The Domestication of Animals." *Journal of Anthropological Research* 68 (2): 161–90.

Zeder, Melinda A., Guy Bar-Oz, Scott J. Rufolo, and Frank Hole. 2013. "New Perspectives on the Use of Kites in Mass-Kills of Levantine Gazelle: A View from Northeastern Syria." *Quaternary International* 297 (May): 110–25.

INDEX

affiliation-distinction relations, 57–63, 66, 94–95, 131, 184, 216n6. *See also* authorization-subjection relations; politics

African cattle pastoralism, 52, 135, 149, 212n11

Against the Grain (Scott), 214n16

agriculture, 42, 47, 51, 111, 136, 149–50. *See also* animal husbandry

allocative resources, 149–50, 152, 154

Amazonia, 46

Amazonian perspectivalism, 215n8

Anatolian Plateau, 72

Anderson, Kay, 29–30

animal husbandry, 8, 20–21, 24, 39, 47, 74, 104, 115, 205, 214n1, 220n2. *See also* agriculture; domestication

animals: agency of, 28, 39–40; materiality of, 5, 17, 52–53, 60, 84, 147, 153–54, 158, 190, 199; modern attitudes toward, 17–19; in mortuary rituals, 87–89, 156, 162–63, 179–85, 199; nonmeat products, 75, 111; as political actors, 7–8, 10, 42, 55, 59, 66–68, 115, 212n8; and producing value, 51, 56, 131–32, 147; ritual power of, 60–61, 161. *See also* critical animal studies; faunal remains; herd animals; human nature; livestock; Secondary Products Revolution (SPR); wild animals

animal sacrifice, 15, 168–69, 188

animal traction, 111–12

anthropocentrism, 4, 7–8, 28–29, 38; and human mastery, 18, 23, 25–27, 29, 215n8. *See also* human nature

anthropology, 7–9, 11, 19–20, 25–26, 35–36, 45, 56

anthropo-zoo-genetic practice, 7–8

ants, 28

ArAGATS, 75–76, 87, 176, 218n5

Arbuckle, Benjamin, 20–21

archaeology, 1–2, 5–6, 14–15, 18–20, 25, 31, 55, 69–71, 75, 95, 99, 195, 211n6. *See also* zooarchaeology

Arendt, Hannah, 43, 223n26

assemblage theory, 57

Assyrian empire, 72

astragali: burning of, 177; and gnawing, 172; modification of, 99–100, 173–74, 177, 180–81, 230nn15–16; overabundance of, 100, 164, 166, 228n3; separation from other remains, 141. *See also* faunal remains

Joyce, Rosemary, 170

Kames, Henry Home, 37
killing, 127; and making killable, 44–
45. *See also* slaughter
kivas, 98n2
Kura-Araxes culture, 72
kurgans. See burial mounds

lab mice, 21
labor: of care, 60; costs of, 149; and
defining the human, 4; definitions
of, 43; distinction from work, 43,
223n26; hierarchies of, 43, 48, 195;
and politics, 49; proliferation of,
125, 130; and reproduction, 43–44,
47–48, 66–67, 103–4, 109, 126,
129, 189–90; and technology,
51. *See also* capitalism; foddering;
property; women's work; work
lactase persistence genes, 112–13, 115
Lang, David, 73
Late Bronze Age, 3–5, 9–12, 14, 67,
72–73, 77, 81, 87–88, 92, 96, 176,
217n2. *See also* Early Bronze Age;
Lchashen-Metsamor material culture horizon; Middle Bronze Age
Lchashen-Metsamor material culture
horizon, 72, 89, 218n3. *See also*
Late Bronze Age
Leach, Helen, 26
Leon, Jeffrey F., 99
Levant, 72
livestock, 14, 23, 30, 36, 45, 47, 65,
118–19, 153, 196–97. *See also*
animals; herd animals; industrialization
Locke, John, 43

mandibles: as evidence of age, 155;
overabundance of, 141–42, 162;
representing individual animals,
171

manghals, 96–98. *See also* ceramics
Marshall, Maureen, 88–89, 202
Marx, Karl, 4, 43, 74, 150, 221n14,
223n26, 226n22
materiality, 5, 10, 17, 52–53, 60, 84,
147, 153–54, 158, 190, 199
meat consumption: contemporary
debates over, 203; and mortuary
rituals, 184; as quotidian, 164; and
social status, 143–44, 151–52, 157,
188
meat production: models of, 113–15,
127–28; and preservation, 159; and
social relationships, 151–52
Meggido, 164
Mesopotamia, 72
metallurgy, 90, 129, 230n1
Meyer, Caspar, 189
Middle Bronze Age, 92–94, 98n1,
229n13, 230n2. *See also* Early
Bronze Age; Late Bronze Age
milk production: availability of fresh
milk, 108–9; industrialization
of, 15, 104–5, 109–11, 115–16,
222n22; labor of, 51, 125–26, 130,
194, 222n23; materiality of milk,
131, 197; and preservation, 86, 189,
221n10; and seasonal availability,
2, 103, 109–10, 118–19, 195; and
the US dairy lobby, 116. *See also*
breastfeeding; cattle; Secondary
Products Revolution (SPR)
Mlekuž, Dimitrij, 222n23
Moche, 188
modernity: boundaries of, 4–5, 9, 46,
193; and forms of value, 135, 152;
and labor, 50; origins in domestication, 18–19, 26, 32, 44, 53–54;
perceptions of, 2, 30; and slavery,
38; and technological development, 110–11. *See also* history; industrialization; postdomestication;
premodernity